Engaging God's Story

Engaging God's Story

Weekly Devotions for the Christian Year

Year A

PAXSON JEANCAKE

Foreword by Reggie Kidd

WIPF & STOCK · Eugene, Oregon

ENGAGING GOD'S STORY
Weekly Devotions for the Christian Year (Year A)

Copyright © 2025 Paxson Jeancake. All rights reserved. Except for brief quotations in critical publications or reviews, no part of this book may be reproduced in any manner without prior written permission from the publisher. Write: Permissions, Wipf and Stock Publishers, 199 W. 8th Ave., Suite 3, Eugene, OR 97401.

Wipf & Stock
An Imprint of Wipf and Stock Publishers
199 W. 8th Ave., Suite 3
Eugene, OR 97401

www.wipfandstock.com

PAPERBACK ISBN: 978-1-6667-1843-0
HARDCOVER ISBN: 978-1-6667-1844-7
EBOOK ISBN: 978-1-6667-1845-4

VERSION NUMBER 10/09/25

Scripture quotations are taken from the New Revised Standard Version Updated Edition. Copyright © 2021 National Council of Churches of Christ in the United States of America. Used by permission. All rights reserved worldwide.

Scripture quotations marked ESV are from the ESV® Bible (The Holy Bible, English Standard Version®), copyright © 2001 by Crossway, a publishing ministry of Good News Publishers. Used by permission. All rights reserved.

Scripture quotations marked NLT are taken from the *Holy Bible*, New Living Translation, copyright © 1996, 2004, 2015 by Tyndale House Foundation. Used by permission of Tyndale House Publishers, Inc., Carol Stream, IL 60188. All rights reserved.

Let the word of Christ dwell in you richly.
—Colossians 3:16

Contents

Foreword by Reggie Kidd | xi
Preface | xiii
Introduction | xvii

YEAR A: THE YEAR OF MATTHEW

Advent through Epiphany

First Sunday of Advent | 5
Second Sunday of Advent | 9
Third Sunday of Advent | 13
Fourth Sunday of Advent | 17
Christmas Eve | 21
Christmas Day | 25
First Sunday after Christmas | 29
Second Sunday after Christmas | 35
Epiphany of the Lord | 41
Baptism of the Lord | 47
Second Sunday after Epiphany | 53
Third Sunday after Epiphany | 59
Fourth Sunday after Epiphany | 63
Fifth Sunday after Epiphany | 69
Sixth Sunday after Epiphany | 75
Seventh Sunday after Epiphany | 81
Eighth Sunday after Epiphany | 87
Ninth Sunday after Epiphany | 93
Transfiguration of the Lord | 99

Lent through Pentecost

Ash Wednesday | 107
First Sunday in Lent | 113
Second Sunday in Lent | 117
Third Sunday in Lent | 121
Fourth Sunday in Lent | 127
Fifth Sunday in Lent | 131
Palm Sunday | 137
Maundy Thursday | 141
Good Friday | 147
Easter | 153
Second Sunday of Easter | 157
Third Sunday of Easter | 161
Fourth Sunday of Easter | 165
Fifth Sunday of Easter | 169
Sixth Sunday of Easter | 175
Ascension of the Lord | 181
Seventh Sunday of Easter | 187
Day of Pentecost | 193

Season after Pentecost

Trinity Sunday | 201
Proper 3 (Sunday between May 24 and May 28 inclusive) | 205
Proper 4 (Sunday between May 29 and June 4 inclusive) | 211
Proper 5 (Sunday between June 5 and June 11 inclusive) | 217
Proper 6 (Sunday between June 12 and June 18 inclusive) | 223
Proper 7 (Sunday between June 19 and June 25 inclusive) | 229
Proper 8 (Sunday between June 26 and July 2 inclusive) | 235
Proper 9 (Sunday between July 3 and July 9 inclusive) | 239
Proper 10 (Sunday between July 10 and July 16 inclusive) | 243
Proper 11 (Sunday between July 17 and July 23 inclusive) | 247
Proper 12 (Sunday between July 24 and July 30 inclusive) | 251
Proper 13 (Sunday between July 31 and August 6 inclusive) | 255
Proper 14 (Sunday between August 7 and August 13 inclusive) | 259

Proper 15 (Sunday between August 14 and August 20 inclusive) | 265
Proper 16 (Sunday between August 21 and August 27 inclusive) | 271
Proper 17 (Sunday between August 28 and September 3 inclusive) | 277
Proper 18 (Sunday between September 4 and September 10 inclusive) | 283
Proper 19 (Sunday between September 11 and September 17 inclusive) | 289
Proper 20 (Sunday between September 18 and September 24 inclusive) | 295
Proper 21 (Sunday between September 25 and October 1 inclusive) | 301
Proper 22 (Sunday between October 2 and October 8 inclusive) | 307
Proper 23 (Sunday between October 9 and October 15 inclusive) | 313
Proper 24 (Sunday between October 16 and October 22 inclusive) | 319
Proper 25 (Sunday between October 23 and October 29 inclusive) | 325
Proper 26 (Sunday between October 30 and November 5 inclusive) | 331
Proper 27 (Sunday between November 6 and November 12 inclusive) | 337
Proper 28 (Sunday between November 13 and November 19 inclusive) | 343
Christ the King | 349

Appendix: Summary of My Doctoral Thesis: Inspiration for Parents and a Challenge to Worship Leaders | 353
Bibliography | 363
Subject Index | 365
Scripture Index | 369

Foreword

I so appreciate the gift that my friend and former student Paxson Jeancake is offering the church in the lectionary toolkit he is building for us in this book and in its companion volume *Lectionary Journey: Worship Aids for the Christian Year*. His journey and mine are parallel, and our desires are a match.

Like Paxson, my own background is mixed: a hybrid of Evangelical, Reformed, mainline, and nondenominational churches.

In my case, for some reason Bob Webber recruited me to teach in his Institute for Worship Studies in the early 2000s. Though I had no—I mean zero—background in the liturgy-friendly ethos he was instilling, I eagerly accepted. I did so because I sensed in Bob and in his worship a higher sense of the Lord's living presence in worship—yes, in the preaching but also the singing and praying and especially in the gathering at the table.

One thing that seemed odd was the notion that preaching should be governed by a lectionary, a set of prescribed Scripture readings for each week. I asked a fellow faculty member, a Reformed pastor who taught the lectionary to our students, if he actually used the lectionary in his own preaching.

"Yes, I certainly do," he answered.

"But don't you find it confining?" I queried.

"Not in the least," he quickly responded, "The lectionary has taught me to see preaching as folding people into Jesus' story instead of trying to shoehorn a little Jesus into people's preset lives and agendas. It's freeing not to spend 80 percent of my sermon prep time trying to figure out where I'm going. And it's thrilling to know that my church is united with countless churches all over the globe who are following the same storyline. Not only that, I am amazed how easy it is to see where my people's lives and needs intersect in any given week with where we are in the biblical drama. It's a Holy Ghost thing."

"That's an intriguing notion" was about all I could come up with in the moment. Some twenty-five years after that conversation and following a decade of handling the lectionary-guided preaching at the church in which I serve, I can only say, "Amen!"

Whether you are just now trying on the idea of letting Sunday worship be directed by lectionary readings or whether it already fits you like your favorite well-worn jacket, you will find Paxson's devotions on each week's combination of texts rewarding. His insights are deep, spiritual, and connected to real life. His observations are hard-earned, worked out in deep study, in the overcoming of personal crises, in working through delicate pastoral relationships, and above all, in his own persistent and relentless wrestling with the God who has folded him into his own story of grace.

Dr. Reggie Kidd
Dean of the Cathedral Church of Saint Luke
Author of *With One Voice: Discovering Christ's Song in Our Worship*

Preface

Over the years, I have become quite a fan of Johann Sebastian Bach. I deeply enjoy listening to his cantatas and discovering the inspiration behind the music and the text. When Bach moved to Leipzig, Germany in 1723 and took his position as Thomascantor (with responsibilities at the St. Thomas School and the four city churches), he channeled his energy into writing a cantata each week based on the Lutheran lectionary of his day. He kept up this weekly pace of writing lectionary-based cantatas for several years (1723–1725). His goal was to create "a well-regulated church music to the glory of God."[1] Gardiner writes,

> For, from the moment of his official induction as Thomascantor in Leipzig in the early summer of 1723 Bach set off at a pace of weekly church cantata composition so furious that probably no one—not even he, with his extraordinary reserves of creative energy and powers of concentration—could sustain it for more than a couple of years (as indeed he didn't). . . . Such zeal went far beyond any contractual obligation to compose and perform music to adorn the liturgy of the Lutheran church.[2]

The sheer volume of Bach's creative output is astonishing. The wealth of expression he has left for the church and the world is a gift, and it evokes a sense of admiration and respect in me as a worship leader and songwriter. I feel a kindred spirit with Bach, and his influence sparked a desire in me to create an ordered and comprehensive resource for the church based on the lectionary of my day.

In addition to Bach, I have been greatly influenced by Russell Mitman and his book *Worship in the Shape of Scripture*. Mitman's basic

1. Gardiner, *Bach*, 138.
2. Gardiner, *Bach*, 288–89.

paradigm is "from lectionary to liturgy."[3] Mitman encourages those involved in worship planning to create an "organic liturgy" that flows from the themes and language of Scripture.[4] At a time when biblical literacy is on the decline and the presence of Scripture in our worship services is low, Mitman's paradigm appeared as a timely remedy to these unfortunate situations.

In 2018, inspired by both Bach and Mitman, I developed a vision for an ordered and comprehensive project that would include worship aids, songs, and devotions for each Sunday in the Christian year over the three-year lectionary cycle.[5] I began to write songs and a weekly blog, offering lectionary-based resources for church and home. This book and other endeavors are the fruit of that initial inspiration.[6] It is my hope that these resources will be helpful for those who are involved in planning corporate worship and also for those who are interested in following a regular pattern of Scripture readings for worship and devotion.

A project like this is never created in a vacuum. I would like to acknowledge and thank those who have been a part of this endeavor in some capacity.

I would like to thank the leadership and congregation of Covenant Church for allowing me the opportunity to write and introduce these resources in our local church context.

I would like to thank those who have gone before me, providing resources, inspiration, and insights that have influenced and informed my worship practices and paradigms.

I would like to thank the participants in my doctoral study. The insights from the surveys, interviews, and focus groups were so helpful for my thesis and have informed this project in ways as well.

I would like to thank the dear friends in our small groups as we have engaged God's story together, using these devotions on Wednesday evenings.

I would like to thank my wife, Allison, and my two daughters, Laura Camille and Mallory, for our times together during "dinner and devo" on

---

3. Mitman, *Worship*, 13.

4. Mitman, *Worship*, 33.

5. Though it is the title of this book, "Engaging God's Story" is also the title of the overall project.

6. Jeancake, *Lectionary Journey*; Jeancake and Jeancake, *You Keep Hope Alive* (the first collection of songs for this project).

Monday evenings, reading Scripture and praying as a family. I hope you will engage God's story with your own family one day.

Finally, all praise be to our triune God, whose steadfast love endures forever. To God alone be the glory.

Introduction

In my journey of spiritual growth and formation, I have come to appreciate the fruit of having regular spiritual practices in my life, ordinary means of grace such as spending time in God's word, in prayer, and in worship. I have come to see how consistently engaging God's story through these steady rhythms has impacted, not only my own life but the spiritual vitality of my family and my church.

A BRIDGE BETWEEN CHURCH AND HOME THROUGH WORSHIP

In my previous book, *Lectionary Journey: Worship Aids for the Christian Year*, I provided an ordered, *liturgical* resource for worship leaders and pastors, those planning weekly worship in the context of the local church.[1] I introduced the concept of an organic liturgy, one that flows from the lectionary and follows the cycles and seasons of the Christian year.

Engaging God's Story: Weekly Devotions for the Christian Year is an ordered, *devotional* resource that is a complement and companion to *Lectionary Journey*. Together, the two books serve as a bridge between church and home through worship. *Lectionary Journey* is a liturgical resource for crafting an organic liturgy for corporate worship on Sunday, while *Engaging God's Story* is a devotional resource for cultivating spiritual practices in the home during the week. Both resources share a foundation in the cycles and seasons of the Christian year and the Revised Common Lectionary.[2]

---

1. Jeancake, *Lectionary Journey*.
2. Consultation on Common Texts (CCT), *Revised Common Lectionary*.

Engaging God's Story is a resource for worship leaders and pastors, individuals and families, small group and Bible study leaders. Worship leaders and pastors can use this resource to prepare for their weekly worship planning, a means of engaging the word before crafting their liturgies or writing their sermons. Individuals can use this book for personal devotions, and parents can use it for family devotions during the week. Small group and Bible study leaders can use this resource for weekly Bible study.

Since the Christian year and the Revised Common Lectionary are the foundation for this resource, I will briefly discuss each of these means of engaging God's story. Through them, we are able to see the big picture of God's redemption and his covenant faithfulness with his people.

THE CHRISTIAN YEAR

In Deuteronomy 6, we are encouraged to love the Lord our God with all our heart, all our soul, and all our might. We are encouraged to share the story and commands of God when we are at home and when we are away, when we lie down, and when we rise. In short, we are to immerse ourselves in the redemptive narrative of God. The early Hebrews held festivals throughout the year, recounting and celebrating the ways God had revealed himself to them as a nation.

Similarly, and rooted in this heritage, celebrating the various Sundays and seasons of the Christian year is a way to mark time and to emphasize the various aspects of the life of Christ and the story of redemption. The Christian year allows us the opportunity, week after week and year after year, to engage the various facets of Christ's life. These steady rhythms help to strengthen our union with Christ and transform us more and more into his likeness.

The Christian year begins with the Cycle of Light (Advent, Christmas, Epiphany) in which we anticipate the second coming of Christ, remember and celebrate his first coming and incarnation, and recall the ways he manifested himself to the world. Next, we celebrate the Cycle of Life (Lent, Easter, Pentecost) in which we remember and celebrate the death, resurrection, and ascension of Christ, and his sending of the Holy Spirit. The season after Pentecost has been described as the Cycle of Love, the way we respond to and live out all that we celebrated in the first half of the Christian year regarding the life of Christ.³ The liturgical calendar is a helpful way to visualize God's story through the cycles and seasons of the Christian year.

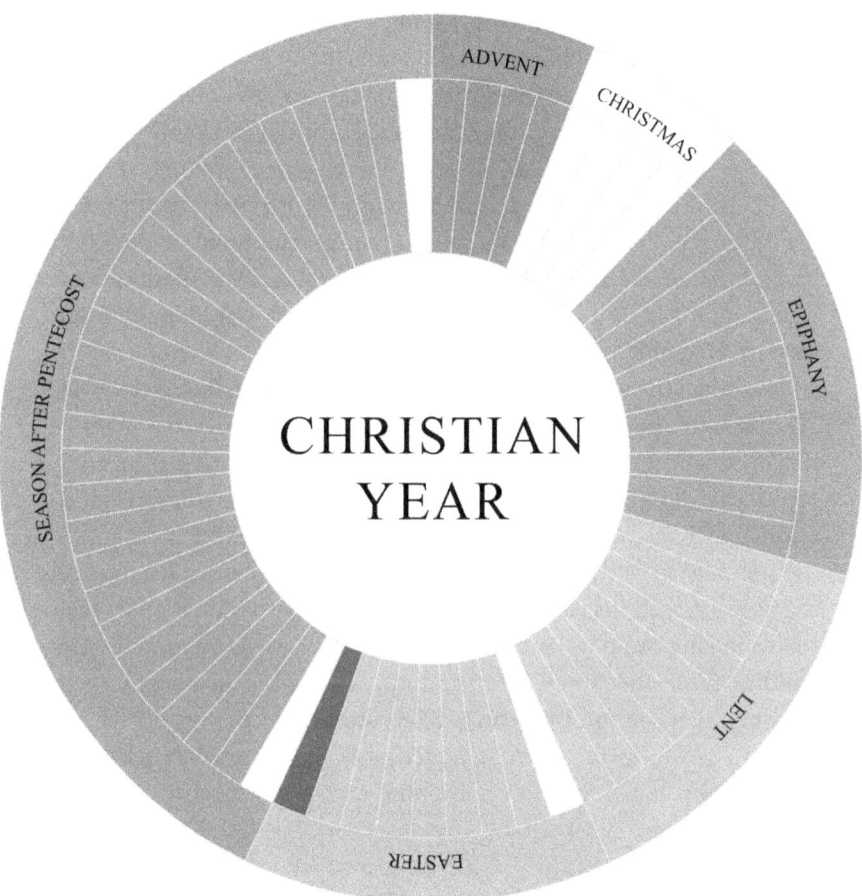

Advent is a time of preparation; a time to remember Christ's first coming and to anticipate his return. During **Christmas** we orient ourselves around the incarnation, the reality that God took on flesh and walked among us. Throughout **Epiphany** we tell about Christ's manifestation to the world. Among other events, we recall the magi who came to see him, his baptism in the Jordan River, and his transfiguration.

3. Gross, *Living the Christian Year*.

Like Advent, **Lent** is a season of preparation. Beginning on **Ash Wednesday**, the season of Lent offers us forty days (not counting Sundays) to orient our lives and prepare for the events of Holy Week and Easter. "Forty" is often a liminal phase in the Bible (forty days, forty years), marking the transition from one significant season or stage of life to the next. Thus, during Lent, we have the opportunity to reflect on those areas of our lives that have too strong a hold on us. We can acknowledge, surrender, and repent over the various idols in our lives such as power, addictions, money, control, and security.

During Holy Week, we walk through the major events of our redemption. On **Palm Sunday** we sing and shout "Hosanna!" to the King of kings; however, we also remember the irony of this day as Jesus wept over Jerusalem for her blindness and hardness of heart. On **Maundy Thursday** we remember how Jesus gave us a new mandate to love one another, and we recall the way he demonstrated this by washing the disciples' feet. We celebrate the Lord's Supper, remembering how Jesus first instituted this meal with the disciples. We walk through the sobering events of his arrest, trial, and crucifixion on **Good Friday**. We rise on **Easter Sunday** to celebrate Christ's resurrection and the hope of new life.

Though it is definitely the forgotten festival among evangelicals, many congregations recognize the **Ascension** (either on a Thursday or the following Sunday) and the reality that Christ is now at the right hand of the Father interceding and advocating for his people. We remember the **Day of Pentecost**, celebrating the coming of the Holy Spirit in power to the church. Pentecost is a time to acknowledge the present ministry of the Holy Spirit who empowers, comforts, fills, and guides us, the people of God.

After celebrating the Day of Pentecost, we enter the long **Season after Pentecost**, celebrating our life in the Spirit as the people of God. We begin this season by celebrating **Trinity Sunday**, acknowledging our worship of one God in three persons. We end the Christian year with **Christ the King** Sunday. As we tell God's story, we are formed and transformed, year after year, by the spiritual realities of a living, sanctifying God.

THE REVISED COMMON LECTIONARY

A lectionary is simply a collection of readings or selections from the Scriptures, arranged and intended for proclamation during the worship of the people of God.[4] The Revised Common Lectionary (RCL) was first published in 1992 and contains readings for the Sundays and major festivals over a three-year cycle (Year A, Year B, Year C). The RCL has its roots in Jewish lectionary systems and in early Christian practice. Among our earliest lectionaries are the lists of readings for Holy Week and Easter in fourth-century Jerusalem.[5]

For each Sunday and for special days in the Christian Year, the RCL assigns a group of four readings: an Old Testament reading (first reading), followed by a psalm of response; a reading from one of the New Testament epistles (second reading); and a Gospel reading. The RCL's three-year cycle centers Year A in Matthew, Year B in Mark, and Year C in Luke. The Gospel of John is woven throughout the three-year cycle.

Even though it is the last reading, the Gospel reading is the primary or governing text; it is the "hermeneutical key" to understanding the relationship of the other readings. From the first Sunday of Advent to Trinity Sunday of each year, the Old Testament reading is chosen to complement the Gospel reading of the day. The psalm is a response to the first reading and follows its themes. The epistle is also related to the Gospel reading and gives us insights into the faith and struggles of the early Christian communities.[6]

For the season after Pentecost, the RCL offers two patterns of readings: the complementary track and the semicontinuous track.[7] Each of these tracks uses the same epistle and Gospel readings, but the Old Testament and psalm readings are different. In the complementary track, the Old Testament readings are related to the Gospel reading of the day. In the semicontinuous pattern, the emphasis is on reading through an Old Testament book. In both cases, the psalm is chosen as a response to the Old Testament reading.[8] Each new cycle in the RCL begins on the first Sunday of Advent and ends on Christ the King.

There are a few times throughout the lectionary cycle in which some adjustments will be needed to stay on track. The first adjustment will be during the Christmas season. Depending on the day of the week in which Christmas falls, there may be one or two Sundays after Christmas, before Epiphany (January 6). The second adjustment will occur during

---

4. CCT, *Revised Common Lectionary*, 185.
5. Green, *Connections*, xv.
6. Green, *Connections*, xv.
7. *Engaging God's Story* follows the complementary track.
8. Long, *Feasting on the Word*, xi.

the Sundays after Epiphany. Transfiguration of the Lord is always the last Sunday after Epiphany, however, the number of Sundays in the season after Epiphany can vary based on the date of Ash Wednesday (the beginning of Lent). The third adjustment will occur after Trinity Sunday, during the season after Pentecost. After Trinity Sunday, find the correct proper (note the inclusive dates) and pick up the readings for the corresponding Sunday based on its date.

In summary, the RCL offers a steady diet of Scripture from the Old and New Testaments, follows the cycles and seasons of the Christian year, and forms us spiritually as we regularly feast on God's word.

SOME PRACTICAL CONSIDERATIONS

In the Gospel of John, Jesus encourages us to "abide" in him and to let his words abide in us (John 15:7). In his Letter to the Colossians, the apostle Paul proclaims, "Let the word of Christ dwell in you richly" (Col 3:16). I encourage you to use these devotions, not just as a means of gaining knowledge, but as a means of abiding in Christ and letting his word dwell in you richly. Each week, begin by first reading the four lectionary readings and the devotion section. Next, engage and find application for the word through the questions for reflection. Finally, make the word your own and place it in your heart through the prayer of response.

Each devotion is meant to prepare you for the designated Sunday. It is meant to be read and engaged during the week *leading up to the designated Sunday*. For example, the devotion for the Third Sunday of Advent would be read and engaged during the week leading up to that Sunday as a means to prepare for worship. The desire for this resource is that it would be a means of *cultivating spiritual practices in the home during the week while preparing for corporate worship with the church on Sunday*.

Worship Leaders and Pastors

If you are a worship leader or pastor, you might engage this resource on Monday by first reading the lectionary readings and devotion section, then spending some time with the questions for reflection, and closing with the prayer of response. After spending time in God's word in this way, you will hopefully feel more equipped, creatively and pastorally, to begin crafting your service and/or your sermon for the upcoming Sunday.

After using *Engaging God's Story* to prepare your heart and mind, you may choose to use *Lectionary Journey* for selecting liturgical elements (e.g., call to worship, prayer of renewal, affirmation of faith).[9]

For each Sunday, the prayer of response in *Engaging God's Story* is the same as the prayer of renewal in *Lectionary Journey*. Thus, each week, the lectionary readings and the prayer can help form a bridge between church and home through worship.[10]

Families

If you are a family, you might consider combining your weekly devotion with a meal. After dinner, for example, you might have a Bible and this book ready to engage. You might consider passing around the Bible to give each member of your family (if they are able) the opportunity to locate and read a given passage of Scripture. You could also take turns reading the devotion section, or you may choose to have one person read that section. You could spend some time with the questions for reflection, applying the word to your own personal lives. You could close your time by having one person pray the prayer of response and then having another person pray for the week, highlighting any personal petitions or broader concerns.

As parents, it will be important to gauge the comprehension levels and attention spans of your younger children. You may choose to spread the devotion over multiple days/evenings, reading and covering less content for each family devotion time. For example, you may choose to cover the first reading and psalm one night, and the epistle and Gospel reading another night. If you are *only* able to read the appointed Scriptures together, that would still be a very fruitful and formative time as a family.[11]

---

9. A "prayer of renewal" is a term I use to describe a prayer that typically combines a confession of sin with a petition for the sanctifying or renewing work of the Holy Spirit (Col 3:10). In thinking carefully about the spiritual formation of my congregation, I felt that a petition for the Spirit's renewal was important to accompany a confession of sin. This concept is in line, theologically, with Paul's paradigm of "putting off and putting on" (Col 3:5–17; Eph 4:22–24; Rom 13:12–14).

10. For more information on building a bridge between church and home through worship, see Appendix.

11. For more information on how these devotions can impact the family, see Appendix.

Small Group and Bible Study Leaders

Small group and Bible study leaders may choose to gather, enjoy some fellowship time, open in prayer, and sing a couple of songs. As you shift into opening the word, you might go around and take turns having different people read from the lectionary readings. Then, as the leader you might read the devotion section, or you may choose to also go around and have others participate in reading this section as well. As the leader, you can lead your group through the questions for reflection, with each person seeking to make personal application to his or her own life. Remember, this is an opportunity, not just to fill our minds with biblical knowledge, but to abide with Christ and to let his word dwell in us richly.

A FEW WORDS ON GRAMMAR AND CONTENT

I have chosen to use the present tense in these devotions to capture the "living and active" quality of Scripture (Heb 4:12). Using the present tense offers an engaging tone and brings a sense of immediacy to the word in its relevance and application to our lives.

In addition, I have mostly refrained from using cultural references and personal anecdotes so that these devotions may have a timeless quality to them. My comments and reflections are in the spirit of Nehemiah 8: "They gave the sense, so that the people understood the reading" (Neh 8:8). My role as the author is simply to help you, the reader, engage God's story. Whether you are using this book as a worship leader, a pastor, an individual, a family, or a small group or Bible study leader, I have tried simply to "give the sense" of the word to invite you into deeper reflection and to allow space for the Holy Spirit to be the true and greater guide.

Lastly, these devotions are more like "devotional commentaries," combining biblical reflection with life application. I believe they have more biblical depth than a typical devotion, but not as much as a scholarly commentary.

In closing, I pray that this book will be a blessing to you in whatever capacity you choose to use it. I also pray that this resource would be like leaven, exerting a subtle but profound force in your heart and soul, and that it would provide a steady and stable rhythm for spiritual growth and formation.

The Year of Matthew

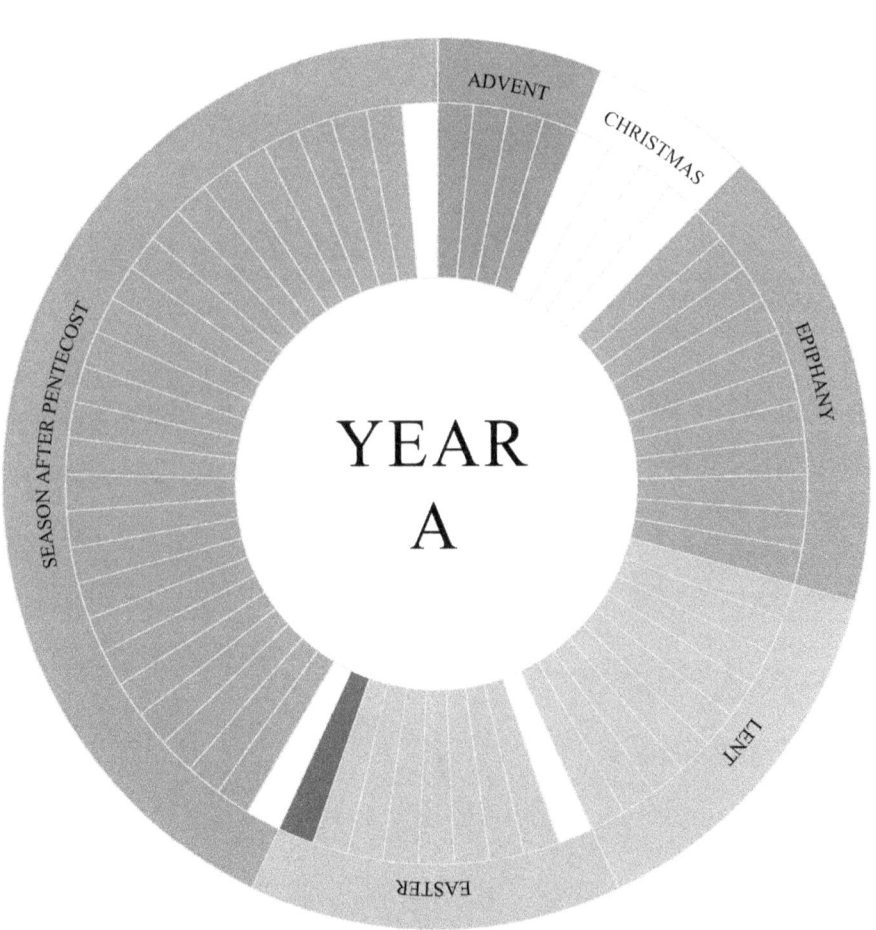

Advent through Epiphany

First Sunday of Advent

LECTIONARY READINGS

>Isaiah 2:1–5
>
>Psalm 122
>
>Romans 13:11–14
>
>Matthew 24:36–44

DEVOTION

In the readings for this Sunday, the first Sunday of Advent, we hear of a time of peace through the prophet Isaiah. The apostle Paul calls us to live wide awake as we anticipate the Lord's return. Jesus also teaches us to be awake and alert, for we do not know the day or hour of his return. Thus, anticipation of Christ's second coming is a common theme in the readings.

Each year, the first Sunday of Advent highlights Christ's second coming, his second advent. The first reading from Isaiah 2 describes a time when nations will flock to the mountain of the Lord. Isaiah describes a time of profound peace. Speaking for the Lord, he declares,

> He shall judge between the nations
> and shall arbitrate for many peoples;
> they shall beat their swords into plowshares
> and their spears into pruning hooks;
> nation shall not lift up sword against nation,
> neither shall they learn war any more. (Isa 2:4)

In this description, the nations are at peace with one another. Weapons for war are transformed into farming tools. Isaiah is describing a time in the future, a time when the kingdom of God will be made manifest in a powerful way. We live now in anticipation of that day, in the "already and not yet" of the kingdom. We do not experience the profound peace of the fullness of God's kingdom, but one day we will. For now, we live each day as instruments of God's peace, making choices that bring his light into this dark world. We live today as Christ's ambassadors of reconciliation.

Psalm 122 is an appropriate psalm of response for it calls us to pray for peace. The psalmist sings,

> Pray for the peace of Jerusalem:
> "May they prosper who love you.
> Peace be within your walls
> and security within your towers."
> For the sake of my relatives and friends
> I will say, "Peace be within you."
> For the sake of the house of the Lord our God,
> I will seek your good. (Ps 122:6–9)

The psalmist is singing about peace within Jerusalem. As New Testament believers, we pray for peace around the world as God's kingdom goes forth powerfully in word and deed. As we enter the Advent season, we should ask how we are living today as instruments of God's peace in the world. Do we pray regularly for our city, our country, and our world? Do we intercede on behalf of world leaders, for nations in conflict, and for struggles within our families, neighborhoods, schools, and our local church? Advent calls us to be a people of prayer, praying for the peace of God's kingdom to be made manifest among us.

The second reading from Romans 13 is a wake-up call from the apostle Paul. Because the Lord's return could be drawing near, Paul writes,

> Let us then throw off the works of darkness and put on the armor of light; let us walk decently as in the day, not in reveling and drunkenness, not in illicit sex and licentiousness, not in quarreling and jealousy. Instead, put on the Lord Jesus Christ, and make no provision for the flesh, to gratify its desires. (Rom 13:12–14)

Paul is calling us to live as if the Lord could return tomorrow. He admonishes us to live honorably and decently, not indulging ourselves in various forms of sin and self-pleasure, but clothing ourselves in the

Lord Jesus Christ. Over and over in his epistles, Paul uses the language of stripping off the old self and clothing ourselves in the new self; laying aside the old and putting on the Lord Jesus Christ.

Too often, we forget our new identity, that we are a new creation in Christ. We are no longer slaves to our former way of life, a life of sin and self-gratification. During Advent, we are reminded to live in light of our Lord's return. We are reminded to live in light of our true identity as sons and daughters of the King.

In the Gospel reading from Matthew 24, Jesus teaches that the day and hour of his return will come at an unexpected time like the flood during Noah's day. People were eating and drinking and had no idea that judgment was about to come upon them. Thus, Jesus exhorts us to be ready and alert. He teaches,

> Keep awake, therefore, for you do not know on what day your Lord is coming. But understand this: if the owner of the house had known in what part of the night the thief was coming, he would have stayed awake and would not have let his house be broken into. Therefore you also must be ready, for the Son of Man is coming at an unexpected hour. (Matt 24:42–44)

The admonition to us is clear: live today as if Jesus could return tomorrow. The exhortation is the same as that of Paul: live wide awake! During the season of Advent, we anticipate the return and judgment of Christ. As believers, we do not need to fear the Lord's return; however, it should inform the way we live. It is all too easy for us to fall into a sense of complacency, to forget about the second coming of Christ and live as if his return is in the distant future. Living in this way would be unwise.

Advent calls us to a sense of urgency and preparation. May we live wide awake, praying for God's kingdom peace and living as Christ's ambassadors of reconciliation. During this season of Advent and throughout the year, may we bring the light of Christ into the darkness of our world.

QUESTIONS FOR REFLECTION

1. What kind of language does Isaiah use to describe a time of peace in the future? How are we to live as instruments of God's peace in the world?

2. For what does the psalmist call us to pray as God's people? Do you intercede for your community, city, nation, and the world? How can you begin to incorporate a rhythm of intercessory prayer into your life?

3. Paul calls us to come awake as the day of Christ's return draws near. What admonitions does Paul give us in Romans 13 that demonstrate what wide-awake living looks like? What is the connection between personal ethics and the reality of Christ's return?

4. Jesus tells us that the day and hour of his return is unknown. Like Paul, he exhorts us to be alert and ready. Have you become complacent in your walk, or do you live with a healthy sense of urgency regarding the day of the Lord? Why does Jesus refer to the days of Noah? How is that relevant to us? How would you live differently today if you knew Christ would come back tomorrow?

PRAYER OF RESPONSE
Based on Matthew 24:36–37, 44

Lord Jesus,
we do not know the day or hour of your return.
Keep us awake and ready,
for your coming will be unexpected.
Help us to lay aside the works of darkness
and put on the armor of light.
By your grace, may we live honorably,
making no provision for sinful desires.
In the name of Jesus we pray. Amen.

Second Sunday of Advent

LECTIONARY READINGS

Isaiah 11:1–10

Psalm 72:1–7, 18–19

Romans 15:4–13

Matthew 3:1–12

DEVOTION

In the readings for this Sunday, we find John the Baptist in the wilderness proclaiming, "Repent, for the kingdom of heaven has come near" (Matt 3:2). Isaiah prophesies of the "stump" and "root" of Jesse who will rule with justice and usher in the peaceable kingdom (Isa 11:1, 10). The apostle Paul speaks of Christ as the one who confirms the promises given to the patriarchs and brings hope to the gentiles. Thus, the themes of hope in Christ, justice, and the root of Jesse are common threads throughout the readings.

In the first reading, we hear of the one who will come from the line of David to rule and reign. Isaiah proclaims,

> A shoot shall come out from the stump of Jesse,
> and a branch shall grow out of his roots.
> The spirit of the Lord shall rest on him,
> the spirit of wisdom and understanding,
> the spirit of counsel and might,
> the spirit of knowledge and the fear of the Lord. (Isa 11:1–2)

This ruler will be filled with wisdom and might, and he will have a heart for the marginalized of society for "with righteousness he shall judge for the poor and decide with equity for the oppressed of the earth" (Isa 11:4). This coming ruler will not favor the rich and powerful, but will bring justice to the oppressed.

Isaiah also describes the peace and harmony that this coming king will bring. He writes,

> The wolf shall live with the lamb,
> the leopard shall lie down with the kid,
> the calf and the lion will feed together,
> and a little child shall lead them.
> The cow and the bear shall graze;
> their young shall lie down together;
> and the lion shall eat straw like the ox. (Isa 11:6–7)

This description should astound and amaze us and fill us with hope. This coming king will bring harmony and restoration, not only to humanity, but to all of creation. This ruler will bring about the redemption for which creation has been longing (Rom 8:19–21).

Psalm 72 is a fitting response to the first reading. Like the ruler in Isaiah 11, the psalmist prays to God, asking for a king who would judge "with righteousness" and "with justice" (Ps 72:2). Also like Isaiah 11, the psalmist prays for righteousness to flourish and for peace to abound under this king. The psalmist is acting as an intercessor for his people as he pours out his heart to God. We all, like the psalmist, long for justice, righteousness, and peace. May our prayers be full of these kinds of petitions, that the kingdom of God would come today in power.

In the second reading, the apostle Paul desires for God's word to bring instruction, encouragement, and hope to God's people. Paul desires unity among the believers so that Christ will be glorified among all peoples of the earth. Paul uses Isaiah's imagery of Christ as the "root of Jesse" in whom "the gentiles shall hope" (Rom 15:12). Indeed, hope is a key theme for Paul in this passage. Paul uses the word twice in his closing prayer that the "God of hope" would fill us with joy and peace and that our hope would abound by "the power of the Holy Spirit" (Rom 15:13). We recognize that, ultimately, hope is a gift from God.

Finally, in the Gospel we read about John the Baptist, the voice in the wilderness calling God's people to repentance for "the kingdom of heaven has come near" (Matt 3:2). John prophesies about Jesus and prepares the way for the one who will come after him, the one who is more powerful than him. He declares:

> I baptize you with water for repentance, but one who is more powerful than I is coming after me, and I am not worthy to carry his sandals. He will baptize you with the Holy Spirit and fire. His winnowing fork is in his hand, and he will clear his threshing floor and will gather his wheat into the granary, but the chaff he will burn with unquenchable fire. (Matt 3:11–12)

John describes the ministry of Jesus as one that divides the wheat from the chaff: the righteous from the unrighteous, the insiders from the outsiders, and those who think they know God from those who humbly know him by faith. Matthew lets us know that John and his message were prophesied by the prophet Isaiah. Many were coming to John, confessing their sins and receiving a baptism of repentance. When the Pharisees and Sadducees arrive, John rebukes them for their righteous arrogance. He speaks of the coming one who will baptize with the Holy Spirit and with fire.

We should take these words to heart and let them convict us of any sense of self-righteousness or superiority. If we know Jesus by faith, we should be grateful that his grace and mercy softened our hard hearts that we would repent and believe that he is our Savior and Lord.

As we reflect on the imagery and truth of these readings, we can find great hope. First, we can place our hope in the fact that God keeps his promises. All of his prophecies will one day be fulfilled. Some of them have already come true. The prophecies of Isaiah and John the Baptist have been fulfilled: the root of Jesse has appeared as Jesus was born from the line of David and on the day of Pentecost, Jesus baptized his church with the promised Holy Spirit. Indeed, everyone who places his or her faith in Jesus Christ receives the gift of the Holy Spirit.

Second, we can find hope in the peaceable kingdom, the day when all of creation will be restored. Isaiah's prophecy of a kingdom that is characterized by peace and harmony should bring us hope. In the midst of the trials, the discord, and the injustice of our current circumstances, we can live expectantly, anticipating the day of ultimate restoration when Jesus returns.

Third, we can rest in the God of hope himself and the promised hope that will abound through the power of the Holy Spirit who dwells within us. Ultimately, our hope is the gift of a gracious, loving, and merciful God who knows our every need. May these promises fill us with hope during this Advent season.

QUESTIONS FOR REFLECTION

1. How does the ancient prophecy and imagery of the "stump" and "root" of Jesse bring you hope and comfort today (Isa 11:1, 10)? Describe the imagery of the peaceable kingdom (Isa 11:6–9). What is God going to renew and restore in the new heaven and the new earth? Do you long for this coming kingdom, its peace and harmony? Explain.

2. The psalmist acted as an intercessor for his people, praying for justice and peace. Do you regularly intercede and pray for the presence and power of God's kingdom to come in our world, our country, our churches, and our homes?

3. Paul talks about hope in Romans 15. How would you define the word hope? Has your understanding of hope been enriched by the passages you read today? Explain.

4. Describe the ministry and baptism of John the Baptist. How did he prepare the way for Jesus? Describe the ministry and baptism of Jesus. What is the meaning of the wheat and the chaff in Matthew 13:12? If you are a believer, how do you live differently today because Jesus has baptized you with the Holy Spirit and fire (Matt 13:11)?

PRAYER OF RESPONSE
Based on Isaiah 11:1–2, 4, 6–7, 9; Matthew 3:1–3

Lord Jesus,
you are the root of Jesse upon whom rests
the spirit of wisdom and understanding, the spirit of counsel and might.
You judge the meek and the poor with righteousness and equality.
As it was prophesied, John came as a voice in the wilderness,
calling us to repentance for your kingdom is near.
We long for the fullness of this peaceable kingdom,
when the wolf shall live with the lamb,
and the cub and the calf shall lie down together.
We place our hope in your promises and look forward to the day
when the earth will be full of the knowledge of the Lord.
In the name of Jesus we pray. Amen.

Third Sunday of Advent

LECTIONARY READINGS

>Isaiah 35:1–10
>
>Psalm 146:5–10
>
>James 5:7–10
>
>Matthew 11:2–11

DEVOTION

In the readings for this Sunday, we hear Isaiah's prophecy of transformation. In the Gospel reading, Jesus quotes from this same passage to assure John the Baptist that he is the Messiah. James calls us to be patient as we await the Lord's return. These are themes for the third Sunday of Advent.

In the first reading from Isaiah 35, the prophet describes the coming of God's kingdom and the restoration that will take place. He declares,

> Then the eyes of the blind shall be opened,
> and the ears of the deaf shall be opened;
> then the lame shall leap like a deer,
> and the tongue of the speechless sing for joy.
> For waters shall break forth in the wilderness,
> and streams in the desert;
> the burning sand shall become a pool, and the thirsty ground springs of water;
> the haunt of jackals shall become a swamp,
> the grass shall become reeds and rushes. (Isa 35:5–7)

The coming of the Lord's kingdom will bring healing and wholeness to those who suffer. The blind shall see, the lame shall walk, and the deaf shall hear. Moreover, creation itself will be transformed and renewed. The dry and thirsty ground shall become "springs of water." Such imagery paints a picture of the redeeming effect that Christ brings to the world.

Psalm 146 echoes this same picture of restoration. The psalmist sings,

> The Lord sets the prisoners free;
> the Lord opens the eyes of the blind.
> The Lord lifts up those who are bowed down;
> the Lord loves the righteous.
> The Lord watches over the strangers;
> he upholds the orphan and the widow,
> but the way of the wicked he brings to ruin. (Ps 146:7b–9)

The theme of physical restoration is prevalent throughout the Scriptures. Jesus came to seek and to save the lost, and he came to heal all that is broken in our world. All of creation has felt the devastating effects of the fall. Jesus came to redeem the world from death and decay. Indeed, the book of Revelation tells us that he is "making all things new" (Rev 21:5). His work of redemption, prophesied in the Old Testament, has begun in his first advent, his first arrival as the child born in Bethlehem. When Jesus put on flesh and walked among us, his ministry of restoration began and his kingdom was inaugurated.

In the second reading from James 5, we are exhorted to be patient as we wait for the Lord to return. James writes,

> Be patient, therefore, brothers and sisters, until the coming of the Lord. The farmer waits for the precious crop from the earth, being patient with it until it receives the early and the late rains. You also must be patient. Strengthen your hearts, for the coming of the Lord is near. Brothers and sisters, do not grumble against one another, so that you may not be judged. (Jas 5:7–9)

James, Jesus' brother, speaks a word of admonition and calls us to exercise patience as we anticipate the Lord's return. He compares such waiting to that of a farmer, waiting for the rains to water the earth. James also calls us to strengthen our hearts as we wait. How does one strengthen his or her heart? Certainly spending regular time in God's word and in prayer, participating each Sunday in corporate worship, building relationships with other Christians, sharing the gospel with friends and neighbors, and serving those in need are all various ways that we strengthen our hearts and our souls. These practices are sometimes referred to as "means of grace" because they feed and nourish our faith; they sustain us in our spiritual journey with Christ as we wait for his return.

Lastly, James offers the exhortation not to grumble with one another. His epistle is filled with much practical wisdom, as exemplified in this simple but profound admonition. How often do we grumble, gossip, and complain about one another? In the context of patiently waiting for Christ's return, James encourages us to love and be patient with one another. May we heed this exhortation during this Advent season and throughout our lives.

In the Gospel reading from Matthew 11, we find John the Baptist sending some of his disciples to question Jesus to make sure that he is truly the Messiah. Jesus sends the disciples back with this response:

> Go and tell John what you hear and see: the blind receive their sight, the lame walk, those with a skin disease are cleansed, the deaf hear, the dead are raised, and the poor have good news brought to them. And blessed is anyone who takes no offense at me. (Matt 11:4–6)

Jesus wants to assure John that he is the one for whom they have been waiting. Using the imagery of Isaiah 35 (the first reading), Jesus describes the healing and restoration that are taking place as his kingdom draws near. The brokenness of the world is being redeemed and restored because the King, the Messiah, has come.

Jesus has commissioned us to bring gospel restoration to those in need. By the power of the word and Spirit, God's healing power reaches those who need physical and spiritual healing. We are the hands and feet of Jesus in this world, sharing the good news of the gospel in word and in deed with our neighbors, our friends, and our families. During this Advent season, may we see brokenness restored and lives transformed even as we await the coming of our King.

QUESTIONS FOR REFLECTION

1. Describe the scope of restoration portrayed in Isaiah 35:1–10. When should we expect this transformation to take place? Do you see this kind of restoration in your own life?

2. Psalm 146 echoes many of the themes in Isaiah 35. Reread Psalm 146:7–9. Can you relate to one of the specific types of restoration mentioned by the psalmist? Explain.

3. James call us to wait patiently for the Lord's return. Do you struggle with waiting on the Lord's timing in your life? What types of practices help to strengthen our hearts (Jas 5:8)? Are any of these practices part of the regular rhythm of your day and week? Do you ever indulge in grumbling with others? What might be a more edifying and God-honoring practice?

4. John the Baptist doubted if Jesus was truly the long-awaited Messiah. Do you ever doubt your faith? Do ever wonder if Jesus is actually present and working in your life? Explain.

PRAYER OF RESPONSE
Based on James 5:7–10; Matthew 11:2–6

Lord Jesus,
give us patience as we wait for your return.
Like John, sometimes we doubt and wonder if your promises are true.
Strengthen our hearts and reassure us for
the blind receive their sight, the lame walk,
the sick are healed, the deaf hear, the dead are raised,
and the poor have good news brought to them.
By your grace, help us not to grumble against one another,
but take the prophets, who spoke in the name of the Lord,
as examples of suffering and patience.
In the name of Jesus we pray. Amen.

Fourth Sunday of Advent

LECTIONARY READINGS

Isaiah 7:10–16

Psalm 80:1-7, 17–19

Romans 1:1–7

Matthew 1:18–25

DEVOTION

In the readings for this Sunday, the prophet Isaiah speaks of a young woman who will give birth to a son, whose name shall be Immanuel. In the Gospel reading from Matthew 1, Joseph has a dream revealing that Mary's child has been conceived by the Holy Spirit and that he is the fulfillment of Isaiah's prophecy, that God is with us. The apostle Paul articulates the gospel message in the opening of his Letter to the Romans. Thus, the good news that God is with us is the common thread in the readings for the fourth Sunday of Advent.

In the first reading from Isaiah 7, the prophet announces that a "young woman" or "virgin woman" will give birth to a son. The context is that King Ahaz is fearful of being invaded, and the Lord gives him a sign. Isaiah declares, "Therefore the Lord himself will give you a sign. Look, the young woman is with child and shall bear a son and shall name him Immanuel" (Isa 7:14).

We see the fulfillment of this prophecy in the birth of Jesus. Jesus is our Immanuel; he is God with us. This is the good news of the gospel. Our God is not distant or aloof. He took on flesh and walked among us. Even now, he is still present and with us through the indwelling Holy

Spirit. During Advent, we remember Jesus' first coming and we anticipate his second coming. During Christmas, we celebrate the reality of the incarnation, the powerful truth that God came down from heaven to dwell with his people and to inaugurate his kingdom on earth.

Psalm 80 is a fitting response as the psalmist pleads that God would come to save his people. The psalmist sings,

> Give ear, O Shepherd of Israel,
> you who lead Joseph like a flock!
> You who are enthroned upon the
> cherubim, shine forth
> before Ephraim and Benjamin and Manasseh.
> Stir up your might,
> and come to save us. (Ps 80:1–2)

On this fourth Sunday of Advent, we embrace the answer to this plea as we remember the promise of Immanuel, that God is with us and that he did come to save us. God will never leave or forsake his people. He loves us so much that he came to earth to redeem and restore all that was broken and in need of salvation. Jesus, our Good Shepherd, came to tend to his flock. One day he will gather his flock together from every tribe and tongue. We will all dwell together in the new heavens and the new earth. Until that time, we wait patiently for his return and serve as his ambassadors on earth.

In the second reading from Romans 1, the apostle Paul articulates the breadth of the gospel in one long sentence. The reality of the incarnation is declared within the third verse. Paul writes,

> Paul, a servant of Jesus Christ, called to be an apostle, set apart for the gospel of God, which he promised beforehand through his prophets in the holy scriptures, the gospel concerning his Son, who was descended from David according to the flesh and was declared to be Son of God with power according to the spirit of holiness by resurrection from the dead, Jesus Christ our Lord. (Rom 1:1–4)

Paul describes the gospel concerning God's Son, "who was descended from David according to the flesh" (Rom 1:3). This reference is about the incarnation, of Immanuel, of God taking on flesh and walking among us. Paul moves quickly from the incarnation to the resurrection as he shares the gospel succinctly with the Romans. This is significant for us as we reflect on the purpose of God coming to his people. His took on flesh to become one of us, to die on the cross to atone for our sins, and to rise from the dead to bring us new life. Our Lord came to this earth to defeat the power of death and to open for us the way to eternal life.

In the Gospel reading from Matthew 1, Joseph encounters an angel of the Lord in a dream. As he is considering how to separate from Mary (who was pregnant) without disgracing her, he is given these words, "Joseph, son of David, do not be afraid to take Mary as your wife, for the child conceived in her is from the Holy Spirit. She will bear a son, and you are to name him Jesus, for he will save his people from their sins" (Matt 1:20–21). Then Matthew adds this commentary: "All this took place to fulfill what had been spoken by the Lord through the prophet: 'Look, the virgin shall become pregnant and give birth to a son, and they shall name him Emmanuel,' which means, 'God is with us'" (Matt 1:22–23).

Matthew's Gospel centers on Joseph while Luke recounts the story of an angel visiting Mary (Luke 1:26–38). Together, Matthew and Luke paint a full picture of the annunciation of Jesus' birth. Matthew gives us a window into Joseph's experience; Luke gives us a window into Mary's experience. Both accounts, however, reveal the promise of one who shall be called Jesus, which means, "God saves." Matthew adds the promise from Isaiah 7 that he shall be called Immanuel, "God is with us."

The good news of the gospel is that, in Jesus, God is with us and God has come to save us. Names are significant, and the names given to our Savior tell us much about his divine mission. During this Advent season, we can embrace the name of Jesus. We know that our Lord came to save his people. He came to defeat the power of death and bring us new life. He has come to redeem and restore us and all of creation.

We also know that he is Immanuel. He is with us and has experienced all that we experience on earth: all the trials, all the sorrows, all the joy, and all the pain. On this fourth Sunday of Advent, we rest in who God is and what he has done for us.

QUESTIONS FOR REFLECTION

1. In the Old Testament, Isaiah declared the promise of Immanuel to King Ahaz. How has that promise been fulfilled in the New Testament? Does the fulfillment of Old Testament promises help you trust in the authority of God's word? Explain.

2. The psalmist pleads for God to save his people (Ps 80:2). How did Jesus fulfill this plea? There is a refrain in Psalm 80: "Restore us, O God; let your face shine, that we may be saved" (Ps 80:3, 7, 19). How is this refrain particularly appropriate during this season?

3. Paul expresses a lot of biblical truth in Romans 1:1–7. What are the major truths that he highlights? Why is the incarnation such a vital aspect of our redemption? How would you share the gospel in one sentence with a nonbeliever?

4. Have you considered how the Scriptures offer us two windows into the annunciation of Jesus' birth: Joseph's experience and Mary's experience? What divine message and guidance did Joseph need to hear? How does God guide us today?

PRAYER OF RESPONSE
Based on Matthew 1:21–23

Lord Jesus,
we thank you for coming to us,
and for saving us from our sins.
During this Advent season,
we stand in awe and wonder
of the fulfillment of your gospel promise:
"The virgin shall conceive and bear a son,
and they shall name him Emmanuel,"
which means, "God is with us."
Help us to walk in faith,
knowing your mighty presence is among us.
In the name of Jesus we pray. Amen.

Christmas Eve

LECTIONARY READINGS

Isaiah 9:2–7

Psalm 96

Titus 2:11–14

Luke 2:1–20

DEVOTION

In the readings for Christmas Eve, we remember the mystery of the incarnation. The Gospel reading from Luke 2, with its familiar storyline, brings us into the wonder and awe of this beloved season of the Christian year. The reading from Isaiah 9 reminds us that the promise of Immanuel was prophesied long ago and found its fulfillment in the birth of Jesus. Psalm 96 fills us with a sense of praise and adoration, like that of the shepherds. The reading from Titus 2 reminds us that the birth of Jesus was the first step in bringing us salvation and transforming us into the likeness of Christ. Thus, the themes of wonder and awe, prophecy and fulfillment, salvation and transformation are threads in the readings for this evening.

In the first reading from Isaiah 9, the prophet declares the words that are so familiar to us now:

> For a child has been born for us,
> a son given to us;
> authority rests upon his shoulders,
> and he is named
> Wonderful Counselor, Mighty God,
> Everlasting Father, Prince of Peace. (Isa 9:6)

Each year, we remember and recall this prophecy. When we pause, however, and reflect on the fact that this prophecy was declared hundreds of years before Christ's birth, our faith is strengthened in the faithfulness of God and his divine word.

Christmas is a time to rest in the covenant faithfulness of our God. For centuries, the people of God waited for the messiah, the one who would bring salvation and establish his kingdom. On this Christmas Eve, we praise God for fulfilling his promises and sending us the one who is our Wonderful Counselor, Mighty God, Everlasting Father, Prince of Peace.

Jesus is the one who leads us and guides us; the one who fights for us and goes before us in his strength and might. He is the one who remains faithful and cares for us forever; the one who shepherds us and brings us peace. On this Christmas Eve, we praise him for who he is and for all of his mighty deeds.

Psalm 96 is fitting for this evening when we stand in awe and wonder before the Prince of Peace. The psalmist sings, "Sing to the Lord; bless his name; tell of his salvation from day to day. Declare his glory among the nations, his marvelous works among all the peoples" (Ps 96:2–3). Songs of praise are the appropriate response on Christmas Eve, the night that we remember the newborn King.

The nativity of Jesus is full of songs, and our own voices simply join the heavenly host as well as the saints before us who have expressed their own praise throughout the centuries. As we remember the birth of Jesus, we sing a new song to the Lord and ascribe to him the glory due his name. And throughout the year, we seek to tell others about Jesus, sharing "his marvelous works among the peoples" (Ps 96:3).

In the second reading from Titus 2, the apostle Paul references the birth of Christ when he declares, "For the grace of God has appeared, bringing salvation to all" (Titus 2:11). This grace and salvation, however, do not leave us unchanged. The birth of Jesus is a first step in our spiritual transformation. The salvation of Christ is "training us to renounce impiety and worldly passions" and "to live lives that are self-controlled, upright, and godly" (Titus 2:12).

As Jesus took on flesh and walked among us, he showed us the example we are to follow, and he provided the means of our transformation. By sending us the Holy Spirit, we have the necessary power to lead lives that are upright and godly; we have the grace to renounce what is evil in this world. The reality of the incarnation is part of the divine plan of salvation, sanctifying us into the likeness of Christ.

Finally, in the Gospel reading from Luke 2, we find the familiar narrative and cast of characters that fill us with wonder and awe each year. We remember the shepherds, who were first given the message of good news by one angel and then received a chorus of praise by a host of angels, declaring, "Glory to God in the highest heaven, and on earth peace among those whom he favors" (Luke 2:14). It is hard for us to imagine the beauty and power of this encounter, but we know the shepherds' response was one of joy and urgency.

We also remember Mary and Joseph, who received the report from the shepherds about the baby Jesus. We sit with Mary on this Christmas Eve and treasure the message of Christ and ponder it in our hearts. We reflect on this joy of salvation and the wonder of the incarnation on this Christmas Eve. May we not leave this night unchanged, but continue to be transformed by the power of the Spirit at work within us. May we share this good news of great joy, telling others about our Wonderful Counselor, Mighty God, Everlasting Father, and Prince of Peace.

QUESTIONS FOR REFLECTION

1. How does Isaiah's prophecy affect your view of the Bible and God's promises? Do you see God's covenant faithfulness in Isaiah 9:2–7? Explain. Which of the titles stands out to you (Wonderful Counselor, Mighty God, Everlasting Father, Prince of Peace) and why?

2. In Psalm 96, the psalmist exhorts us to sing a new song to the Lord. Why is song such a vital part of the lives of the people of God? Why is song so prevalent during this time of year?

3. In Titus 2:11–14, Paul describes how we are changed by the grace of God and salvation. How does he describe how we are to live? Can you see these changes in your own life? Describe.

4. In the familiar narrative of Luke 2:1–20, what stands out to you this year? Do you relate to the shepherds, their praise and joy? Do you resonate with Mary who "treasured all these words and pondered them in her heart" (Luke 2:19)? Describe.

PRAYER OF RESPONSE
Based on Luke 2:15–20

Lord Jesus, on this holy night,
fill us with anticipation as we celebrate your birth.
Like the shepherds, may we seek you
with a sense of urgency and joy;
may we glorify and praise you
for your faithfulness and goodness to us.
Your word and your promises are true.
Out of an overflow of joy in our hearts,
help us to share our faith with boldness,
and may all who hear it be amazed by your great deeds.
As we sing and pray and remember the incarnation, like Mary,
we have much to treasure and ponder in our hearts.
You are Immanuel, the God who is with us. Amen.

Christmas Day

LECTIONARY READINGS

    Isaiah 52:7–10

    Psalm 98

    Hebrews 1:1–12

    John 1:1–14

DEVOTION

In the readings for Christmas day we celebrate both the humanity and the divinity of Christ. The Gospel reading from John 1 echoes the first words of the Bible from Genesis 1: "In the beginning" (Gen 1:1 ESV). John then describes Jesus as the eternal Word. The author of Hebrews also writes a very eloquent and rich introduction to his epistle, describing Jesus as the Son who is the reflection of God's glory. The first reading from Isaiah 52 speaks of the one who will bring salvation to God's people. Thus, the common thread for Christmas Day is that Jesus is the eternal Word, the Son of God, and the salvation of the world.

In the first reading from Isaiah 52, the prophet speaks of a future day when God will bring salvation to his people. He declares,

> Break forth; shout together for joy,
> you ruins of Jerusalem,
> for the Lord has comforted his people;
> he has redeemed Jerusalem.
> The Lord has bared his holy arm
> before the eyes of all the nations,
> and all the ends of the earth shall see
> the salvation of our God. (Isa 52:9–10)

The prophet was promising the restoration of God's people from their time in exile in Babylon. Ultimately, this restoration was brought about through the life, death, resurrection, and ascension of Jesus. He is the one who has brought redemption and salvation to all the nations of the world. One day every tribe and tongue will bow before the King of kings and Lord of lords, for the child born in Bethlehem is the Savior of the world.

Psalm 98 is a joyful response to this first reading. The psalmist calls for a symphony of praise unto God. He sings,

> Make a joyful noise to the Lord,
> all the earth;
> break forth into joyous song and sing praises.
> Sing praises to the Lord with the lyre,
> with the lyre and the sound of melody.
> With trumpets and the sound of the horn
> make a joyful noise before the King, the Lord. (Ps 98:4–6)

Indeed, song was the way in which Mary and Simeon expressed their joy in the reality of the Messiah. The angels burst forth into song, heralding the birth of Jesus to the shepherds. In Luke's Gospel, the exhortation of Psalm 98 is fulfilled. Song is a gift given to us by our Creator to express the depths of the gospel, the intimacy that we share with him, and the fellowship that we enjoy with one another. Christmas is certainly a time and a season to sing and make a joyful noise for all of these reasons!

The second reading from Hebrews 1 is an eloquent description of the humanity and divinity of Christ. The author of Hebrews writes,

> Long ago God spoke to our ancestors in many and various ways by the prophets, but in these last days he has spoken to us by a Son, whom he appointed heir of all things, through whom he also created the worlds. He is the reflection of God's glory and the exact imprint of God's very being, and he sustains all things by his powerful word. (Heb 1:1–3)

These opening words to the book of Hebrews are a nice complement to the opening of John's Gospel. Both speak of Jesus as the final Word. Once God spoke through prophets, now he has spoken through his Son. This Son is the creator and sustainer of all things. Moreover, he is the "reflection of God's glory and the exact imprint of God's very being." This is a straightforward articulation of the divinity of Christ.

The child born in Bethlehem is also fully human. He cried, wet his diaper, and nursed from Mary's breasts; and yet, the baby in her arms is the one who created her. This is the mystery of the incarnation. This is the grace and glory of a God who would become one of us so that he could save us.

In the Gospel reading from John 1, we hear the echo of Genesis 1. Unlike Matthew, Mark, and Luke, John begins his Gospel in a more poetic fashion. John was written after the Synoptics, and he offers us a different perspective on the incarnation. Rather than an earth-bound nativity scene, John gives us a cosmic perspective. He writes,

> In the beginning was the Word, and the Word was with God, and the Word was God. He was in the beginning with God. All things came into being through him, and without him not one thing came into being. (John 1:1–3)

Jesus is the eternally-begotten Son, with the Father from the beginning. He is the one through whom all things have come into existence. The wonder of the incarnation is that eternity stepped into time. God put on flesh and walked among us. The light of the world came quietly into the darkness of night.

The baby born in Bethlehem came with a mission, to bring light and life to all people. He came, full of grace and truth, so that we might understand the nature of God. The great message of Christmas is this: to all who receive him, who believe in his name, he gives the power to become children of God, born, not of blood or of the will of the flesh or of the will of man but of God. Will you receive him this Christmas?

QUESTIONS FOR REFLECTION

1. What is the immediate context for Isaiah 52? What is the ultimate fulfillment of Isaiah's prophecy? What are the "ruins" that Jesus came to restore?

2. The psalmist exhorts God's people to sing and make a joyful noise in Psalm 98. How did singing fill the air at the news of Christ's birth? Song is a gift to us for expressing the depth of our relationship with the Lord. Is song a regular part of your daily and weekly worship? Explain.

3. Reflecting on Hebrews 1:1–12, how does God speak to us today? How does the author of Hebrews describe Jesus as being God? Why would the author of Hebrews need to make this clear, even describing Jesus as superior to the angels? How does knowing that Jesus is fully God and fully human affect the way you approach him in your own life?

4. John offers a cosmic perspective of Jesus in the opening of his Gospel. How is this different from the other Gospel accounts? Why would John open with the phrase "In the beginning"? Why would an echo from Genesis 1 be important for John? What does being a child of God mean to you this Christmas season?

PRAYER OF RESPONSE
Based on John 1:1–5, 9, 14

Lord Jesus,
on this day we celebrate the incarnation;
we remember that though you were born in time as a baby,
you were in the beginning as the Word.
You are the light that shines in the darkness,
and you are the true light, which enlightens everyone.
You became flesh and lived among us,
and we have seen your glory,
the glory as of a father's only son, full of grace and truth.
In the name of Jesus we pray. Amen.

First Sunday after Christmas

LECTIONARY READINGS

Isaiah 63:7–9

Psalm 148

Hebrews 2:10–18

Matthew 2:13–23

DEVOTION

In the readings for this Sunday, the prophet Isaiah recounts the gracious deeds of the Lord. The author of Hebrews teaches how Jesus became like one of us, his brothers and sisters, so that he could be our faithful high priest. Matthew describes the way the child Jesus was protected from Herod. Thus, remembrance, mediation, and protection are themes in the readings for the first Sunday after Christmas.

In the first reading from Isaiah 63, the prophet remembers the acts of God. He proclaims,

> I will recount the gracious deeds of the Lord,
> the praiseworthy acts of the Lord,
> because of all that the Lord has done for us
> and the great favor to the house of Israel
> that he has shown them according to his mercy,
> according to the abundance of his steadfast love. (Isa 63:7)

The prophets often played the role of covenant historians for the people of God, reminding them and recounting all of the ways the Lord had acted and intervened on their behalf. In this passage, Isaiah seems to recount the time after the exodus as God was present among his people while they were in their distress. He declares, "It was no messenger or angel but his presence that saved them; in his love and pity it was he who redeemed them; he lifted them up and carried them all the days of old" (Isa 63:9).

The language of Isaiah reminds us of how the Lord appeared to the people of Israel in a pillar of cloud by day and a pillar of fire by night (Exod 13:21) and how his glory, his divine presence, filled the tabernacle (Exod 40:34). Divine presence is the all throughout the Christmas story. The Gospel narrative for this Sunday recounts how an angel of the Lord guided Joseph and his family to Egypt, to Israel, and then to Galilee. The Lord was with them, leading and guiding them to safety. The Lord's divine presence was made known to us through the incarnation as Jesus took on flesh and "tabernacled" among us (John 1:14).

The Lord still leads, guides, and protects us today. Through his word and through the Spirit, we receive direction and guidance. Moreover, his presence is made known to us through the Spirit who dwells within us, individually and corporately (1 Cor 3:16; 2 Cor 6:16), and he protects us in countless ways through his divine intercession (Heb 7:25; Rom 8:31–34). We serve a gracious and merciful God who is not distant, but intimately involved in the lives of his covenant children.

Psalm 148 fills us with praise in response to God's gracious acts, recounted in the first reading from Isaiah 63. The psalmist sings,

> Let them praise the name of the Lord,
> for his name alone is exalted;
> his glory is above earth and heaven.
> He has raised up a horn for his people,
> praise for all his faithful,
> for the people of Israel who are close to him.
> Praise the Lord! (Ps 148:13–14)

God has raised up a horn for his people, a horn of salvation (Luke 1:69), Jesus Christ our Lord. This is the basis of our praise and our joy. Think of all the music and praise that surrounded the birth of Jesus. Praise and worship are the most natural responses to our Lord and Savior.

The psalmist also speaks of how we are brought close to God. This is the climax of this psalm and of the gospel: "And I heard a loud voice from the throne saying, 'Behold, the dwelling place of God is with man. He will dwell with them, and they will be his people, and God himself will be with them as their God'" (Rev 21:3, ESV). In the new heaven and the new earth, we will dwell with God forever. As his people, we will praise and worship the King of kings and Lord of lords. People from every tribe and tongue will bow before the Lamb of God. Our eternal praise begins now as we remember God's might deeds, past, present, and future.

In the second reading from Hebrews 2, the author uses familial language in describing our relationship with Jesus and with God. He writes,

> For the one who sanctifies and those who are sanctified all have one Father. For this reason Jesus is not ashamed to call them brothers and sisters, saying, "I will proclaim your name to my brothers and sisters; in the midst of the congregation I will praise you." (Heb 2:11–12)

The author of Hebrews teaches us a profound message. First, we are Jesus' brothers and sisters; we are part of the family of God. Second, Jesus is our true worship leader, the one who proclaims the Lord to us and a voice singing in our midst. Jesus is our prophet and our priest. After proclaiming that Jesus defeated death, the author of Hebrews describes how he had to become one of us. He writes,

> Therefore he had to become like his brothers and sisters in every respect, so that he might become a merciful and faithful high priest in the service of God, to make a sacrifice of atonement for the sins of the people. Because he himself was tested by what he suffered, he is able to help those who are being tested. (Heb 2:17-18)

Jesus is both the sacrifice and our high priest. Through his death, he atoned for our sin; through his life of suffering, he is qualified to be our high priest and to intercede on our behalf. This is why Jesus had to come and dwell among us. He had to be the perfect, spotless Lamb of God who takes away the sin of the world. He also had to face all of the trials and temptations that we do, yet without sin, so that he could be our great high priest, able to sustain us and help us in our time of need. And his priesthood is eternal. We are known by Jesus throughout our entire life on earth and into eternity in the new heaven and the new earth.

In the Gospel reading from Matthew 2, we read of the Lord's guidance and protection of the child Jesus. First, Joseph receives the divine word to flee to Egypt to escape the atrocities of King Herod. Seeking to destroy the young Jesus, Herod had commanded that children two years old or under were to be murdered. These are remembered as the "holy innocents." Next, Joseph is given divine guidance to return to Israel and then to go to Galilee.

The Lord was merciful and gracious to Joseph and Mary in protecting the young Jesus. God still protects his children today. This is the message of the first Sunday after Christmas. The child born in Bethlehem, protected and sustained by God, is now at the Father's right hand, where he ever lives to make intercession for us.

QUESTIONS FOR REFLECTION

1. The prophet Isaiah recounts the gracious deeds of the Lord. What were some of these mighty acts and deeds? What are some of the great things the Lord has done in your own life?

2. The psalmist is full of praise in Psalm 148. First the psalmist directs humans, animals, and all of the cosmos to praise the Lord, and then he gives the reasons why we should praise him. What are some of the reasons we are called to praise and worship the Lord?

3. How is it that we are called Jesus' brothers and sisters? How is Jesus both the sacrifice for our sins and our high priest? What does it mean that Jesus proclaims the Lord's name to us and sings among us (Heb 2:12)?

4. God gave Joseph divine guidance and protection. How does God guide, sustain, and protect you today?

PRAYER OF RESPONSE
Based on Isaiah 63:7–9; Matthew 2:19–23

Redeeming Lord,
we will recount your gracious deeds,
praiseworthy acts, and all that you have done for us.
In all of our distress, it is your presence that saves and comforts us.
You lift us up and carry us; you sustain us all the days our lives.
Like Joseph, you protect us and guide us
though there is evil and warfare all around us.
When we face temptation, you provide a way of escape.
We thank you for your mercy and the abundance of your steadfast love.
In the name of the Father, Son, and Holy Spirit. Amen.

Second Sunday after Christmas

LECTIONARY READINGS

> Jeremiah 31:7–14
>
> Psalm 147:12–20
>
> Ephesians 1:3–14
>
> John 1:1–18

DEVOTION

In the readings for the second Sunday after Christmas, the prophet Jeremiah describes the faithfulness of God in bringing the exiled people of God back home. The psalmist sings of God's sovereign care and control of all his creation. The apostle Paul reminds us of all of the spiritual blessings we have in Christ, that we are adopted sons and daughters. The Gospel narrative from John 1 gives us, not a nativity story like Matthew and Luke, but a beautiful and rich picture of Jesus as the Word, who has been from the beginning. All of these images and narratives allow us to further ponder the reality of the incarnation.

The first reading from Jeremiah 31 offers us the description of the people of God returning from exile back to the promised land. The prophet declares,

> For thus says the Lord:
> Sing aloud with gladness for Jacob,
> and raise shouts for the chief of the nations;
> proclaim, give praise, and say,
> "Save, O Lord, your people,
> the remnant of Israel."

> See, I am going to bring them from the land of the north
> and gather them from the farthest parts of the earth,
> among them the blind and the lame,
> those with child and those in labor, together;
> a great company, they shall return here. (Jer 31:7–8)

The prophet offered hope to God's people during a time of darkness and despair. God brought about the salvation of his people and brought back all those who had suffered under the hands of their enemies. The prophet does not shy away from the grief and sorrow they experienced, for he states, "With weeping they shall come, and with consolation I will lead them back" (Jer 31:9); however, the Lord will remain faithful to shepherd his people. He will provide for them and restore them once again.

The Lord deals with us in the same way. Though we may not be physically exiled to a foreign country, we can sometimes feel distanced from God through the various trials we face and through the various patterns of sin that squelch our intimacy with the Lord. Our sin can cause us to hide from God, living in guilt and shame, rather than drawing close to the loving embrace of our Father. The season of Christmas reminds us, however, that God came near. He came to earth to ransom sinners, to bring us home, and restore our fellowship with him.

In Psalm 147, the psalmist sings of God's sovereign care over all of his creation, including his people, saying,

> He sends out his command to the earth;
> his word runs swiftly.
> He gives snow like wool;
> he scatters frost like ashes.
> He hurls down hail like crumbs—
> who can stand before his cold?
> He sends out his word and melts them;
> he makes the wind blow, and the waters flow. (Ps 147:15–18)

The Lord is faithful in his governance of all his creation, guiding and sustaining the wind as well as streams, river currents, and ocean tides. The amazing aspect of this psalm, however, is that the same God who sustains creation also provides sustained and loving care for his people. The psalmist sings, "For he strengthens the bars of your gates; he blesses your children within you. He grants peace within your borders; he fills you with the finest of wheat" (Ps 147:13–14).

During this Christmas season, as we ponder the reality of the incarnation, may we remember that this baby is the King of the earth. He is the Word who was from the beginning, creating and sustaining the earth; yet, he came to save his chosen people, to bring them his word (Ps 147:19–20), and to *be* the living Word to them.

In the second reading from Ephesians 1, the apostle Paul reminds us of all of the spiritual blessings that are ours in Christ. He writes,

> He predestined us for adoption to himself as sons through Jesus Christ, according to the purpose of his will, to the praise of his glorious grace, with which he has blessed us in the Beloved. In him we have redemption through his blood, the forgiveness of our trespasses, according to the riches of his grace, which he lavished upon us, in all wisdom and insight. (Eph 1:5–8, ESV)

In Christ, we are adopted children, sons and daughters of God. In addition, we have redemption and forgiveness; we are no longer slaves to sin, but live in the freedom and grace of our loving Savior. Christmas is the beginning of the unveiling of God's plan, "the mystery of his will" (Eph 1:9). Through the incarnation, God began the rescue and salvation of his people. In Jeremiah 31, we saw God restore his people and bring them back home. In Ephesians 1, we see the ultimate restoration plan, beginning with the incarnation. God became one of us so that he could redeem us and adopt us as his sons and daughters.

Finally, in the Gospel reading from John 1, we hear the beautiful, eloquent, and profound description of Jesus as the Word. John writes,

> In the beginning was the Word, and the Word was with God, and the Word was God. He was in the beginning with God. All things came into being through him, and without him not one thing came into being. What has come into being in him was life, and the life was the light of all people. The light shines in the darkness, and the darkness did not overtake it. (John 1:1–5)

The season of Christmas reminds us that light has come into the darkness. Jesus, the one through whom all things were created, has come to bring life to all people. The prologue to John's Gospel is unlike the birth narratives found in Matthew and Luke. John takes us all the way back to the beginning. He reveals that Jesus was with God and that Jesus is God.

The wonder of the incarnation is the reality that God "became flesh and lived among us" and showed us his glory, "the glory as of a father's only son, full of grace and truth" (John 1:14). Jesus dwelt among his people and revealed the glory of God to us. Christmas reminds us that the baby born in a manger is our creator and our redeemer; he is the obedient son who came to shine light into the darkness and save his people. As we celebrate the days of Christmas, may we linger in the reality of our salvation and shine Christ's light to those around us who need to hear the gospel of freedom and forgiveness.

QUESTIONS FOR REFLECTION

1. The prophet Jeremiah brings the hope of restoration to the people of God in exile. What does exile look like in your own life? How does God restore you and lead you back home when you try to isolate and hide from him?

2. In Psalm 147, the psalmist describes God's sovereign care over creation and over his people. How does God's control and authority comfort you? Describe God's sovereign care over your own life? How does God reveal that he is concerned about the details of your life?

3. In Ephesians 1, Paul enumerates the spiritual blessings we have in Christ. Which of these blessings stands out to you in particular? Why? What is the "mystery" of God's will that Paul expresses in Ephesians 1:9? What does it mean that we are "marked with the seal of the promised Holy Spirit" (Eph 1:13)? How does this encourage you?

4. The prologue to John's Gospel is different from the birth narratives in Matthew and Luke. What language does John use to describe Jesus? How does this description complement the narratives of Matthew and Luke? Does your life shine Christ's light into the darkness of our world? Describe.

PRAYER OF RESPONSE
Based on Ephesians 1:3–5

Our Father,
we praise you for blessing us in Christ
with every spiritual blessing in the heavenly places,
and for choosing us in Christ before the foundation of the world
to be holy and blameless before you in love.
We thank you that you predestined us for adoption
as your children through Jesus Christ,
according to the good pleasure of your will.
In the name of Jesus we pray. Amen.

Epiphany of the Lord

LECTIONARY READINGS

Isaiah 60:1–6

Psalm 72:1–7, 10–14

Ephesians 3:1–12

Matthew 2:1–12

DEVOTION

Epiphany (January 6) is the original celebration of Christ's birth in the East.[1] This festival celebrated the baptism of Jesus; later, in the West, it incorporated the visit of the wise men.[2]

In the readings for Epiphany, we hear the prophecy from Isaiah 60 that nations would be drawn to the light of the Lord and would bring gifts of gold and frankincense. The psalmist sings of kings bringing gifts and falling down in worship before the Lord. In Ephesians 3, the apostle Paul speaks of the "mystery of Christ," that the gentiles have become part of the family of God. The Gospel reading from Matthew 2 recalls the visit of the wise men (or magi) to Bethlehem, bringing gifts from afar and bowing before the baby Jesus. Thus, the themes of kingship, worship, and the light of Christ to the nations are common threads in the readings for this Sunday.

In the first reading from Isaiah 60, the prophet declares,

> Arise, shine, for your light has come,
> and the glory of the Lord has risen upon you.

---

[1] Adam, *Liturgical Year*, 144.

[2] Adam, *Liturgical Year*, 145.

> For darkness shall cover the earth
> and thick darkness the peoples,
> but the Lord will arise upon you,
> and his glory will appear over you.
> Nations shall come to your light
> and kings to the brightness of your dawn. (Isa 60:1–3)

In this portion of Isaiah (chapters 40–66), the prophet is speaking about the future restoration of God's people. In this particular passage, he is speaking of the reality of God's light reaching the nations. This promise if fulfilled in the visit of the wise men to Bethlehem.

In addition, the prophet states that people from foreign lands "shall bring gold and frankincense and shall proclaim the praise of the Lord" (Isa 60:6). Isaiah provides us with many specific descriptions of events connected to the life of Christ (Isa 9:6–7; 53:1–12). This verse is one such example.

When we connect the dots between Isaiah 60:1–6 and the coming of the wise men to Bethlehem to see the baby Jesus, we discover the covenant faithfulness of God. We see how God fulfills his promises, made to the people of God hundreds of years before the events took place. Here, we understand how the visit of the wise men was part of bringing the nations to the light of Christ.

Psalm 72 is an appropriate psalm of response. The psalmist sings,

> May the kings of Tarshish and of the isles
> render him tribute;
> may the kings of Sheba and Seba bring gifts.
> May all kings fall down before him,
> all nations give him service. (Ps 72:10–11)

Such actions are displayed by the wise men. They brought him gifts and bowed before him. Such actions would be expected when one is in the presence of the Lord. The psalmist offers the reasons why such worship is a natural response. He writes, "For he delivers the needy when they call, the poor and those who have no helper. He has pity on the weak and needy and saves the lives of the needy. From oppression and violence he redeems their life, and precious is their blood in his sight" (Ps 72:12–14).

The psalmist is prophetically expressing the messianic mission of Christ. The language of Psalm 72:12–14 finds echoes in Luke 4. Luke writes,

When he came to Nazareth, where he had been brought up, he went to the synagogue on the Sabbath day, as was his custom. He stood up to read, and the scroll of the prophet Isaiah was given to him. He unrolled the scroll and found the place where it was written:

> "The Spirit of the Lord is upon me,
> because he has anointed me
> to bring good news to the poor.
> He has sent me to proclaim release to the captives
> and recovery of sight to the blind,
> to set free those who are oppressed,
> to proclaim the year of the Lord's favor."

And he rolled up the scroll, gave it back to the attendant, and sat down. The eyes of all in the synagogue were fixed on him. Then he began to say to them, "Today this scripture has been fulfilled in your hearing." (Luke 4:16–21)

The baby born in Bethlehem and baptized in the Jordan has rescued his people. Because of the nature of who he is and what he has done, worship is the only response. When we truly reflect on and recall who Jesus is and how he has saved us and freed us, our lives should be a living sacrifice of praise to him (Rom 12:1).

In the second reading from Ephesians 3, the apostle Paul writes about the inclusive nature of the kingdom, how all nations, not just the Jews, are part of the family of God. He writes,

> In former generations this mystery was not made known to humankind, as it has now been revealed to his holy apostles and prophets by the Spirit: that is, the gentiles have become fellow heirs, members of the same body, and sharers in the promise in Christ Jesus through the gospel. (Eph 3:5–6)

In this passage, Paul is making it clear that the message of forgiveness, adoption, and restoration is for all people. The Epiphany of the Lord is a time to celebrate and remember this truth. As we remember the visit of the wise men, we celebrate the far reach of the gospel to people of every tribe and tongue.

Finally, in the Gospel reading from Matthew 2, we continue the story of the birth of Jesus by reading of the amazing journey of the wise men. Matthew writes,

> In the time of King Herod, after Jesus was born in Bethlehem of Judea, magi from the east came to Jerusalem, asking, "Where is the child who has been born king of the Jews? For we observed his star in the east and have come to pay him homage." (Matt 2:1–2)

We do not know all of the details of their journey, but we can imagine it was long and arduous. These men, however, were on a mission. They were following a star to find one born king of the Jews. Matthew informs us of the evil intentions of Herod to kill this child; however, the wise men were able to avoid his schemes and find the Christ child. Matthew writes,

> When they saw that the star had stopped, they were overwhelmed with joy. On entering the house, they saw the child with Mary his mother, and they knelt down and paid him homage. Then, opening their treasure chests, they offered him gifts of gold, frankincense, and myrrh. And having been warned in a dream not to return to Herod, they left for their own country by another road. (Matt 2:10–12)

This Gospel narrative is the fulfillment of what we have read and discussed in the previous readings. We find the nations being drawn to the light of God; we find them offering gifts and bowing in worship before the baby Jesus. As we have discussed, this narrative reminds us of the steadfast love of the Lord and his commitment to fulfilling all of his promises to his people.

The steadfast love of the Lord should bring us hope no matter our circumstances. We can rest in knowing that the Lord will protect us and go before us as he did with the wise men (Matt 2:12). Moreover, the faithfulness of God should bring us to kneel before our loving Savior and offer our praise and adoration. And though we do not need to bring gifts of gold, incense, and myrrh, we do bring him our lives. We offer our time, treasure, and talents to him who is worthy of our whole-life devotion.

As we remember the Epiphany of the Lord, may we seek to bring the light of Christ to those around us. By the grace of God and the power of the Spirit, may we lead lives of humble submission to the one true King, and may we worship and adore him every day we draw breath.

QUESTIONS FOR REFLECTION

1. Why would the message of Isaiah 60:1–6 be of comfort and encouragement to the people of God long ago? How does this passage prophesy of the coming of the wise men in Matthew 2? How does this passage find application in our lives today? Are those around you drawn to the light of Christ within you? Describe.

2. In Psalm 72, we read of kings worshiping the messianic king. How do such prophecies bring you hope today? The psalmist qualifies our worship by connecting it to the life of the King: how he delivers the needy, has pity on the weak, and saves us. How is this passage connected to Luke 4:16–21 (which was referenced earlier)? How has Jesus brought freedom and restoration to your life? How does his work in you bring about worship and gratitude in your life?

3. Paul reveals the "mystery of Christ" (Eph 3:4). In your own words, what is this mystery that has now been revealed? Why is this significant for us today?

4. What motivated and inspired the wise men from the East to take on such a long journey? What were some of their obstacles? How did God guide them and protect them? What was their response to the baby Jesus? How does God guide and protect us today? How does your life reveal your love and devotion to King Jesus? What gifts do you offer him?

PRAYER OF RESPONSE
Based on Matthew 2:1–2, 10–12

Lord Jesus,
during this Epiphany season,
we recognize you as King.
Like the wise men from the East, may we seek you,
find you, and be overwhelmed with joy.
By your grace, help us to offer our very lives to you,
and to love you with all of our heart, soul, mind, and strength.
Forsaking the many idols that tempt us, may we bow our knees
before you each day, yielding and surrendering to your grace and mercy.
In the name of Jesus we pray. Amen.

Baptism of the Lord

LECTIONARY READINGS

>Isaiah 42:1–9
>
>Psalm 29
>
>Acts 10:34–43
>
>Matthew 3:13–17

DEVOTION

In the readings for Baptism of the Lord Sunday, we find Jesus being baptized by John. We see the Spirit descend upon him like a dove, and we hear the voice of the Lord revealing Jesus as his beloved Son. The prophet Isaiah declares the first of four servant songs. This servant song is ultimately fulfilled in the person and life of Jesus, the one who sets the prisoners free and who is a light to the nations. The apostle Peter delivers a sermon to a Roman centurion (Cornelius), recounting the life and ministry of Jesus and then shares the gospel of salvation to Cornelius's household. Thus, baptism, sonship, daughterhood, and being a light to the nations are common threads in the readings for this Sunday.

In the first reading from Isaiah 42, the servant of the Lord is described. The prophet declares,

> Here is my servant, whom I uphold,
> my chosen, in whom my soul delights;
> I have put my spirit upon him;
> he will bring forth justice to the nations.
> He will not cry or lift up his voice
> or make it heard in the street;

> a bruised reed he will not break,
> and a dimly burning wick he will not quench;
> he will faithfully bring forth justice.
> He will not grow faint or be crushed
> until he has established justice in the earth;
> and the coastlands wait for his teaching. (Isa 42:1–4)

The description of the servant of the Lord is fulfilled in the life and ministry of Jesus. He is the one who will bring forth justice to the nations; he is the one who is compassionate toward the broken and the hurting, the "bruised reeds" and the "dimly burning wicks." Whenever Jesus encountered people with chronic ailments and disease, he always demonstrated kindness and compassion. He never avoided asking hard, probing questions, but he always maintained a posture of mercy and love. We can learn much from Jesus' ministry to the bruised reeds and dimly burning wicks of this world, people who may be holding on by a thread. Jesus made time for these people.

Moreover, with regard to Jesus' baptism, one of the key descriptions of that event was how the spirit descended upon him like a dove. This fulfills the prophecy that states, "I have put my spirit upon him" (Isa 42:1). Jesus was anointed by God and filled with the Spirit for his ministry on earth.

Psalm 29 is a strong response to the first reading as the "voice of the Lord" thunders and displays its power over all creation. The psalmist sings,

> The voice of the Lord is over the waters;
> the God of glory thunders,
> the Lord, over mighty waters.
> The voice of the Lord is powerful;
> the voice of the Lord is full of majesty. (Ps 29:3–4)

The psalmist does not hold back in describing the power of God. The voice that hovers over the waters, that is full of majesty and power, and that strips the forest bare is the same voice that declared to Jesus and all those who were around him, "This is my dearly loved Son, who brings me great joy" (Matt 3:17, NLT). In his humanity, Jesus needed to hear those words, and the people who were witnesses to this event heard the public acknowledgment of Christ's divinity.

Indeed, the voice of the Lord is powerful. When we hear the voice of our Good Shepherd, it often comes in the form of a still, small voice (1 Kgs 19:12; John 10:27), but it is crystal clear and undeniable. The Lord speaks clearly to us through his word and through the Holy Spirit.

The second reading from Acts 10 recounts Peter's sermon in the household of a Roman centurion named Cornelius. The Holy Spirit brought Peter and Cornelius together and once it became clear that this was a divine engagement, Peter began to preach with boldness. Luke records this sermon in which Peter clearly and succinctly recounts the life and ministry of Jesus and the good news of the gospel to Cornelius's household. Regarding the gospel of Jesus, Peter declared,

> That message spread throughout Judea, beginning in Galilee after the baptism that John announced: how God anointed Jesus of Nazareth with the Holy Spirit and with power; how he went about doing good and healing all who were oppressed by the devil, for God was with him. (Acts 10:37–38)

It is interesting that Luke gives us the detail that Jesus' message began to spread "after the baptism that John announced." Historically, the baptism of Jesus was a watershed event, one that brought his ministry and identity out of obscurity and into public awareness. Peter affirms what the Gospel writers have recorded, that at Jesus' baptism, God anointed him "with the Holy Spirit and with power." This was a profoundly significant moment in redemptive history. And as Peter was sharing this message, "the Holy Spirit fell upon all who heard the word" (Acts 10:44). And so, they were all baptized with water in the name of Jesus.

This is the story of all who have placed their faith in the Lord Jesus Christ. When we hear the word and are regenerated by the Holy Spirit, we either have our infant baptism confirmed, or we are baptized with water as adults. The sacrament of baptism is our entrance into the family of God as sons and daughters of the King.

The Gospel reading from Matthew 3 recounts the event of Jesus' baptism, which we have already been discussing. Interestingly, Matthew gives us the detail of John initially resisting Jesus' desire to be baptized. Matthew writes,

> Then Jesus came from Galilee to John at the Jordan, to be baptized by him. John would have prevented him, saying, "I need to be baptized by you, and do you come to me?" But Jesus answered

him, "Let it be so now, for it is proper for us in this way to fulfill all righteousness." Then he consented. (Matt 3:13–15)

John could not say no to the Son of God! Jesus assured John that it was proper for him to be baptized "to fulfill all righteousness." The baptism of Jesus was a significant and appropriate way for him to begin his public ministry. First of all, it made it clear that Jesus was the Son of God, the anointed one who would fulfill all of the promises of Isaiah 42 (the first reading). Second, Jesus was anointed for his ministry with the power of the Holy Spirit, which descended upon him like a dove. He would need this power as his next forty days would be in the wilderness facing the temptations of the enemy. Thirdly, Jesus would be affirmed by the Father as he heard the words, "This is my Son, the Beloved, with whom I am well pleased" (Matt 3:17).

We, too, need to be regularly renewed and affirmed in our own baptism, recalling the vows we took as we became members of a local church. The waters of baptism mark us as sons and daughters of God and remind us that we are his dearly loved children who bring him great joy.

QUESTIONS FOR REFLECTION

1. Who is the servant of the Lord? What are some of the defining characteristics of this servant? How did Jesus' life and ministry fulfill this prophecy? How does Jesus use us to minister to the "bruised reeds" and "dimly burning wicks" in our lives?

2. The psalmist describes the voice of the Lord. What are some of the images he uses? How have you experienced the voice of the Lord in your own life? How does the Lord speak to us today?

3. Peter proclaimed the life and ministry of Jesus and the good news of the gospel to Cornelius's household. What were the main themes that Peter highlighted? Peter identified the baptism of Jesus as the beginning of his public ministry. Why was Jesus' baptism such a significant event? What would you highlight about Jesus' life if you were sharing the gospel with someone?

4. Why was John initially hesitant to baptize Jesus? Why did Jesus need to be anointed by the Holy Spirit? Why did Jesus need to hear the voice of the Lord? Why were these moments significant for his ministry and in the scope of redemptive history? Do you find peace and rest in your identity as a child of God, knowing that you are dearly loved by the Father? Explain.

PRAYER OF RESPONSE
Based on Acts 10:38–40; Isaiah 42:1–3, 5–7

Holy God
you sent your beloved Son to be baptized;
to be anointed with the Holy Spirit and with power.
We praise you that he was sent to bring forth justice to the nations,
and that he went about doing good and healing all who were oppressed;
as was prophesied: a bruised reed he will not break
and a dimly burning wick he will not quench.
He was put to death, but you raised him on the third day.
We praise you for you created the heavens and stretched them out;
you spread out the earth and give breath and spirit to the people upon it.
You take us by the hand and keep us as your covenant people;
you open the eyes of the blind, and you set the prisoners free.
We worship and adore you, triune God. Amen.

Second Sunday after Epiphany

LECTIONARY READINGS

>Isaiah 49:1–7
>
>Psalm 40:1–11
>
>1 Corinthians 1:1–9
>
>John 1:29–42

DEVOTION

In the readings for the second Sunday after Epiphany, we continue to linger around the Jordan River and Jesus' baptism. Jesus approaches John the Baptist the day after his baptism, and John greets him as "the Lamb of God who takes away the sin of the world" (John 1:29). Jesus also begins to call his disciples, including Andrew and Peter. The prophet Isaiah offers another of his "servant songs," ultimately fulfilled in the life and ministry of Jesus. The apostle Paul writes to the church in Corinth and expresses his gratitude that the "testimony of Christ" is strengthened among them. Thus, who Jesus is and what he came to do are common threads in the readings for this Sunday.

In the first reading from Isaiah 49, the prophet offers the second of his collection of servant songs. Here, he describes the servant as being a redeemer and a light to the nations. He proclaims,

>And now the Lord says,
>who formed me in the womb to be his servant,
>to bring Jacob back to him,
>and that Israel might be gathered to him,
>for I am honored in the sight of the Lord,

and my God has become my strength—
he says, "It is too light a thing that you should be my servant
to raise up the tribes of Jacob
and to restore the survivors of Israel;
I will give you as a light to the nations,
that my salvation may reach to the end of the earth." (Isa 49:5–6)

Isaiah describes this servant as one who will bring redemption both to Israel and to the nations. The prophet speaks for God, saying that it is "too light a thing" for him just to gather and restore Israel; he will also be a light to the nations. Israel was supposed to be this light, but she failed. Jesus fulfilled the mandate that God had given to his people.

Psalm 40 is an appropriate response as David's language resonates with Isaiah's servant song. He writes,

Sacrifice and offering you do not desire,
but you have given me an open ear.
Burnt offering and sin offering
you have not required.
Then I said, "Here I am; in the scroll of the book it is written of me.
I delight to do your will, O my God;
your law is within my heart." (Ps 40:6–8)

Interestingly, the author of Hebrews has Jesus quoting this verse, referring to himself (Heb 10:5–9). Clearly, these verses are fulfilled in the life and ministry of Jesus. He is the one who obeyed the Lord and about whom the Scriptures prophesy. Isaiah sang about Jesus in the servant songs; David sings about Jesus in Psalm 40. Both passages paint a similar picture of the servanthood and obedience of Jesus.

In the second reading from 1 Corinthians 1, Paul encourages the believers in Corinth and gives thanks to God that "the testimony of Christ" has been strengthened among them so that they are not "lacking in any spiritual gift" (1 Cor 1:6, 7). Though Paul does not say exactly "how" the testimony of Christ was strengthened among the Corinthians, we can assume that it was through the same means as God uses among us today: regularly gathering and worshiping together, regularly spending time in prayer and in the Word, and regularly receiving the ministry and power of the Holy Spirit.

In his Letter to the Colossians, Paul writes, "Let the word of Christ dwell in you richly; teach and admonish one another in all wisdom; and with gratitude in your hearts sing psalms, hymns, and spiritual songs to God" (Col 3:16). Having the testimony of Christ strengthened among us and letting the word of Christ dwell richly within us seem to be very similar practices. The means of grace (e.g., word, song, prayer, preaching) and the work of the Spirit strengthen the truth of the gospel in our hearts and lives.

Because the Corinthians were strengthened by the gospel, they were not lacking in any spiritual gift. They were equipped for ministry to one another and to the world. The same is true of us. As we are edified, enriched, and strengthened by the testimony of Christ (the gospel), we are equipped for the work of ministry.

Paul also states that God will strengthen us "to the end" (1 Cor 1:8). This verse relates to the doctrine of the perseverance of the saints. As believers, God is the one who began a good work in us, and he will be the one to bring it to completion (Phil 1:6). God is the one who will strengthen and carry us to the end so that we will be "blameless" on the day of Christ's return. We do not depend on our own strength or righteousness, but in the God who is forever faithful to sustain us in every season of our lives.

In the Gospel reading from John 1, we encounter John the Baptist for a second week in a row. This time, we hear John declare, "Here is the Lamb of God who takes away the sin of the world!" (John 1:29). This is the mission of Jesus in one of its most concise articulations. At the end of John the Baptist's declarations, he states, "And I have seen and have borne witness that this is the Son of God" (John 1:34, ESV). The season of Epiphany is about manifestation and asks questions about Jesus' identity. In John 1 it is clear, Jesus is the Lamb of God who saves us from our sin and the Son of God who speaks and acts with divine authority.

Jesus also begins to call his disciples and offers three simple words that can change a person's life forever: "Come and see" (John 1:39). Jesus calls Andrew and in their conversation, we receive further insight into Jesus' identity. In addition to being the Lamb of God and the Son of God, he is also Teacher (rabbi) and Messiah. Andrew is so excited to have found the long-awaited Messiah that he goes and finds his brother Simon. When Jesus meets Simon, he gives him a new name; he calls him "Cephas (which is translated Peter)" (John 1:42). The choice of this name will be explained further, but in his first encounter, Peter's identity is transformed by Jesus.

During this season of Epiphany, may we recognize Jesus for who he is: Lamb of God, Son of God, Teacher, and Messiah. Let us remember that he is the servant in Isaiah who delights in doing the Father's will; he is the light to the nations whose ministry goes beyond just the people of Israel. He is the one who strengthens us, sustains us to the end, and completes his work of redemption within us. To God be the glory.

QUESTIONS FOR REFLECTION

1. Jesus is the servant of the Lord described in Isaiah 49. How is Jesus a light to the nations?

2. The author of Hebrews has Jesus quoting Psalm 40:6–7 in reference to himself. Do the narratives and testimonies in the New Testament fulfill this declaration? Give some examples.

3. Paul gives thanks to God that the testimony of Christ is being strengthened among the Corinthians. Would you say the same about yourself or your church? How and for what purpose is the testimony of Christ strengthened among us? Does it bring you comfort that it is God who sustains us "to the end" (1 Cor 1:8). Explain.

4. What are some of the titles given to Jesus in John 1:29–42? Which one speaks to you most meaningfully today? Why are the words, "come and see," so powerful? Do you invite others into the journey of knowing and following Christ?

PRAYER OF RESPONSE
Based on 1 Corinthians 1:4–9

Loving Father,
in our own strength, we often fall short,
but you have enriched us in every way,
in speech and knowledge of every kind.
Because of your grace, we are not lacking in any spiritual gift
as we wait for the return of our Lord Jesus Christ.
Though we grow weary, we know you will strengthen us to the end,
so that we may be blameless on the day of our Lord Jesus Christ.
We trust in your faithfulness, O God, and we thank you for calling us
into the fellowship of your Son, Jesus Christ our Lord. Amen.

Third Sunday after Epiphany

LECTIONARY READINGS

Isaiah 9:1–4

Psalm 27:1, 4–9

1 Corinthians 1:10–18

Matthew 4:12–23

DEVOTION

In the readings for the third Sunday after Epiphany, light is a common thread. The first reading from Isaiah 9 is usually read during Advent and Christmas. In this season after Epiphany, light refers to Jesus' ministry. In the second reading from 1 Corinthians 1, Paul laments the various factions that have arisen in Corinth and calls for Christian unity. In the Gospel reading, Matthew quotes from Isaiah 9, revealing how Jesus' ministry shined light into the darkness of "Galilee of the nations" (Isa 9:1). Matthew also recounts the calling of the first disciples. Thus, Christian unity, the light of Christ, and the cost of discipleship are common threads in the readings for this Sunday.

In the first reading from Isaiah 9, the prophet announces that a light will dawn in the midst of gloom and despair. The northern tribes of Israel have experienced the attack of the Assyrian army, but Isaiah offers hope to the people of God. He declares,

> The people who walked in darkness
> have seen a great light;
> those who lived in a land of deep darkness—
> on them light has shined. (Isa 9:2)

The book of Isaiah is full of war and devastation, but the prophet always declares a ray of hope in the midst of ruin. In our own day and time, we experience global pandemics, war, violence, and various kinds of abuse and injustice. And yet, we place our hope in the dawning light of our Savior, Jesus Christ. He has come to bring justice to the nations and salvation to those he has called his own. During this season of Epiphany, we live in the "already and not yet" of God's kingdom. We wait with patience for the light of Christ to shine in every nation and bring justice to all who are oppressed.

Psalm 27 continues in the theme of light and salvation. The psalmist sings,

> The Lord is my light and my salvation;
> whom shall I fear?
> The Lord is the stronghold of my life;
> of whom shall I be afraid? (Ps 27:1)

When we have the Lord as our light and salvation, we need not fear people or circumstances. As followers of Christ, we find ourselves in the grip of God's amazing grace. The psalmist continues, "For he will hide me in his shelter in the day of trouble; he will conceal me under the cover of his tent; he will set me high on a rock" (Ps 27:5). The Lord is our shelter and the protection we need from our enemies and our fears. Because it can be hard to truly believe this in the midst of trials and hard circumstances, we must reorient ourselves daily in the truth of the gospel and live, not as orphans or slaves but as beloved children of God. God's grace allows us to face our enemies and our fears and find peace in times of trial. The Lord gives us enough light for each new day, sustaining us in our present circumstances.

The second reading from 1 Corinthians 1 recounts the divisive climate within the church at Corinth. Paul writes,

> For it has been made clear to me by Chloe's people that there are quarrels among you, my brothers and sisters. What I mean is that each of you says, "I belong to Paul," or "I belong to Apollos," or "I belong to Cephas," or "I belong to Christ." Has Christ been divided? Was Paul crucified for you? Or were you baptized in the name of Paul? (1 Cor 1:11–13)

The people in Corinth gravitated to certain leaders. Some followed Paul, others followed Apollos or Cephas (Peter). Paul exhorts them not to place their hope in man, but in Christ. Divisions occur in churches to this day. Some follow the lead pastor while others gravitate toward a different pastor or ministry leader. Some may even follow a television evangelist or a popular pastor/teacher who has written influential books.

Paul is calling us to unity. He states how "the message about the cross is foolishness to those who are perishing, but to us who are being saved it is the power of God" (I Cor 1:18). The gospel is not about who is delivering the message, but the one who is the subject of the message, Christ himself. May we not lose sight of our call to unity and love for one another. Factions and divisions send a bad message to the culture around us, but unity, peace, and mutual love shine brightly in the context of a dark world.

In the Gospel reading from Matthew 4, we find Jesus leaving for Galilee after the arrest of John the Baptist. Matthew tells us that this was done "so that what had been spoken through the prophet Isaiah might be fulfilled" (Matt 4:14). Matthew then quotes from Isaiah 9 (the first reading). He writes,

> Land of Zebulun, land of Naphtali,
> on the road by the sea, across the Jordan,
> Galilee of the gentiles—
> the people who sat in darkness
> have seen a great light,
> and for those who sat in the region and
> shadow of death light has dawned. (Matt 4:15–16)

The coming of Jesus and the inauguration of his kingdom was the light that began to shine in the darkness. Matthew shares, "Jesus went throughout Galilee, teaching in their synagogues and proclaiming the good news of the kingdom and curing every disease and every sickness among the people" (Matt 4:23). Jesus' kingdom comes with power, healing the afflicted, opening the eyes of the blind, and setting prisoners free.

Matthew also describes how Jesus began to call his first disciples, including Peter and Andrew, James and John. These four men were all fishermen and left their possessions (boats, nets) to follow Jesus. Jesus told them that they if they followed him, he would make them "fishers of people" (Matt 4:19).

Jesus calls us to this same task. He calls us to surrender our lives and our possessions and follow him. We leave behind the things that have a hold on us in this world and follow wherever he may lead us. We fish for people by loving our neighbors, breaking bread with unbelievers, serving those in need, and sharing the gospel with those who need to hear it. There is an indescribable joy in sharing the gospel in word and in deed.

During this season of Epiphany, may we be light bearers in this world, shining brightly with the grace, mercy, and love of God.

QUESTIONS FOR REFLECTION

1. Isaiah offered the hope of a dawning light to the people who were in darkness and despair. How is our own context like "Galilee of the nations"? How can we be the light of Christ to those around us?

2. The imagery of light continues in Psalm 27. How is light significant for the psalmist? How does God's light help remove our fears? Why does God often give us enough light for each day, each new step rather than the whole journey (Ps 119:105)?

3. Paul exhorted the church in Corinth not to become divisive over which leader they preferred. How do we experience this same issue in the church today? How does God call us to be peacemakers within the church?

4. Matthew quotes Isaiah 9 in the text for this Sunday. How is light to be associated with Jesus' ministry? How would you describe the "kingdom of heaven" to someone? Read Matthew 4:18–22. What did Jesus ask Peter, Andrew, James, and John to do? Does Jesus ask the same of us today? Explain.

PRAYER OF RESPONSE
Based on Isaiah 9:2–3; Matthew 4:16, 18–23

Lord Jesus,
we thank you for bringing the light of the gospel
into the darkness of our lives.
Increase our joy for you and break the power
of enemies and idols that seek to oppress us.
Help us to follow you and your ways each day.
As your disciples, may we be light bearers
in this world, bringing the good news of the kingdom
to family, friends, and neighbors in need.
In the name of the Father, Son, and Holy Spirit. Amen.

Fourth Sunday after Epiphany

LECTIONARY READINGS

Micah 6:1–8

Psalm 15

1 Corinthians 1:18–31

Matthew 5:1–12

DEVOTION

In the readings for the fourth Sunday after Epiphany, Jesus calls for a radical way of living based on kingdom values, not worldly values. This way of life is also portrayed in the Old Testament reading from Micah 6 where the prophet exhorts the people to do justice, love kindness, and walk humbly with their God. The apostle Paul calls the Corinthians to see that God's foolishness is wiser than human wisdom, and God's weakness is stronger than human strength. Thus, living wisely and humbly according to God's kingdom values will bring us a blessed life, one that is contrary to the values of this world. This concept is a common theme in the readings for this Sunday.

In the first reading from Micah 6, the prophet describes the kind of life to which God is calling his people. Micah wrote during the eighth century BC, spanning Israel's troubled years before its invasion by Assyria. The prophet is writing to the people of God who are living unjustly and facing judgment. They have turned their covenant relationship with the Lord into a means of religious manipulation. Micah declares,

> "Will the Lord be pleased with thousands of rams,
> with ten thousands of rivers of oil?

> Shall I give my firstborn for my transgression,
> the fruit of my body for the sin of my soul?"
> He has told you, O mortal, what is good,
> and what does the Lord require of you
> but to do justice, and to love kindness
> and to walk humbly with your God? (Mic 6:7–8)

Micah rebukes Israel's empty religious actions and describes what God truly desires from his people: to do justice, love kindness, and walk humbly with our God. We can live very much like the people of long ago, trying to bargain with God or looking for God to bless us because we are doing what we think will please him. God will not tolerate this kind of manipulation. He knows our hearts better than we do and can distinguish between true and false worship.

Micah pleaded for the people to remember how loving and faithful God had been in their lives. Such remembrance should stir our own hearts towards gratitude and should evoke genuine praise. Viewing our relationship with God like a contract ("You do this for me, and I'll do this for you") will only lead to empty obedience and unhealthy expectations of God.

Psalm 15 provides a natural response to Micah 6 and further affirms the kind of life that God desires of his people. The psalmist offers a question and response. He writes,

> O Lord, who may abide in your tent?
> Who may dwell on your holy hill?
> Those who walk blamelessly and do what is right
> and speak the truth from their heart;
> who do not slander with their tongue
> and do no evil to their friends
> nor heap shame upon their neighbors. (Ps 15:1–3)

In asking, "Who may dwell on your holy hill?" the psalmist raises a question very similar to that of Micah: "What does the Lord require of you?" The psalmist's answer is very similar to Micah's answer. The psalmist describes a way of life that is full of integrity, love for neighbor, and restraint of tongue. We would expect these two responses (one from the psalmist and one from the prophet) to be similar because our God does not change. His heart has never been for us to offer him empty praise. He surely does not desire for us to show up at church on Sunday while harboring hatred and bitterness in our hearts toward others. God wants us to have pure hearts, to love and honor our neighbors, and to seek justice and mercy toward others.

In the second reading from 1 Corinthians 1, the apostle Paul distinguishes between the wisdom of the world and the wisdom of God. He summarizes by stating,

> God chose what is foolish in the world to shame the wise; God chose what is weak in the world to shame the strong; God chose what is low and despised in the world, things that are not, to abolish things that are, so that no one might boast in the presence of God. (1 Cor 1:27–29)

The greatest demonstration of God's upside-down kingdom is the cross of Christ. For Paul and for believers, the cross is the power of God; for those opposed to God, it is a stumbling block. We should not expect the world to understand the way we live our lives. We should not expect our unbelieving friends or family members to understand how we raise our children, how we make financial decisions, or how we choose our vocations. To the world, our wisdom may seem like foolishness. We know, however, that as we seek to live according to God's wisdom and God's ways, we will find a blessing and a joy that are beyond measure.

In the Gospel reading from Matthew 5, Jesus further articulates the blessed life, what it looks like to live according to God's kingdom values. As he introduces his well-known Sermon on the Mount, Jesus begins with the Beatitudes, a list of divine blessings on a way of life that expresses the heart of God. He teaches,

> Blessed are the poor in spirit, for theirs is the kingdom of heaven.
> Blessed are those who mourn, for they will be comforted.
> Blessed are the meek, for they will inherit the earth.
> Blessed are those who hunger and thirst for righteousness, for they will be filled.
> Blessed are the merciful, for they will receive mercy.
> Blessed are the pure in heart, for they will see God.
> Blessed are the peacemakers, for they will be called children of God.
> Blessed are those who are persecuted for the sake of righteousness, for theirs is the kingdom of heaven. Blessed are you when people revile you and persecute you and utter all kinds of evil against you falsely on my account. Rejoice and be glad, for your

> reward is great in heaven, for in the same way they persecuted the prophets who were before you. (Matt 5:3–12)

In the previous readings, Micah, David, and Paul all expressed a way of life that God truly desires of his people. In many ways, this way of life is counterintuitive to us. We do not typically think that blessing comes from poverty and meekness. In God's kingdom economy, however, the character traits that Jesus articulates bring an eternal joy and satisfaction that no earthly reward can match. Being merciful to others and being poor in spirit are desired character traits in the kingdom of God.

This kind of life is only a work of the Spirit within us. We cannot manufacture purity of heart, but the Spirit within us is purifying us and sanctifying us so that we are being transformed more and more into a reflection of God's own glory (2 Cor 3:18). During this season of Epiphany, may we seek to live according to God's kingdom values. May we know the eternal joy and peace of practicing justice, loving kindness, and walking humbly with our God.

QUESTIONS FOR REFLECTION

1. What was so offensive about how the people of God were living during Micah's time? How did Micah, speaking for the Lord, call them to live? How can we sometimes mistake empty, religious practices for true worship?

2. What are the characteristics that the psalmist highlights in Psalm 15 that enable one to abide with God? How are these similar to the godly way of life that Micah describes? The psalmist mentions speaking truth from one's heart and not slandering with one's tongue. How can these two practices spare us from much discord with others? Do you practice restraint of tongue or do you speak without thinking of the consequences of your words?

3. How does Paul contrast the wisdom of God with the wisdom of the world? What does Paul point out specifically as a stumbling block to those opposed to Christ? Why do believers see the cross as the power of God? How would you explain the power of the cross to someone opposed to the gospel?

4. Jesus opens his Sermon on the Mount with the Beatitudes. Why? What do the Beatitudes teach us about God's kingdom values? Are these traits we can work on, a function of our circumstances, or the fruit of the Spirit within us?

PRAYER OF RESPONSE
Based on Matthew 5:3–12

Holy God,
your ways are so different from our ways.
Help us, by your grace, to live the kind of life
that reveals the values of your kingdom.
Help us to find your blessing through a poverty in spirit;
through meekness and mourning.
May we hunger and thirst for righteousness;
may we seek to be merciful, pure in heart
and peacemaking in our relationships.

May we know your presence and reward
through persecution and false accusation.
We pray for this kind of life in the name of
the Father, the Son, and the Holy Spirit. Amen.

Fifth Sunday after Epiphany

LECTIONARY READINGS

Isaiah 58:1–12

Psalm 112:1–10

1 Corinthians 2:1–16

Matthew 5:13–20

DEVOTION

In the readings for the fifth Sunday after Epiphany, we are called to be the light of Christ in the world. In one of the key verses in the Gospel reading from Matthew 5, Jesus states that our righteousness must exceed "that of the scribes and Pharisees" (Matt 5:20). The Old Testament reading from Isaiah 58 echoes this exhortation as the prophet condemns the people of God for thinking that their empty fasts and religious rituals were pleasing to God. The Lord makes it clear that without a concern for justice and freedom for the oppressed, their fasts were meaningless. According to the prophet, when they expressed their love and worship through deeds of mercy, then their light would shine before the world.

The psalmist also expresses the light that comes from this kind of generous and merciful lifestyle. The apostle Paul teaches that we need the Spirit to comprehend spiritual things. Thus, being the light of Christ, loving God in word and deed, and living with the Spirit's discernment are common threads in the readings for this Sunday.

In the first reading from Isaiah 58, the prophet condemns the people of God for going through the motions of worship (e.g., a day of fasting) while neglecting to seek justice and mercy for the oppressed. Speaking for the Lord, Isaiah proclaims,

> Is such the fast that I choose,
> a day to humble oneself?
> Is it to bow down the head like a bulrush
> and to lie in sackcloth and ashes?
> Will you call this a fast,
> a day acceptable to the Lord?
> Is not this the fast that I choose:
> to loose the bonds of injustice,
> to undo the straps of the yoke,
> to let the oppressed go free,
> and to break every yoke? (Isa 58:5–6)

It can be all too easy for us to compartmentalize our worship of God. We can go to church on Sunday and feel as though we are doing what is pleasing to God; however, God is always more concerned about the condition of our heart than our outward expression of worship. Our life of worship *inside* the walls of the church should reflect our life of worship *outside* the walls of the church as we seek to love our families and our neighbors and bring the gospel in word and deed to those around us. Such lifestyles of genuine love and mercy will bring the light of Christ into our homes, neighborhoods, and cities.

The psalmist also speaks into the idea of bringing light into the darkness, singing,

> Praise the Lord!
> Happy are those who fear the Lord,
> who greatly delight in his commandments.
> Their descendants will be mighty in the land;
> the generation of the upright will be blessed.
> Wealth and riches are in their houses,
> and their righteousness endures forever.
> They rise in the darkness as a light for the upright;
> they are gracious, merciful, and righteous.
> It is well with those who deal generously and lend,
> who conduct their affairs with justice. (Ps 112:1–5)

Those who delight in following and obeying God's commands will be happy and blessed. They will be "a light for the upright" as they are gracious, merciful, generous, and just toward others. This is the kind of life the Lord desires for his people. When we reflect generosity, grace, mercy, gentleness, kindness, and compassion, we demonstrate the kingdom of God to those around us. We do not have to do something "big" for God; rather, we are called to live each day in a manner that reveals the fruit of the Spirit to others.

In the second reading from 1 Corinthians 2, the apostle Paul teaches about spiritual discernment. He writes,

> Now we have received not the spirit of the world, but the Spirit that is from God, so that we may understand the gifts bestowed on us by God. And we speak of these things in words not taught by human wisdom but taught by the Spirit, interpreting spiritual things to those who are spiritual. Those who are unspiritual do not receive the gifts of God's Spirit, for they are foolishness to them, and they are unable to understand them because they are spiritually discerned. (1 Cor 2:12–14)

Once our hearts have been regenerated by the Holy Spirit, and we place our hope and trust in the Lord Jesus by faith, we begin to understand spiritual things. We are able to understand the Scriptures; we see the things of God as wise and powerful, not foolish and weak. However, those whose hearts have not been regenerated by the Holy Spirit are unable to discern spiritual things. Unbelievers cannot read the Scriptures by faith and with spiritual discernment. The Bible may sound confusing and, as Paul describes, foolish to those who do not know Christ.

For this reason, we should not be surprised or intimidated by those who think the Bible is irrelevant, outdated, or just one religious story among many. We should not expect an unbeliever to fully discern things that can only be comprehended through the power of the Holy Spirit within us. Sometimes it is best not to try to persuade someone about the truth of the Bible or the claims of our faith, but to invite that person simply to read the Scriptures for him or herself. In this way, the inspired word can bring about conviction, the awakening of one's heart, and the awareness and confession of one's need of Christ.

If you have placed your faith and hope in Christ, be grateful that you have the person of the Holy Spirit within you as a Counselor, Guide, Teacher, and Advocate. Jesus fulfilled his promise to send the

Holy Spirit (John 14:26) who indwells his people, reminding us and leading us into all truth.

In the Gospel reading from Matthew 5, Jesus calls us to be light in this world. He declares,

> You are the light of the world. A city built on a hill cannot be hid. People do not light a lamp and put it under the bushel basket; rather, they put it on the lampstand, and it gives light to all in the house. In the same way, let your light shine before others, so that they may see your good works and give glory to your Father in heaven. (Matt 5:14–16)

As part of his Sermon on the Mount, Jesus exhorts us not to remain quiet about the message of the gospel, but to offer our testimony to those who need to hear it. We should not hide our faith, but share it with those around us. As a church, we are to be a light in our city, proclaiming the good news of the gospel in both word and deed. It is easy for us to become insulated as the people of God, keeping our light contained within the walls of our church building. Jesus, however, calls us to take our light out into the world as a beacon of hope to our neighbors, our friends, our family members, and our coworkers.

When we realize the depth of grace and love that has been shown to us, we cannot help but share it with others who are lost and in need of salvation and restoration. During this season of Epiphany, may we be the light of Christ to the broken and hurting among us. Empowered by the Spirit, may we bring the hope of the gospel to those who are yet unable to discern spiritual things.

QUESTIONS FOR REFLECTION

1. What message was the prophet trying to convey to the people of God in Isaiah 58? Do you, at times, practice outward demonstrations of worship while inwardly being prideful and complacent, neglecting the needs of those around you? Explain.

2. Read Psalm 112:4–5 again. What character traits allow our lives to shine in the darkness of this world? Do you pray for God to make you more gracious, merciful, generous, and just in dealing with others? Why do we often want to do something "big" for God instead of simply loving others well each day?

3. Paul describes the topic of spiritual discernment. Why do unbelievers think the gospel is foolish? How should this affect our interactions and conversations with friends and family members who do not have the Holy Spirit within them?

4. Jesus calls us to be light in this world. How do we shine brightly in our schools, workplaces, and homes? How can we, as a church, be a light to our city? If our church closed its doors tomorrow, would our community know it?

PRAYER OF RESPONSE
Based on Matthew 5:14–20; Isaiah 58:6–7

Merciful God,
as your people, may our light shine before others,
so that they may see the fruit of the Spirit
in our lives and give you glory.
Help us to live righteously in this world,
bringing the gospel, in word and in deed,
to those who are in bondage;
to those who are homeless and poor;
to those who are suffering physically, spiritually, and emotionally.
In the name of Jesus we pray. Amen.

Sixth Sunday after Epiphany

LECTIONARY READINGS

>Deuteronomy 30:15–20
>
>Psalm 119:1–8
>
>1 Corinthians 3:1–9
>
>Matthew 5:21–37

DEVOTION

In the readings for the sixth Sunday after Epiphany, Jesus quotes the law given to Moses in his Sermon on the Mount and then intensifies it and moves it to the level of the heart. We hear Moses exhorting the people of God and reminding them of the law and the covenant before they enter the promised land. The apostle Paul continues to admonish the church at Corinth for quarreling and choosing one leader over another. Thus, obeying the law in our heart and with our actions and seeking peace within the church are themes in the readings for this Sunday.

In the first reading from Deuteronomy 30, Moses reminds the people of God about keeping the law before they enter the land of Canaan. He proclaims,

>See, I have set before you today life and prosperity, death and adversity. If you obey the commandments of the Lord your God that I am commanding you today, by loving the Lord your God, walking in his ways, and observing his commandments, decrees, and ordinances, then you shall live and become numerous, and the Lord your God will bless you in the land that you are entering to possess. (Deut 30:15–16)

At this point in redemptive history, the people of God have been wandering in the desert for forty years and are now on the brink of entering the promised land. Though Moses will not be their leader in this new season, he is exhorting them to renew their covenantal relationship with the Lord. He reminds them that if they keep God first and live according to his ways, they will be blessed; however, if they forget about God and live as they desire, they will be cursed.

When we follow the Lord with all of our heart, soul, mind, and strength, we will live a life of peace and joy. This does not mean that we will not have trials and hardship, but when we follow the Lord, we experience the close and intimate relationship with him that sustains us through the highs, the lows, and the ordinary seasons of life.

When our hearts are led astray, and we make idols of lesser things, the Holy Spirit can convict us of our sin and bring us back to a right relationship with God. Living openly and transparently with other Christians helps us to remain accountable so that we do not fall readily into sin and idolatry. Though we will be tempted in various ways, regular worship, Christian fellowship, and personal devotions will help to keep us on the narrow way, full of blessing and peace.

The psalmist expresses a similar way of life, singing,

> O that my ways may be steadfast
> in keeping your statutes!
> Then I shall not be put to shame,
> having my eyes fixed on all your commandments. (Ps 119:5–6)

Eugene Peterson describes this way of life as "a long obedience in the same direction."[1] The psalmist expresses a longing to be "steadfast" in his ways and for his eyes to be "fixed" on all of God's commandments. This way of life puts the Lord above everything; it involves walking with him day by day, trusting in his provision and protection.

Living in this way protects us from the guilt and shame that weigh on us when we indulge in sinful behavior. The enemy tempts us and lures us into places we think will bring us satisfaction, but his ways always end in shame. The Lord's ways never lead to guilt and shame; his ways bring us blessing and peace.

---

1. Peterson, *Long Obedience*.

In the second reading from 1 Corinthians 3, the apostle Paul admonishes the believers for their spiritual immaturity, causing quarrels and divisions over leadership. He writes,

> For as long as there is jealousy and quarreling among you, are you not fleshly and behaving according to human inclinations? For when one says, "I belong to Paul," and another, "I belong to Apollos," are you not all too human? (1 Cor 3:3–4)

Paul rebukes the believers in Corinth for living according to the flesh and not understanding things from a spiritual point of view. Paul and Apollos each have a role in the kingdom; thus, there should not be jealousy or quarrels over leaders. Paul reminds the Corinthians, "For we are God's coworkers, working together; you are God's field, God's building" (1 Cor 3:9).

Each one of us has a role in God's kingdom. No one is greater than or less than the other. Stirring up divisions goes against our calling as servants of God. We should take this message to heart as believers today. In the modern church, we can get into quarrels over leadership, worship styles, and a host of other issues. God wants us to be mature followers, seeking to build up and encourage one another as we seek his kingdom.

In the Gospel reading from Matthew 5, Jesus teaches about the Ten Commandments in his Sermon on the Mount. He intensifies the law and shows how obeying God is rooted in the heart, not in mere outward behavior. He teaches,

> You have heard that it was said, "You shall not commit adultery." But I say to you that everyone who looks at a woman with lust has already committed adultery with her in his heart. (Matt 5:27–28)

Jesus takes the outward expression of the law and turns it inward. In the case of adultery, Jesus causes us to look inward at how we lust in our hearts. His teaching should demonstrate to us that it is impossible for us to keep the law. Jesus was revealing to the followers then and to his people today how desperately we need a Savior. Only the atoning power of the blood of Christ shed on the cross at Calvary can wash away the sin inside our hearts.

The gospel teaches us that we need a new heart, not just outward obedience. Once our hearts are regenerated by the power of the Holy Spirit, we can then begin to live according to the Spirit within us; then our outward behavior can reflect the redeeming, sanctifying work of the Spirit.

The law and the prophets always pointed to Christ. In the Sermon on the Mount, Jesus shows us our need of his sacrifice on the cross. During this Epiphany season, may we live as redeemed sons and daughters of God. May we be light in this world as we obey God in our hearts and through our actions, seeking peace with one another and sharing the good news of God's redeeming grace.

QUESTIONS FOR REFLECTION

1. Why would Moses need to remind the people of God's law and covenantal stipulations? Are we still called to follow God's law today? What are the consequences of obeying or disobeying God?

2. What words does the psalmist use to describe his relationship with the Lord? Do these words describe your own relationship with God? Explain.

3. Why is Paul having to admonish the Corinthians? How are they stirring up divisions within the church? How can we stir up division today? What are some signs of spiritual maturity?

4. How does Jesus intensify the Ten Commandments in his Sermon on the Mount? Give examples. What is the take-home message in this passage? How does Jesus cleanse our hearts? See Hebrews 10:1–22.

PRAYER OF RESPONSE
Based on Matthew 5:21–37

Lord Jesus,
we confess that your standard is much higher than ours,
and that we battle the flesh in more subtle ways than we often realize.
Your word tells us that we not only sin when we murder,
but when we insult or harbor anger towards another person,
we have committed murder in our heart.
Your word tells us that we not only sin when we commit adultery,
but when we look with lust at another person,
we have committed adultery in our heart.
Your word tells us that we not only sin
when we fail to keep our vows to the Lord,
but when we fail to keep our word with anyone,
we have sworn falsely before you.
Help us to have integrity with our vows and commitments.
Transform our hearts, O Lord, by the power of the Holy Spirit;
may we seek you with our whole heart.
In the name of Jesus we pray. Amen.

Seventh Sunday after Epiphany

LECTIONARY READINGS

> Leviticus 19:1–2, 9–18
>
> Psalm 119:33–40
>
> 1 Corinthians 3:10–11, 16–23
>
> Matthew 5:38–48

DEVOTION

In the readings for the seventh Sunday after Epiphany, we hear the teaching of Jesus to be perfect, as our heavenly Father is perfect. We hear the command from Leviticus 19 to be holy as the Lord our God is holy. In Psalm 119, the psalmist prays that he would keep the law and observe it with his whole heart. In the second reading from 1 Corinthians 3, the apostle Paul reminds us that we are God's temple and that the Holy Spirit dwells within us. Thus, the themes of love, holiness, and obedience to the Lord are common threads in the readings for this Sunday.

In the first reading from Leviticus 19, Moses teaches us that we are to be holy as God is holy. He then reveals what such holiness looks like with regard to treating others with love and kindness. He proclaims:

> You shall not hate in your heart anyone of your kin; you shall reprove your neighbor, or you will incur guilt yourself. You shall not take vengeance or bear a grudge against any of your people, but you shall love your neighbor as yourself: I am the Lord. (Lev 19:17–18)

Moses describes a lifestyle that is void of greed, deceit, false accusation, prejudice, hatred, theft, and murder. When we treat others with respect, generosity, love, kindness, and justice, we are doing what is pleasing to the Lord. Living in such a way is what holiness is all about in God's economy. Holiness means being set apart. When we love our enemies, for example, we are living contrary to the world's values. Living this way, however, is only possible through the power of the Spirit who dwells within us. We cannot attempt a life of holiness apart from the grace of God.

The psalm of response comes from Psalm 119:33–40. It is an appropriate response to the first reading for we find the psalmist asking God to turn his heart toward the ways of the Lord. He prays,

> Teach me, O Lord, the way of your statues,
> and I will observe it to the end.
> Give me understanding, that I may keep your law
> and observe it with my whole heart.
> Lead me in the path of your commandments,
> for I delight in it.
> Turn my heart to your decrees
> and not to selfish gain.
> Turn my eyes from looking at vanities;
> be gracious to me according to your word. (Ps 119:33–37)

The psalmist knows that he needs the Lord to help him turn from his selfish and vain ways. He needs guidance and direction to obey the Lord's commands with his whole heart. We need this same guidance and understanding in our lives. Too often, our hearts are prone to looking after our own needs and desires without a care or concern for others in our lives. We try to live according to our own wisdom and with our own resources, neglecting the Lord's instructions and kingdom values. Like the psalmist, we need the Lord to "turn" our hearts to his ways, his word, and his commandments.

In the second reading from 1 Corinthians 3, the apostle Paul reminds us that we are God's temple. He writes, "Do you not know that you are God's temple and that God's Spirit dwells in you?" (1 Cor 3:16). Knowing that the Spirit dwells within us is crucial to living a life of holiness.

In his Letter to the Philippians, Paul shares his desire "to know Christ and the power of his resurrection" (Phil 3:10). This power is available to us through the Spirit who dwells within us. It is the Spirit's power that enables us to love our enemies, to let go of a grudge, and to deal with others justly and mercifully. We cannot live in this manner on our own.

Moreover, it is this divine power within us through the Holy Spirit that transforms us, little by little, into the likeness of Christ (2 Cor 3:18).

In his Letter to the Corinthians, Paul also reminds us of the contrary nature of living a life of holiness and obedience to the Lord. He writes,

> Do not deceive yourselves. If you think that you are wise in this age, you should become fools so that you may become wise. For the wisdom of this world is foolishness with God. (1 Cor 3:18-19)

The ways of the Lord and his kingdom are contrary to the ways and values of this world. A way of living that is honest, void of greed, vanity, grudges, and false accusation is foreign to the world. According to the world's values, we should be striving to get ahead and make a name for ourselves no matter the cost to others. Kingdom living is foolish to this world; it does not make sense. As believers, faith tells us otherwise. Faith and obedience to God's ways bring us a joy and a peace that fame, fortune, and power cannot give us. It takes the power of the Spirit within us, however, to turn our hearts in a godly direction.

Finally, in the Gospel reading from Matthew 5, Jesus expounds upon kingdom living. In his familiar Sermon on the Mount, Jesus teaches,

> You have heard that it was said, "You shall love your neighbor and hate your enemy." But I say to you: Love your enemies and pray for those who persecute you, so that you may be children of your Father in heaven, for he makes his sun rise on the evil and on the good and sends rain on the righteous and on the unrighteous. For if you love those who love you, what reward do you have? Do not even the tax collectors do the same? And if you greet only your brothers and sisters, what more are you doing than others? Do not even the gentiles do the same? Be perfect, therefore, as your heavenly Father is perfect. (Matt 5:43-48)

Jesus reveals the upside-down nature of the kingdom in his famous sermon. In this particular passage, he teaches us that we are to love our enemies. The plain meaning of Jesus' teaching is that anyone can love people who love them back. Jesus is calling his followers to a radical way of life; he is calling us to love the people who hate us. And with a similar command, found in Leviticus 19 (to be holy for the Lord our God is holy), Jesus calls us to "be perfect" as our heavenly Father is perfect.

We will never be perfect in our life on earth. Through the Spirit's power within us, however, we can learn to love others in the radical way that Jesus describes. We can begin to live according to the way of Jesus as we express kingdom values such as justice, kindness, mercy, love, peace, and patience with and toward others in our lives.

The call to radical love is a needed reminder to us during this season of Epiphany. As we seek to bring the light of Christ to this dark world by living in obedience to the ways of the Lord, we do so by learning to love with Christ's love, through the power of the Holy Spirit who dwells within us.

QUESTIONS FOR REFLECTION

1. In Leviticus 19:2, Moses tells the people of God that they are to be holy for the Lord is holy. How would you define holiness? What are some of the ways that holiness is expressed through God's people? That is, what kind of lifestyle does Leviticus 19:9–18 describe? How are you able to lead a holy life in this way?

2. In Psalm 119:33–40, the psalmist prays for God to turn his heart to his ways and commandments. What are some verbs and/or phrases that stand out to you in this passage? In seeking to live a life of holiness, do you pray in this manner? Explain.

3. In his Letter to the Corinthians, Paul reminds the people of God that their bodies are a temple of God and that the Holy Spirit dwells within them. Are you prone to forget this truth? Explain. How does this inform our call to holiness? How might the reality that the Holy Spirit dwells within you cause you to make different choices at times (Eph 4:30–31)? Why does living a life of holiness, one that seeks kingdom values, seem like foolishness to the world?

4. In Matthew 5, Jesus teaches us about a radical kind of love. How does he describe this kind of love? Does your life reflect this kind of love? Explain.

PRAYER OF RESPONSE
Based on Matthew 5:40–44

Merciful God,
help us to be gracious to others
as you have been gracious to us.
Give us hearts to go out of our way
to serve and minister to someone else.
May the Spirit be at work in us,
allowing us to love even our enemies,
and to pray for those who persecute us.
Refine us and sanctify us, O Lord,
that we would shine as bright lights in this broken world.
In the name of Jesus we pray. Amen.

Eighth Sunday after Epiphany

LECTIONARY READINGS

Isaiah 49:8–16a

Psalm 131

1 Corinthians 4:1–5

Matthew 6:24–34

DEVOTION

In the readings for the eighth Sunday after Epiphany, Jesus comforts his people with a message about the love and care of the Father in the Gospel reading from Matthew 6. In the first reading from Isaiah 49, God's love for his people is understood as greater than the love of a mother towards her nursing child. Psalm 131 builds on this theme of nurturing love through the psalmist's expression of contentment in God being like that of a weaned child. In the second reading from 1 Corinthians 4, the apostle Paul teaches on the judgment of God, exposing the purposes of each of our hearts. Thus, the love and care as well as the judgment of God are common themes in the readings for this Sunday.

In the first reading from Isaiah 49, the prophet brings hope and encouragement to the people of God who are in exile. Through the prophet, God promises that his covenant will remain true as the people return to and reestablish the land (Isa 49:8). Moreover, the Lord describes his role as shepherd in leading the people out of darkness and exile. Speaking for the Lord, Isaiah declares,

> They shall feed along the ways;
> on all the bare heights shall be their pasture;

> they shall not hunger or thirst,
> neither scorching wind nor sun shall strike them down,
> for he who has pity on them will lead them
> and by springs of water will guide them.
> And I will turn all my mountains into a road,
> and my highways shall be raised up. (Isa 49:9b–11)

God will guide his people home and will make sure their journey is successful, providing food, protection, and a safe path. Though the prophet is speaking of a future return from Babylonian exile, he is also revealing how the Lord continues to lead and guide his people today as the Good Shepherd. God is still faithful to restore his people.

The prophet also describes the profound, divine love that God has for his people. Speaking for the people of God and the Lord himself, Isaiah proclaims,

> But Zion said, "The Lord has forsaken me;
> my Lord has forgotten me."
> Can a woman forget her nursing child
> or show no compassion for the child of her womb?
> Even these might forget,
> yet I will not forget you.
> See, I have inscribed you on the palms of my hands;
> your walls are continually before me. (Isa 49:14–16)

Isaiah responds to the people's doubts about God's love by revealing how God's love surpasses even that of a mother for her nursing child. Such language offers us a window into the profound love that God has for us, his children. Moreover, God encourages us with the language that we are inscribed "on the palms" of his hands. We are ever before him, and he cares for us more than we often realize. Such tender expressions from God's word reveal the depth and consistency of his love for his people.

Psalm 131 is an appropriate response to the first reading from Isaiah 49. Here, David speaks of his contentment in the Lord. He does not occupy himself with things too great for him to understand, but simply finds rest in the tender love of God. David sings,

> But I have calmed and quieted my soul,
> like a weaned child with its mother;
> my soul is like the weaned child that is with me. (Ps 131:2)

An unweaned child will often cry for food and nourishment and is satisfied only when his or her cravings have been met. A weaned child has learned to trust in and rest in the mother who has proven that she will take care of her child's needs. A weaned child has a deeper sense of his mother's love. As those who first learned to trust God for our physical and felt needs, we also learn to trust him during times of trial and suffering. This is the kind of trust that David is expressing. He has learned to rest and be content in the love of his Good Shepherd, the one who is with him through all of life's circumstances.

Learning to trust the Lord is a journey for all of those who have put their faith in God. We must rest in the one who gives us, not all that we want, but all that we truly need. Moreover, we learn that we can trust in the Lord's steadfast love, his covenant faithfulness towards his children. Though we walk through valleys, God is with us in all things. Our souls can rest in his divine love and care.

In the second reading from 1 Corinthians 4, the apostle Paul reveals the role of God as judge. He writes,

> Therefore do not pronounce judgment before the time, before the Lord comes, who will bring to light the things now hidden in darkness and will disclose the purposes of the heart. Then each one will receive commendation from God. (1 Cor 4:5)

In the context of this passage, Paul is expressing what a "very small thing" (1 Cor 4:3) it is to be judged by humans. As an apostle, Paul was defending his role as a leader in the church; however, in the midst of his defense, he encourages the Corinthians to be concerned about the Lord's judgment of each of us. Only God can expose the true nature of our hearts.

This reading complements the previous expressions of God's nurturing love and care as our Good Shepherd with the reality that he is also our Judge, the one who brings "to light the things now hidden in darkness." For those who have placed their hope in the Lord, we should not feel worried or anxious about this reality. Though our hearts will be exposed, we will not be condemned. In God's economy, bringing truth to light brings relief to those who know him as Lord (Ps 32:1-5).

Finally, in the Gospel reading from Matthew 6, we hear the comforting words of Jesus who reminds us not to worry, but to rest in God's constant love and care for his children. Jesus declares,

> But if God so clothes the grass of the field, which is alive today and tomorrow is thrown into the oven, will he not much more clothe you—you of little faith? Therefore do not worry, saying, "What will we eat?" or "What will we drink?" or "What will we wear?" For it is the gentiles who seek all these things, and indeed your heavenly Father knows that you need all these things. But seek first the kingdom of God and his righteousness, and all these things will be given to you as well. (Matt 6:30–33)

Jesus encourages us with the Father's sovereign care for his creation. As Isaiah encouraged the people of God in his day by expressing that God's love and care is greater than that of a mother; here, Jesus expresses God's care for his people as greater than that of the birds of the air and the lilies and grass of the field. If God feeds and clothes them, how much more will he feed and clothe us, his beloved children? Jesus even describes how we lack faith when we fail to trust in God's steadfast love for us.

Jesus' deeper point, however, is that the Father not only provides for our physical needs; he provides for our spiritual needs as well. More than food and shelter, the Lord provides the righteousness we need that can only be found in Christ. We find true contentment and rest from worry and anxiety when we seek the kingdom of God. The apostle Paul offers a similar message to the Colossians. He writes,

> So if you have been raised with Christ, seek the things that are above, where Christ is, seated at the right hand of God. Set your minds on the things that are above, not on the things that are on earth, for you have died, and your life is hidden with Christ in God. (Col 3:1–3)

We must remember our baptismal identity as sons and daughters of God. With this knowledge, we are able to put earthly concerns in their proper perspective. We do not need to worry about physical needs when we trust the goodness of our loving God. He knows what we need. He is our Good Shepherd who guides us, loves us, protects us, and provides for us. His love for us is greater than a mother's love for her child. This is the good news of the gospel. During this season of Epiphany, may we rest in the nurturing love and care of our heavenly Father, the one who has given us his one and only Son to make us righteous.

QUESTIONS FOR REFLECTION

1. The prophet Isaiah reveals the guidance and protection of God (Isa 49:9–11). How does God guide and protect you today? Isaiah also reveals that God's love for his people is greater than the love of a mother for her child. How does this image encourage you?

2. In Psalm 131, David describes his contentment in God. Put the imagery of David's soul being like that of a weaned child in your own words. Is your soul at rest in this way? Explain.

3. In his Letter to the Corinthians, Paul reminds the people that God is the judge who will expose the true nature of our hearts. Does this bring you comfort or fear? Explain. How is God's love both tender (greater than the love of a mother for her child) and just (bringing to light things that are now hidden)?

4. In Matthew 6, Jesus teaches us about God's sovereign care for his creation and for his beloved children. Knowing how much he loves us, why do we still doubt that he will care for us and provide for our needs? What is our greatest need? How has God provided for that need? Do you find rest and contentment by setting your heart and mind on the kingdom of God and on things that are above? Explain.

PRAYER OF RESPONSE
Based on Matthew 6:25–34

Lord Jesus,
our hearts long for rest.
Help us not to worry about our life,
what we will eat or what we will drink,
or about our bodies, what we will wear.
We know that you care for all of your creation,
providing food and nourishment for all living things.
When we become anxious and fearful, by your grace,
help us to trust in your provision for each new day.
May we strive first for your kingdom and your righteousness,
knowing that all of these earthly concerns will be given to us as well.
In the name of Jesus we pray. Amen.

Ninth Sunday after Epiphany

LECTIONARY READINGS

>Deuteronomy 11:18–21, 26–28
>
>Psalm 31:1–5, 19–24
>
>Romans 1:16–17; 3:22b–31
>
>Matthew 7:21–29

DEVOTION

In the readings for the ninth Sunday after Epiphany, we hear the final words of Jesus' Sermon on the Mount in Matthew 7. In his teaching, he offers sobering words about the day of judgment and exhorts us to live out what we hear. In the first reading from Deuteronomy 11, we hear the words of Moses on the plains of Moab, instructing the people to teach the next generation about the faith and to obey God's commands. In Psalm 31, the psalmist looks to God as his rock. In the second reading from the book of Romans, the apostle Paul teaches us that we are justified by faith and not by works. Thus, the themes of hearing and doing the word and of living by faith and obedience are common threads in the readings for this Sunday.

In the first reading from Deuteronomy 11, Moses is instructing the people of God and renewing God's covenant with them before they cross the Jordan River and enter the promised land. He exhorts the people of God:

>You shall put these words of mine in your heart and soul, and you shall bind them as a sign on your hand and fix them as an emblem on your forehead. Teach them to your children, talking

about them when you are at home and when you are away, when
you lie down and when you rise up. (Deut 11:18–19)

Moses gave the people of God this same instruction in Deuteronomy 6. Evidently, it is so important that he is repeating himself for emphasis. Moreover, Moses is exhorting the people of God to make God's word a part of their heart and soul. These commandments are not meant to be mere information, but words that shape who we are and inform how we live our lives. Through Moses, the Lord tells the people of the blessing for living according to God's word and the curse for disobeying God's word.

We should take these words to heart. Like the Israelites long ago, we are to pass on God's story to our children and to future generations. We should talk about all that God has done in the Bible and in our own lives when we are at home and when we are away, when we lie down and when we rise. The story of God should permeate our homes. Having spiritual conversations should be a normal and natural rhythm of our lives. God blesses us in countless ways when we live genuine, humble lives of faith and obedience.

In Psalm 31, the psalm of response, David sings of the Lord as his rock:

> Be a rock of refuge for me,
> a strong fortress to save me.
> You are indeed my rock and my fortress;
> for your name's sake lead me and guide me;
> take me out of the net that is hidden for me,
> for you are my refuge. (Ps 31:2b–4)

The imagery and stability of a rock will be discussed in the Gospel reading from Matthew 7. Here, David describes the Lord as his "rock of refuge." He knows his God is faithful and unchanging and that he can trust the Lord for guidance and protection.

Moreover, David placed his hope and trust in the steadfast love of the Lord. He sings,

> Blessed be the Lord,
> for he has wondrously shown his steadfast love to me
> when I was beset as a city under siege.
> I had said in my alarm,
> "I am driven far from your sight."
> But you heard my supplications
> when I cried out to you for help. (Ps 31:21–22)

David knew that the Lord would protect him, even as he felt "beset as a city under siege." The Lord heard David's prayers and cries for help. We can look to the Lord as our rock of refuge still today. He keeps his covenant with his children and is faithful even when we are unfaithful. As our rock of refuge, we cling to him by faith and rely on the Holy Spirit to lead us and guide us in the way we should go. The Lord is our advocate who protects us and reveals his steadfast love in countless ways. Like David, our lives are lived by faith and in humble reliance upon the Lord.

In the second reading from the book of Romans, the apostle Paul teaches about the power of the gospel. He writes,

> For I am not ashamed of the gospel; it is God's saving power for everyone who believes, for the Jew first and also for the Greek. For in it the righteousness of God is revealed through faith for faith, as it is written, "The one who is righteous will live by faith." (Rom 1:16–17)

Here, we find that the gospel is "God's saving power" and that it contains instructions for living "by faith." Those who are righteous live by faith. It is vital that we understand this truth: "The one who is righteous will live by faith." As we will see in the Gospel reading from Matthew 7, many people do good things, even things that appear to be of the Spirit (prophesying, casting out demons, performing deeds of power). These actions alone, however, do not mean that a person truly knows the Lord. This is a sobering reality, but one that we need to hear. All is in vain if we are not saved by faith, to live by faith.

Paul further writes, "For we hold that a person is justified by faith apart from works prescribed by the law" (Rom 3:28). We are declared right before God, not by works, but by faith. As Moses stressed to the people of God in Deuteronomy 11, we do not take in the word for knowledge alone or merit before God, but as a means of informing our heart and soul. As we teach our children and the future generations about faith and the story of God, our hope is that one day, by the power of God's grace, they will make this faith their own.

Finally, in the Gospel reading from Matthew 7, Jesus finishes his Sermon on the Mount by offering a sobering message about the day of the Lord. He teaches,

> Not everyone who says to me, "Lord, Lord," will enter the kingdom of heaven, but only the one who does the will of my Father in heaven. On that day many will say to me, "Lord, Lord, did we not prophesy in your name, and cast out demons in your name, and do many mighty works in your name?" Then I will declare

to them, "I never knew you; go away from me, you who behave lawlessly." (Matt 7:21–23)

As he brings his message (Sermon on the Mount) to a close, Jesus speaks candidly about those who thought they were doing things in his name, but were never actually saved by faith in him. This message should not cause us to doubt our salvation for we have the inner witness of the Spirit with our spirit that we are sons and daughters of God (Rom 8:16). It should cause us to be more discerning, however, and to realize that not everyone who has the outward signs of faith is truly a child of God. In other words, not everyone who preaches, teaches, sings, attends church on Sunday, or goes to a small group during the week is a true believer.

Jesus also teaches about those who are both hearers and doers of the word versus those who are hearers only. Regarding the hearers and doers, he declares,

> Everyone, then, who hears these words of mine and acts on them will be like a wise man who built his house on rock. The rain fell, the floods came, and the winds blew and beat on that house, but it did not fall because it had been founded on rock. (Matt 7:24–25)

As Moses and the apostle Paul taught, the word is not for knowledge alone. It should be in our hearts and souls; it should inform our lives; it is the power to live by faith. Like David, Jesus is exhorting us to know God as our rock of refuge. Those who live in such a way are wise. Those who are wise are able to persevere through trials and the various circumstances of life because their faith and hope are in Christ. Those who are foolish, Jesus taught, build their houses on sand. The word of God has not changed their hearts and souls; it is not the foundation of and source of their faith. Ultimately, those who are foolish put their faith and hope in themselves.

During this season of Epiphany, may we live by faith in Christ. Like Paul, may we not be ashamed of the gospel for it is God's saving power for those who believe. May the wisdom of God be evident to the world as we live in humble obedience to the Lord.

QUESTIONS FOR REFLECTION

1. In Deuteronomy 11, Moses teaches the people of God to put the word of God in their hearts and souls and to teach this word to their children and future generations. What does it mean to put God's word in your heart and in your soul? How do you teach your child or children about the story of God?

2. In Psalm 13, David describes the Lord as his "rock of refuge." How would you express this metaphor in your own words? How is God your rock of refuge? How do you experience the steadfast love of the Lord in your life? Do you cry out to the Lord in prayer for help? Describe.

3. In his Letter to the Romans, Paul teaches about the power of the gospel. How would you articulate the gospel in your own words? What does this statement mean: "The one who is righteous will live by faith" (Rom 1:17)? What does living by faith look like in your own life?

4. In Matthew 7, Jesus teaches us about the day of the Lord and of being hearers and doers of the word. Is it sobering to you that not everyone who appears to be a Christian is one? Explain. How can we have assurance of our own faith? What does the message about building one's house on rock versus sand mean? Why is it foolish to build one's house on sand?

PRAYER OF RESPONSE
Based on Deuteronomy 11:18–21; Matthew 7:24–27

Lord Jesus,
help us to put your word in our heart and soul,
feasting on it in such a way that it would nourish us and fill us.
May we be diligent to teach our children about your mighty deeds,
talking about them when we are at home and when we are away,
when we lie down and when we rise.
By your grace, let the truth of the gospel
bring abundant blessing upon our lives.
Forgive us when we foolishly neglect your word and commandments,
finding ourselves vulnerable to temptation; lacking in faith, hope, and love;
and quenching our fellowship with the Holy Spirit.
For our desire is to be like a wise man who built his house on a rock,

able to withstand the storms and trials of this life,
and drawing ever closer to you.
In the name of Jesus we pray. Amen.

Transfiguration of the Lord

LECTIONARY READINGS

> Exodus 24:12–18
>
> Psalm 2
>
> 2 Peter 1:16–21
>
> Matthew 17:1–9

DEVOTION

In the readings for Transfiguration of the Lord Sunday, we are taken to the mountain of the Lord. First, in Exodus 24, we read of Moses receiving the tablets with the Ten Commandments and experiencing the glory of the Lord. Second, we read about the transfiguration of Jesus on the mountaintop with Peter, James, and John. Peter also refers to this event in his second epistle, recounting the voice of God referring to Jesus as his Son on the "holy mountain." Thus, the glory of the Lord, the holy mountain, and the divinity of Jesus are common themes in the readings for this Sunday.

In the first reading from Exodus 24, we follow Moses up to Mount Sinai where he received the law and commandments of God and also experienced his presence and glory as it covered the mountain. Moses writes,

> Then Moses went up on the mountain, and the cloud covered the mountain. The glory of the Lord settled on Mount Sinai, and the cloud covered it for six days; on the seventh day he called to Moses out of the cloud. Now the appearance of the glory of the Lord was like a devouring fire on the top of the mountain in the sight of the Israelites. Moses entered the cloud and went up on the mountain. Moses was on the mountain for forty days and forty nights. (Exod 24:15–18)

Moses spent forty days and forty nights in the presence of the Lord. This was a significant moment in the history of the people of God. Moses, as the mediator between God and the people, received the law and commandments, the instruction of the Lord on how the people were to live. He also experienced the glory and the presence of God in a way that is beyond our full comprehension. We read this narrative with the eyes of faith and recognize the mercy of God in coming to speak and dwell with Moses in this way.

The incarnation of Jesus represents another moment in redemptive history in which God chose to live and dwell with his people in a close and intimate way. And the Holy Spirit, who indwells his people (corporately and individually) is a further step in the intimate relationship between God and his people. The new heavens and the new earth represent the final restoration of all things when we will see the Lord face to face and dwell with him in all his glory forever.

Psalm 2 is the response to the first reading from Exodus 24. Here, the psalmist tells of how the Lord has placed his Son, the King, on his "holy hill." He sings,

> He who sits in the heavens laughs;
> the Lord has them in derision.
> Then he will speak to them in his wrath
> and terrify them in his fury, saying,
> "I have set my king on Zion, my holy hill." (Ps 2:4–6)

The mountain of the Lord is echoed in the psalm, and the true King, Jesus, is foreshadowed as the one who will rule the nations. The psalm also echoes the language of the Father to the Son both at Jesus' baptism and on the Mount of Transfiguration. The psalmist prophetically describes the Lord as saying "You are my son; today I have begotten you" (Ps 2:7). At Jesus' baptism and at his transfiguration, Jesus hears the Father say, "You are my Son, the Beloved." Jesus' sonship is prophesied in the psalms. We recognize in passages such as this one that the story of God has always pointed to Jesus, the true King and Son of God. This is why Jesus spoke to the disciples, interpreting the Scriptures for them and showing them how he fulfills all that is written in the "law of Moses, the prophets, and the psalms" (Luke 24:27, 44).

In the second reading from 2 Peter 1, the apostle recounts to us what took place on the Mount of Transfiguration. Clearly, it had an impact on Peter because he still remembers the majesty as well as the words that were spoken by God. Peter's testimony affirms the validity and trustworthiness of the Scriptures. Everything holds together and all the various prophecies and testimonies complement one another, filling us with faith as we hear of different accounts telling the same story. Speaking of Jesus, Peter writes,

> For he received honor and glory from God the Father when that voice was conveyed to him by the Majestic Glory, saying, "This is my Son, my Beloved, with whom I am well pleased." We ourselves heard this voice come from heaven, while we were with him on the holy mountain. (2 Pet 1:17–18)

The main thrust of Peter's message and the reason for his recounting this moment in redemptive history is to validate the reality of the events he is describing. Peter makes it clear that he and the other disciples did not cleverly make up these stories about Christ. They are not "myths," they really happened (2 Pet 1:16). Peter, James, and John were eyewitness.

Our faith is not built on myths or philosophies, but on real, historical events that demonstrate the power and majesty of God. Jesus Christ lived among real people whose lives were utterly transformed by his presence and power. Thus, we can be strengthened in our own faith as we read about the accounts of others who walked with Jesus. And Jesus still works and moves among his people in mighty ways today.

Through the Holy Spirit and the various means of grace (word, sacrament, prayer), we can experience the presence, the power, and the majesty of God. As we gather to worship corporately, we, in a sense, ascend the holy mountain and receive a taste of God's divine glory among his people. Regular worship and the various means of grace sustain us and strengthen us in our journey of faith.

In the Gospel reading from Matthew 17, we read of the mysterious account of Jesus being transfigured on the holy mountain. Matthew writes,

> Six days later, Jesus took with him Peter and James and his brother John and led them up a high mountain, by themselves. And he was transfigured before them, and his face shone like the sun, and his clothes became bright as light. Suddenly there appeared to them Moses and Elijah, talking with him. (Matt 17:1–3)

We are encouraged to read this narrative with the eyes of faith as well as an informed imagination. A moment such as this is not part of our normal, daily experience. To have Jesus' face shining "like the sun" and to see his clothes as "bright as light" would have been startling, but then to have him speaking with Moses and Elijah would have been beyond immediate comprehension.

Peter is clearly confused and baffled as he offers clumsily, "Lord, it is good for us to be here; if you wish, I will set up three tents here, one for you, one for Moses, and one for Elijah" (Matt 17:4). Peter does not seem to fully know what he is even saying. We probably would not have responded much differently. We would have been grasping to comprehend what we were witnessing.

The presence of Moses and Elijah are thought to represent the Law and the Prophets. There are many interpretations of why these two men are before Jesus; however, the main point is that Jesus is clearly divine in nature. Aside from his divine appearance, we hear the very words of the Father declare, "This is my Son, the Beloved; with him I am well pleased; listen to him!" (Matt 17:5).

Peter and the other apostles would eventually heed these words. Because of this event as well as the cross, the resurrection, the ascension, and the sending of the Holy Spirit, the disciples would believe that Jesus is Lord, the Son of God. And their testimony to these realities would spread and transform the world.

Jesus also calls us to share the good news that he is Lord. We believe events such as the transfiguration and the resurrection by faith, for we were not eyewitnesses like Peter; yet, the Lord will use our testimony to bring others to salvation. The Holy Spirit works in the hearts and lives of those with whom we share the message of the gospel. On this last Sunday after Epiphany, the transfiguration of the Lord, may we be gripped by the majesty and glory of God. May we know Jesus as the beloved Son of God who came to bring light and salvation to the world.

QUESTIONS FOR REFLECTION

1. What do you think it was like for Moses to dwell for forty days in the presence of the Lord? What does it say about God that he would choose to draw near to his people and reveal his glory to Moses on the mountain, to a nation through the tabernacle and the temple, to many followers who walked with Jesus, and to us today who know the indwelling presence of the Holy Spirit?

2. How does Psalm 2 speak prophetically about Jesus? How does Jesus fulfill all that was written in the law, the prophets, and the psalms?

3. Why do you think Peter so clearly remembered the experience of Jesus' transfiguration? Does Peter's testimony about that event strengthen your own faith? Explain.

4. Why would the Father speak the words, "This is my Son, the Beloved; with him I am well pleased; listen to him!" Who needed to hear that message? How should that message impact us today?

PRAYER OF RESPONSE
Based on Psalm 2; 2 Peter 1:19

Lord Jesus,
you are the beloved Son of God
who reigns from heaven.
All the nations of the earth are subject to you;
you rule over all.
Help us to be attentive to the message
of your glory and salvation;
may it influence our lives until the day of your return.
In the name of Jesus we pray. Amen.

Lent through Pentecost

Ash Wednesday

LECTIONARY READINGS

Joel 2:1–2, 12–17

Psalm 51:1–17

2 Corinthians 5:20b—6:10

Matthew 6:1–6, 16–21

DEVOTION

Ash Wednesday begins the season of Lent, our forty-day journey to orient our lives and prepare for the events of Holy Week and Easter. Lent is an opportunity to discern those areas of our lives that have too strong of a hold on us. As Jesus spent forty days in the wilderness, we have forty days in which to acknowledge, surrender, and repent over the various idols and sin patterns in our lives such as power, addictions, money, control, and security. Lent is a time to repent and return to the Lord.

In the readings for Ash Wednesday, we will hear Joel's call to return to the Lord. We will resonate with the heart-felt cry of David's prayer of repentance and renewal from Psalm 51. In Paul's Letter to the Corinthians, we will celebrate the work of Christ, the one who has reconciled us to God. In the Gospel reading from Matthew 6, we will learn from Jesus what true giving, prayer, and fasting look like. May these readings open the door to a season of repentance, reflection, and renewal as we heed Joel's call and return to the Lord with our whole heart.

In the first reading from Joel 2, the prophet exhorts the people of God to "sound the alarm" (Joel 2:1) and be reminded that the Day of the Lord is coming. He is calling the people to repent and return to the Lord. Joel proclaims:

> Yet even now, says the Lord,
> return to me with all your heart,
> with fasting, with weeping, and with mourning;
> rend your hearts and not your clothing.
> Return to the Lord your God,
> for he is gracious and merciful,
> slow to anger, abounding in steadfast love,
> and relenting from punishment. (Joel 2:12–13)

Joel is encouraging the people of God to return to the Lord "with all your heart." He invites them to a season of fasting, weeping, and mourning. He exhorts them to this level of bold and raw repentance in light of God's grace, mercy, and steadfast love. What a difference it makes when we know we can come to God with all of our shortcoming and failures, all of our idols and sin, and know that he will not condemn us for he is "slow to anger, abounding in steadfast love" (Joel 2:13).

We come to Ash Wednesday and the whole season of Lent, not with fearful hearts, doubtful that God will still love us when we confess our true hearts to him. We come boldly to the throne of grace, knowing that we will "receive mercy and find grace to help in time of need" (Heb 4:16).

Psalm 51 is an appropriate response to the first readings as we find David pouring out his heart to God in raw, real repentance. He prays,

> Have mercy on me, O God,
> according to your steadfast love;
> according to your abundant mercy,
> blot out my transgressions.
> Wash me thoroughly from my iniquity,
> and cleanse me from my sin. (Ps 51:1–2)

If we recall the context of David's confession, we will remember that his repentance did not come immediately. His repentance came after the prophet Nathan told him a parable which opened his eyes to the depth of his sin: having an affair with Bathsheba, followed by having her husband, Uriah, killed in battle (2 Sam 11–12). David was in a season of sin and despair, and he sought the Lord with tears of sorrow and repentance over what he had done.

As we enter the season of Lent, may we have the same openness to what the Lord may reveal to us that David had when the Lord used Nathan to open his eyes to his sin. May we, like David, be open to times of tears and sorrow over our sin and idolatry. Lent is a season to come before the Lord, broken over the areas of our lives that have a tight hold on us. We come, asking God to have mercy according to his steadfast love.

In the second reading from 2 Corinthians, we find the apostle Paul teaching about the way in which we have been reconciled to God. He writes,

> We entreat you on behalf of Christ: be reconciled to God. For our sake God made the one who knew no sin to be sin, so that in him we might become the righteousness of God. (2 Cor 5:20–21)

Ash Wednesday invites us to be reconciled to God. If we have placed our faith in Christ, we know that we are justified and made right with God; we do not have to doubt our salvation. When we try to hide from our sin, however, or when (like David) we are not fully aware of the ways in which we have sinned against God, we are not able to experience the intimate fellowship and union with our triune God that we were designed to have. In this sense, we need to be reconciled and restored once again to God, knowing intimate fellowship and union with him. The season of Lent invites us into this reconciled and restored relationship.

Finally, in the Gospel reading from Matthew 6, Jesus teaches his followers what true giving, prayer, and fasting look like. He begins his teaching on these areas by declaring,

> Beware of practicing your righteousness before others in order to be seen by them, for then you have no reward from your Father in heaven. (Matt 6:1)

Whether in giving alms, praying, or fasting, we should seek to do these things in private, not looking for people's approval. When we give, pray, and fast in secret, "the Father who sees in secret" will reward us (Matt 6:4, 6, 18). I cannot speak definitively regarding the "reward" of the Father, but I believe it would entail things like peace, blessing, union, and intimate fellowship with God. These are rewards that no amount of money, prestige, or human approval can buy. As we cultivate spiritual practices in secret with our heavenly Father, we will know and experience priceless spiritual blessings.

On this Ash Wednesday, and as we journey throughout this season of Lent, may we know the blessings of returning to the Lord with our whole hearts, pouring out our confessions to God, and being reconciled and restored to him once again.

QUESTIONS FOR REFLECTION

1. The prophet Joel called the people of God to return to the Lord in his day. He was sounding the alarm and calling them to repentance. How is the Lord calling you to return to him on this Ash Wednesday? How might the Holy Spirit be sounding the alarm in your own heart?

2. David poured out his heart to the Lord in confession and repentance in Psalm 51. Why was David unable to see the depth of his sin at first, needing the help of the prophet Nathan? What may be blinding you to the sin and idols of your heart? Our God is full of mercy and steadfast love. Does this help draw you into true confession and repentance? Explain.

3. Have you been reconciled to God as Paul describes in his Letter to the Corinthians? If you have been justified by faith, are you experiencing rich intimacy and union with Christ? Are sin and idolatry squelching your relationship with Christ and the Holy Spirit? Describe. How might the season of Lent be an invitation to deeper fellowship with God in your life?

4. Are you cultivating the regular spiritual practices of giving, praying, and fasting? Are you doing these practices for people's approval or for the unseen rewards from the Father? Explain. What are the rewards we receive when we cultivate spiritual practices?

PRAYER OF RESPONSE
Based on Psalm 51:1–2, 6–12

Have mercy on us, O God, according to your steadfast love;
according to your abundant mercy blot out our transgressions.
Wash us thoroughly from our iniquity, and cleanse us from our sin.
You desire truth in the inward being;
therefore teach us wisdom in our secret heart.
Purge us with hyssop, and we shall be clean;
wash us, and we shall be whiter than snow.
Let us hear joy and gladness; let the bones that you have crushed rejoice.
Hide your face from our sins, and blot out our iniquities.
Create in us a clean heart, O God, and put a new and right spirit within us.
Do not cast us from your presence, and do not take your Holy Spirit from us.
Restore to us the joy of your salvation, and sustain in us a willing spirit.
Amen.

First Sunday in Lent

LECTIONARY READINGS

> Genesis 2:15–17; 3:1–7
>
> Psalm 32
>
> Romans 5:12–19
>
> Matthew 4:1–11

DEVOTION

The first Sunday in Lent always includes a Gospel account of Jesus' temptation in the wilderness. This year, we read Matthew's account as Jesus was led into the wilderness following his baptism in the Jordan River. As a contrast to this narrative, we read of the fall of Adam and Eve in the garden, being tempted by the serpent. The apostle Paul compares the first Adam with the second Adam, Christ. Thus, the themes of wilderness, temptation, and identification with Christ, our true Adam, are common themes in the readings for this Sunday.

In the first reading from Genesis 3, we find the enemy, the serpent, tempting Eve and twisting what the Lord had told her and Adam. The enemy asked Eve if God said, "You shall not eat from any tree in the garden" (Gen 3:1). Eve responded by saying that they were not to eat of the tree that was in the middle of the garden, for if they did, they would die. Then the serpent responded, "You will not die, for God knows that when you eat of it your eyes will be opened, and you will be like God, knowing good and evil" (Gen 3:4–5). Falling prey to the enemy's temptation to eat of the fruit God told them not to, their eyes were opened and they experienced nakedness and shame.

This is the tragic fall of humankind. The experience of Adam and Eve is the same for us today. When we give into the temptations of the enemy, we feel naked and ashamed and try to hide from God.

Psalm 32 offers a fitting response to the first reading. In this psalm of David, we discover that confessing to God, rather than trying to hide from him, is always the healthiest response to sin. The psalmist sings,

> While I kept silent, my body wasted away
> through my groaning all day long.
> For day and night your hand was heavy upon me;
> my strength was dried up as by the heat of summer.
> Then I acknowledged my sin to you,
> and I did not hide my iniquity;
> I said, "I will confess my transgressions to the Lord,"
> and you forgave the guilt of my sin. (Ps 32:3–5)

Adam and Eve tried to cover their shame and hide from God. The psalmist tried to keep his sin from God as well, only to find the relief of confession. Before confessing his sin, his body and soul were suffering from guilt and shame. When he acknowledged his sin to the Lord, he experienced the liberating freedom of the forgiveness of God. As we mature in our faith, we should find ourselves more quickly confessing to God and to another human being the sin that weighs heavy on our soul. Healing comes when we name our sin and shortcomings.

In the second reading from Romans 5, the apostle Paul contrasts the first Adam with the second Adam, Christ. He writes,

> Therefore just as one man's trespass led to condemnation for all, so one man's act of righteousness leads to justification and life for all. For just as through the one man's disobedience the many were made sinners, so through the one man's obedience the many will be made righteous. (Rom 5:18–19)

In Adam, we are all sinners, destined to die; in Christ, we find life and are made righteous. Christ did for us what we could not do for ourselves. He lived and experienced all the temptations we do, yet he did not sin. He is the spotless Lamb of God who "takes away the sin of the world" (John 1:29). His blood has atoned for all of our sin. In Adam, all die; in Christ, we are made alive.

In the Gospel reading from Matthew 4, we read of Jesus' temptation in the wilderness by the enemy. Satan approaches Jesus three times, tempting him to turn stones into bread; tempting him to put God to the test; and tempting him to worship someone or something other than God. Each time the devil tempts Jesus, Jesus refutes him with the word of God. Jesus experienced temptations in the wilderness as ancient Israel had, generations before him; yet, Jesus did not sin. He is the true son and servant who perfectly obeys the Father. His life opens the way for our redemption and salvation.

By withstanding the enemy's schemes, Jesus demonstrates the kind of life we are to live. During this season of Lent, Jesus invites us to fight the enemy's schemes and to find true nourishment through God's word.

QUESTIONS FOR REFLECTION

1. What is ironic about the way Satan twisted God's words? To what were Adam and Eve's eyes opened? How does the enemy still twist God's word and tempt us today?

2. The psalmist was weighed down and burdened physically and spiritually by his sin. How did he find relief? Why do we often resist confessing our sin to God and others?

3. How does Paul contrast Adam and Christ? Describe life "in Adam" and life "in Christ."

4. How did Jesus resist Satan's temptations? How did God minister to Jesus in the wilderness? How does God comfort us today?

PRAYER OF RESPONSE
Based on Genesis 3:1–7; Psalm 32:3–5; Matthew 4:1–11

Lord Jesus,
we acknowledge that we often try to hide our sin from you.
Naked and ashamed, our souls grow weary and heavy
and our bodies waste away
while we keep our transgressions to ourselves.
Help us to more readily confess our hearts before you,
finding the forgiveness and healing we truly desire.
May we resist the temptations of the evil one,
protecting ourselves through the power of the Spirit
and the strength of your word.
In the name of Jesus we pray. Amen.

Second Sunday in Lent

LECTIONARY READINGS

Genesis 12:1–4a

Psalm 121

Romans 4:1–5, 13–17

John 3:1–17

DEVOTION

In the readings for the second Sunday in Lent, John presents us with a meditation on Christian baptism through the conversation between Jesus and Nicodemus. Baptism is the sign of the covenant for believers in Christ. Thus, to complement the Gospel reading, the first reading from Genesis 12 recalls God's covenant with Abraham. In the second reading from Romans 4, the apostle Paul teaches that Abraham was blessed by God, not because he obeyed the law but because he had faith in the promises of God. Thus, baptism, covenant blessings, and covenant promises are common themes in the readings for this Sunday.

In the first reading from Genesis 12, God promises to bless Abraham. The Lord told Abraham,

> Go from your country and your kindred and your father's house to the land that I will show you. I will make of you a great nation, and I will bless you and make your name great, so that you will be a blessing. I will bless those who bless you, and the one who curses you I will curse, and in you all the families of the earth shall be blessed. (Gen 12:1–3)

God promised Abraham a land, a people, and a blessing. Abraham trusted God and obeyed. The Lord called Abraham into a journey without all of the details. Abraham did not know the land to which he would be traveling. He did not know just how God would make him into a great nation. He did not know how he would be a blessing, but Abraham believed God and exercised faith.

We are called to the same way of life. God will call us into a gospel journey without giving us all of the directions. Our nature is to question, doubt, or feel that God should choose someone else! Like Abraham, we are simply called to trust God and exercise faith in him. God does not call the equipped; he equips the called.

Psalm 121, as a response to the first reading, offers us orientation and hope for our gospel journey. The psalmist sings,

> I lift up my eyes to the hills—
> from where will my help come?
> My help comes from the Lord,
> who made heaven and earth. (Ps 121:1–2)

In those moments when we feel doubt and fear, we turn our gaze unto the Lord for our help comes from him. Rather than focus our eyes on what seems terrifying, we fix our eyes on the maker of heaven and earth. This shift in focus puts our situations in proper perspective. The psalmist also declares, "The Lord will keep your going out and your coming in from this time on and forevermore" (Ps 121:8).

In both the ordinary seasons of life and in new ventures, God is the one who keeps us. He guides and sustains us in the mundane and in the unknown. God never leaves us alone; his presence is always with us, in our comings and goings. He is always by our side.

In the second reading from Romans 4, the apostle Paul clarifies the nature of Abraham's standing with God. He teaches how Abraham was not justified according to the law, but according to faith in the promises of God. Paul writes,

> For the promise that he would inherit the world did not come to Abraham or to his descendants through the law but through the righteousness of faith. For if it is the adherents of the law who are to be the heirs, faith is null and the promise is void. For the law brings wrath, but where there is no law, neither is there transgression. For this reason the promise depends on faith, in order that it may rest on grace, so that it may be guaranteed to

all his descendants, not only to the adherents of the law but also to those who share the faith of Abraham (who is the father of all of us). (Rom 4:13–16)

The promise precedes the law. "Abraham believed God, and it was reckoned to him as righteousness" (Rom 4:3). Thus, Abraham was not justified by works, but by faith in the promises of God. The same is true of us today. We are not justified by our obedience to the law, but by faith in Christ. We are the spiritual ancestors of Abraham, inheritors of divine promises: a land, a people, and a blessing. The land we look forward to is the new heaven and the new earth; the people of whom we are a part is the body of Christ, the church; and the blessing we receive is Christ. Through Christ, we are blessed, and we are a blessing to the world.

In the Gospel reading from John 3, we find Nicodemus, a Jewish religious authority, coming to Jesus to gain understanding. Jesus teaches him:

> Very truly, I tell you, no one can enter the kingdom of God without being born of water and Spirit. What is born of the flesh is flesh, and what is born of the Spirit is spirit. Do not be astonished that I said to you, "You must be born from above." The wind blows where it chooses, and you hear the sound of it, but you do not know where it comes from or where it goes. So it is with everyone who is born of the Spirit. (John 3:5–8)

Jesus and Nicodemus are having a conversation about the kingdom of God and what it means to be "born from above." This narrative is seen by some scholars as a meditation on baptism. Jesus tells Nicodemus that to enter the kingdom of God, one must be born of "water and Spirit." Baptism is the sign of God's covenant with his people. Along with the Lord's Supper, it is a sacrament—a means of grace through which God acts on our behalf. Baptism is given once; it is the way into God's kingdom. The Lord's Supper is a recurring meal that nourishes and sustains us on our journey as God's pilgrim people.

During this season of Lent, may we be renewed in our baptism and find strength in the promises of God. We are his children who long for our final home in the new heaven and the new earth. Until that day, we seek to be a blessing to the world, living as the light of Christ to those around us.

QUESTIONS FOR REFLECTION

1. Why do you think Abraham trusted in God's promises? Where did he find the faith to leave his own country and move to a foreign land? Do you live with the faith of Abraham, willing to go wherever God may call you?

2. The psalmist knew his help came from the Lord, the maker of heaven and earth. Do you go to God first when you need help? Do you trust in your own resources first or in the one who made heaven and earth? What does it mean that the Lord will "keep your life" (Ps 121:7)?

3. How would you summarize Paul's teaching in Romans 4:1–5, 13–17? Which came first, the promises of God or the law of God? Are we justified by works or by faith? Are the promises to Abraham the same as the promises to us? Explain.

4. Why did Nicodemus search for Jesus in the night? What does it mean to be born of "water and Spirit"? What is the significance of your own baptism? How can we be renewed in our baptismal promises and identity? What are our baptismal promises? How is the sacrament of baptism like the sacrament of the Lord's Supper? How are they different?

PRAYER OF RESPONSE
Based on Romans 4:16; John 3:5, 16

Almighty God,
you are the one who keeps his covenant
to a thousand generations.
By faith, we believe the promise
you made to Abraham long ago.
By grace, we receive all the benefits of that promise
as the spiritual children of Abraham.
As those born of water and Spirit,
we trust in you to guide us and give us eternal life.
In the name of Jesus we pray. Amen.

Third Sunday in Lent

LECTIONARY READINGS

Exodus 17:1–7

Psalm 95

Romans 5:1–11

John 4:5–42

DEVOTION

For the third Sunday in Lent, we continue to read from the Gospel of John and meditate on the sacrament of baptism. Historically, the season of Lent has been a time to train baptismal candidates in the truths of the Christian faith. It is also a time for those who are already in Christ to renew their baptismal identity as children of God.

In the readings for this Sunday, we find Jesus talking with a Samaritan woman about living water. We find the Israelites quarreling because of thirst, so Moses strikes the rock at Meribah and the Lord displays his power and provision for his people. We read from Paul's Letter to the Romans describing justification by faith. Thus, water (a sign of baptism), the grace of God, and justification by faith are common threads in the readings for this Sunday.

In the first reading from Exodus 17, we find the Israelites quarreling with Moses about not having any water. They have been journeying for weeks in the desert and are longing for Egypt. We read,

> The people quarreled with Moses, and said, "Give us water to drink." Moses said to them, "Why do you quarrel with me? Why do you test the Lord?" But the people thirsted there for water,

and the people complained against Moses and said, "Why did you bring us out of Egypt, to kill us and our children and livestock with thirst?" (Exod 17:2–3)

The Israelites had already begun to gather manna, the miraculous bread from heaven, to satiate their hunger. Now, they are crying out because of their thirst. In their despair, they began to romance their time in Egypt, forgetting the cruelty and bondage under Pharaoh. The Lord, in his grace, directed Moses to strike the rock with his staff. Moses obeyed and the Lord displayed his power and his mercy toward his people. They were able to drink of the water that the Lord provided.

One author aptly describes "how much easier it was to get them out of Egypt than it was to get Egypt out of them."[1] We are very much like the Israelites, often idolizing or romanticizing a prior season of life, while neglecting God's goodness, provision, and blessings in the present.

Psalm 95 is an appropriate response to the first reading as it recalls the situation at Meribah. The psalmist sings,

> O come, let us worship and bow down;
> let us kneel before the Lord, our Maker!
> For he is our God,
> and we are the people of his pasture
> and the sheep of his hand.
> O that today you would listen to his voice!
> Do not harden your hearts, as at Meribah,
> as on the day at Massah in the wilderness,
> when your ancestors tested me
> and put me to the proof, though they had seen my work.
> (Ps 95:6–9)

The generation in the wilderness had hardened their hearts before the Lord even though they were recipients of his divine care and provision. They tested the Lord and doubted whether he was with them and for them. Thus, speaking for the Lord, the psalmist concludes by stating,

> For forty years I loathed that generation
> and said, "They are a people whose hearts go astray,
> and they do not regard my ways."
> Therefore in my anger I swore,
> "They shall not enter my rest." (Ps 95:10–11)

---

1. Ryken, *Exodus*, 390.

These are hard words to hear from the Lord. May they remind us not to put God to the test or harden our own hearts against him. Like the psalmist, may we be quick to see that the Lord is good; he is our Shepherd and King. He leads us and cares for us in ordinary and miraculous ways. He is the living water that quenches our thirsty souls.

In the second reading from Romans 5, the apostle Paul teaches us that our justification, our right standing before God, is by faith. It is not something we earn. He writes,

> Therefore, since we are justified by faith, we have peace with God through our Lord Jesus Christ, through whom we have obtained access to this grace in which we stand, and we boast in our hope of sharing the glory of God. And not only that, but we also boast in our afflictions, knowing that affliction produces endurance, and endurance produces character, and character produces hope, and hope does not put us to shame, because God's love has been poured into our hearts through the Holy Spirit that has been given to us. (Rom 5:1–5)

Because of the blood of Christ, we have peace with God. We are seen as righteous before him because of the atoning work of the cross of Christ. Moreover, Paul calls us to hope not only in the future glory that we will share with God, he calls us to hope in our afflictions and sufferings as well. The afflictions we endure will produce endurance, character, and hope. This is a message about kingdom living, not worldly living. The world does not usually endorse or teach us to embrace suffering and affliction. The philosophy of the world is all about comfort and happiness; it does not hold up the sanctifying nature of suffering.

Because we are only temporary citizens of this world, we fix our eyes on a greater destination and a greater reality. We can embrace hard circumstances that we may not fully understand. We can be open to the refining work of God in our lives, helping us to loosen our grip on the things we think we want and to pursue the things God knows we truly need. The Lord's process of getting us to a place of contentment may involve affliction, endurance, character building, and hope in things that are of an eternal nature.

Lastly, Paul calls us to remember how God has reconciled us to himself. He writes,

> For if while we were enemies we were reconciled to God through the death of his Son, much more surely, having been reconciled,

will we be saved by his life. But more than that, we even boast in God through our Lord Jesus Christ, through whom we have now received reconciliation. (Rom 5:10–11)

Paul calls us to boast in God who, through Christ his Son, has reconciled us to himself. We, who were once enemies of God, are now at peace with him. Knowing that we are at peace with God, that we are reconciled with him, should fill us with joy and give us proper perspective on our current circumstances. Wherever we find ourselves, we can rest in knowing that our eternity is secure.

In the Gospel reading from John 4, we find Jesus having a life-changing conversation with a Samaritan woman. She came in the heat of the day to draw water, likely out of shame because of her many husbands. She came on a normal day to fulfill a mundane task. By the end of her time at the well, however, John gives us the detail that she "left her water jar" before heading into town to tell everyone about Jesus (John 4:28). The one thing she came to do that day was greatly overshadowed by the life-giving, life-changing conversation with Jesus. More than her parched lips, her thirsty soul was quenched by the Lord Jesus.

Jesus and the woman spoke about living water and then about worship. Initially, the woman seemed skeptical and defensive. Slowly, her guard came down as Jesus spoke to her as one who truly knew her. Through his divine love and compassion, Jesus touched the wounded and vulnerable places of this woman's soul. John recounts their dialogue about worship with Jesus' words and the woman's response. Jesus told her,

> "God is spirit, and those who worship him must worship in spirit and truth." The woman said to him, "I know that Messiah is coming" (who is called Christ). "When he comes, he will proclaim all things to us." Jesus said to her, "I am he, the one who is speaking to you." (John 4:24–26)

At this point in their conversation, the disciples arrived and the woman left to tell others that she had met the Messiah. The narrative ends with Jesus remaining in the town and with others coming to believe that he is the Savior of the world (John 4:42).

Jesus works in the same way with us today. He reveals himself to those who may be skeptical, defensive, or doubtful of his divine lordship. Jesus is able to meet us in our woundedness, our brokenness, and our sinfulness. He knows our past and comes to heal us and transform us in the deep places of our soul, and he may use us to share with others how we have been healed and changed by his saving grace.

Like the woman at the well, Jesus loves to break into the ordinary places of our lives and fill us afresh with his living water. During this season of Lent, may we remember that we are baptized sons and daughters of God. We have been born again of water and Spirit. May we live each day, renewed in this eternal identity, sharing the hope of the gospel with those who need to hear it.

QUESTIONS FOR REFLECTION

1. Why were the people of God quarreling with Moses? How did God provide for their needs? What are the various ways we quarrel with God in our daily lives? Do you sometimes wonder if God is really for you? What is the lesson for you in Exodus 17?

2. The psalmist recounts the narrative from Exodus 17 and exhorts us not to harden our hearts toward the Lord. How does the psalmist describe God in Psalm 95? Discuss which phrases and descriptions stand out to you and why.

3. How does Paul describe our relationship with God prior to justification by faith? How does he describe our relationship after justification? How does Paul call us to view suffering? What does being reconciled to God mean to you personally?

4. Why does John give us the detail about the woman leaving her water jar? What does this indicate about her time with Jesus? How was Jesus living water to the Samaritan woman? How is Jesus the source of living water in your own life?

PRAYER OF RESPONSE
Based on John 4:5–42

Lord Jesus,
we come to you with thirsty souls.
Like the woman at the well,
we are full of pride and false assumptions about you.
Though our stories are messy and our needs are great,
we often remain at a distance from you.
Grant us joy and peace for you know all we have ever done,
yet you love us with an unfailing love.
Give us boldness to share this good news,
from hearts overflowing with gratitude,
to those around us that need your grace.
In the name of Jesus we pray. Amen.

Fourth Sunday in Lent

LECTIONARY READINGS

1 Samuel 16:1–13
Psalm 23
Ephesians 5:8–14
John 9:1–41

DEVOTION

In the readings for this Sunday, the fourth Sunday in Lent, we read of the man born blind who was healed by Jesus. We read of the young David being anointed by Samuel, and we hear the apostle Paul's exhortation to live as children of light. Thus, living in the light, the anointing of God, seeing, and believing are common themes in the readings for this Sunday.

In the first reading from 1 Samuel 16, we find that the Lord has rejected Saul as king and has sent Samuel to find the new king of Israel. Samuel arrives at the house of Jesse who has eight sons. Samuel has the seven oldest sons pass by him, but none of them are to be the new king. Samuel asks if there is another son and then has someone go and find David, the young shepherd boy. David is chosen as the new king even though he is much smaller than his seven older brothers. A key spiritual paradigm is found in this narrative. Samuel shares, "The Lord does not see as mortals see; they look on the outward appearance, but the Lord looks on the heart" (1 Sam 16:7). God does not judge us by our size or physical strength; he knows our hearts.

Samuel anoints David, and the spirit of the Lord comes upon him. We read, "Then Samuel took the horn of oil and anointed him in the presence of his brothers, and the spirit of the Lord came mightily upon David from that day forward" (1 Sam 16:13). At our baptism, we are filled with the power of the Holy Spirit, chosen by God to live for him and to shine as a light in this world. We should not concern ourselves with what we may deem as strengths or weaknesses, but trust that God will use us for his purposes in his kingdom.

Psalm 23 is the response to the first reading. Here, David poetically expresses the nature of God and how he leads and guides us throughout our lives. David writes,

> You prepare a table before me
> in the presence of my enemies;
> you anoint my head with oil;
> my cup overflows.
> Surely goodness and mercy shall follow me
> all the days of my life,
> and I shall dwell in the house of the Lord
> my whole life long. (Ps 23:5–6)

David's life would prove that Samuel chose according to God's divine providence. When Goliath was taunting the people of God, it was the young David (who did not even fit into the battle armor) who boldly went out and defeated the great enemy (1 Sam 17). Time after time, the Lord proved himself faithful to David. David knew what it meant to have goodness and mercy follow him throughout his life. He knew the joy of dwelling in the house of the Lord.

In the second reading from Ephesians 5, the apostle Paul exhorts us to live as children of light. He writes,

> For once you were darkness, but now in the Lord you are light. Walk as children of light, for the fruit of the light is found in all that is good and right and true. Try to find out what is pleasing to the Lord. Take no part in the unfruitful works of darkness; rather, expose them. (Eph 5:8–11)

As baptized sons and daughters, we are to search out what is "pleasing to the Lord," all that is "good and right and true." Living in this manner not only pleases God, it will bless us as well. Walking and living as children of light is the way we were always meant to live. Unfortunately, we often choose unfruitful and evil practices. Rather than exposing these behaviors, we indulge in them. Paul is admonishing us to wake up and live as children of God, shining the light of Christ into the darkness of this world.

In the Gospel reading from John 9, we read of a man born blind who is healed by Jesus on the Sabbath. After receiving this miraculous healing, the man is then interrogated by the religious leaders. When the Pharisees refer to Jesus as a sinner, the man offers a simple but profound response that has become well-known to our ears: "I do not know whether he is a sinner. One thing I do know, that though I was blind, now I see" (John 9:25).

John Newton wove this statement into his beautiful hymn "Amazing Grace," which has been embraced by the church since the eighteenth century. The man's declaration speaks for all of us in a powerful way. Though we have not all been physically blind, we have all been blinded spiritually. As Paul taught us, we were once in the darkness, but through Christ we have become children of light. Once we were blind, now we see. Once we sought evil, now we seek what is good and right and true.

During this season of Lent, may we be reminded that we are children of light. We have been chosen by God to be his ambassadors in this world. Our testimony is simple but profound: we once were blind, but now we see. May we share this powerful message with those who need to hear it.

QUESTIONS FOR REFLECTION

1. Why did God not choose one of Jesse's seven strong sons? Why did he choose David? What does the spiritual paradigm that humans look "on the outward appearance, but the Lord looks on the heart" mean to you? How has this truth been reflected in your own life?

2. David wrote a beautiful and poetic song about God, our Shepherd. Where do you think he found his inspiration? What does he mean by the line "you anoint my head with oil, my cup overflows" (Ps 23:5)? Do you think he is referring to his anointing by Samuel? How does this verse apply to us?

3. How does the apostle Paul exhort us to live? Name behaviors that would be characterized as "good and right and true." Have you fallen asleep in your faith? Do you need to be awakened to the love of God? Explain.

4. Jesus brings clarity through mud to the man born blind. What are some of the unconventional ways Jesus heals and restores us? Why did healing a man on the Sabbath enrage the religious leaders? What lesson do we learn through this misunderstanding?

PRAYER OF RESPONSE
Based on Psalm 23; 1 Samuel 16:7; John 9:25

Good Shepherd,
we rejoice in you for you restore our souls.
You grant us safety and peace
and protect us from our enemies.
We delight in you for your goodness and mercy
follow us all the days of our lives.
We praise you for you do not see us
by our outward appearances; you look at our hearts.
By your grace, we who were once blind now see.
In the name of Jesus we pray. Amen.

Fifth Sunday in Lent

LECTIONARY READINGS

Ezekiel 37:1–14

Psalm 130

Romans 8:6–11

John 11:1–45

DEVOTION

In the readings for the fifth Sunday in Lent, we find Jesus raising his friend Lazarus from the dead. We can imagine the scene Ezekiel describes of dead bones coming to life. We read from the apostle Paul's letter to the Romans that we are alive through the Spirit. Thus, "from death to life" is a common theme in the readings for this Sunday.

In the first reading from Ezekiel 37, we find the amazing account of the word of God breathing life into a valley of dry bones. The prophet declares,

> So I prophesied as I had been commanded, and as I prophesied, suddenly there was a noise, a rattling, and the bones came together, bone to its bone. I looked, and there were sinews on them, and flesh had come upon them, and skin had covered them, but there was no breath in them. Then he said to me, "Prophesy to the breath, prophesy, mortal, and say to the breath: Thus says the Lord God: Come from the four winds, O breath, and breathe upon these slain, that they may live." I prophesied as he commanded me, and the breath came into them, and they lived and stood on their feet, a vast multitude. (Ezek 37:7–10)

This narrative reveals many truths that are relevant for us today. First, the word of God is powerful, able to bring dead bones to life. For us, God's word is "living and active and sharper than any two-edged sword, piercing until it divides soul from spirit, joints from marrow; it is able to judge the thoughts and intentions of the heart" (Heb 4:12). Indeed, God's word brought creation into existence. Thus, as we feed on the word throughout the day and week, we are strengthened, edified, renewed, and convicted. Moreover, this word is life to us.

Second, though scholars believe this narrative points to the return of God's people from exile and to their restoration, it can also be seen as a picture of the final resurrection when Jesus returns, and we dwell once again with our Lord. Paul writes, "For the trumpet will sound, and the dead will be raised imperishable, and we will be changed. For this perishable body must put on imperishability, and this mortal body must put on immortality" (1 Cor 15:52–53).

John describes the day when God will dwell with us and there will be no more death, mourning, or pain (Rev 21:3-4). One day our mortal bodies will become resurrection bodies, fit for eternal life in the new heaven and the new earth. This is a truth beyond our comprehension, but Scripture speaks to his reality. The valley of dry bones is like a picture of this future reality.

Psalm 130 is the response to the first reading. Like the setting in Ezekiel 37, the psalmist's situation is bleak. He writes,

> Out of the depths I cry to you, O Lord.
> Lord, hear my voice!
> Let your ears be attentive
> to the voice of my supplications! (Ps 130:1–2)

The psalmist cries out from a place of despair—"Out of the depths." Yet, like the valley of dry bones, the psalmist puts his hope in the word of God. He sings,

> I wait for the Lord; my soul waits,
> and in his word I hope;
> my soul waits for the Lord
> more than those who watch for the morning,
> more than those who watch for the morning. (Ps 130:5–6)

The word of the Lord breathed life into dead, dry bones. Here, the heart of the psalmist is renewed in the word of God, his steadfast love, and his power to redeem (Ps 130:7). The same is true for us. The word of God is where we find hope in desperate situations. When we find ourselves in the depths of grief, depression, loneliness, addiction, or fear, we can turn to God's word for hope and life. Like the psalmist, we come to God who is full of steadfast love and the power to redeem.

In the second reading from Romans 8, we find the apostle Paul speaking of the life-giving power of the Spirit. He writes, "If the Spirit of him who raised Jesus from the dead dwells in you, he who raised Christ from the dead will give life to your mortal bodies also through his Spirit that dwells in you" (Rom 8:11). Paul speaks of a profound truth: the same power that raised Christ from the dead lives within us. We can often lose sight of this reality, but it should be a source of strength and encouragement for us. We are no longer slaves to sin and death; we are the beloved children of God, made alive by the Spirit. We can access this power at any time through prayer, worship, God's word, and fellowship with other believers. By God's grace and the power of the Spirit, we can overcome fears, trials, and temptations.

Finally, in the Gospel reading from John 11, we find Jesus at the tomb of Lazarus, his friend. John writes,

> And Jesus looked upward and said, "Father, I thank you for having heard me. I knew that you always hear me, but I have said this for the sake of the crowd standing here, so that they may believe that you sent me." When he had said this, he cried with a loud voice, "Lazarus, come out!" The dead man came out, his hands and feet bound with strips of cloth and his face wrapped in a cloth. Jesus said to them, "Unbind him, and let him go." (John 11:41–44)

There are many lessons to glean from this narrative. First, we know that Jesus was close to Lazarus and his sisters, Mary and Martha. Mary and Martha sent word to Jesus telling him, "Lord, he whom you love is ill" (John 11:3). We also know that when they took Jesus to the tomb, he began to weep (John 11:35). Jesus expressed his own grief at the death of Lazarus. We cannot know for certain what all his tears signified: anger at death itself, grief over his friend's death, grief over the sadness of Mary and Martha. We do know that in his humanity, Jesus wept just like any one of us.

Second, John gives us the detail that this took place, in part, so that the witnesses of this event would believe that Jesus was sent by the Father. John writes, "Many of the Jews, therefore, who had come with

Mary and had seen what Jesus did believed in him" (John 11:45). This miracle demonstrated Jesus' authority over death. In raising Lazarus from the dead, Jesus brought some to faith and led others to plot how they could kill him (John 11:53).

During this season of Lent, may we reflect on how we have been brought from death to life. Like the valley of dry bones, we have the hope of no longer being exiles but citizens in God's eternal kingdom. We have the power of new life already within us through the indwelling Holy Spirit. He is our advocate, our guide, our counselor, and our teacher. Lastly, because he lived and wept just like us, we know that we have a high priest in Jesus who is able to sympathize with us in our weakness and our distress (Hebrews 4:15). We can approach him at any time knowing that he loves us; he is for us; and he is able to restore us and redeem us. This is the good news for those who believe.

QUESTIONS FOR REFLECTION

1. The valley of dry bones paints a vivid picture in our minds. How did this narrative encourage the people of Israel who were in exile at the time? How does this narrative encourage us today? How should the reality of the final resurrection bring us hope for today?

2. How does the psalmist describe his situation in Psalm 130? Where does he turn for hope? The psalmist sings, "My soul waits for the Lord" (Ps 130:6). How do you handle waiting for the Lord?

3. What does Paul mean when he says that the Spirit will bring "life to your mortal bodies" (Rom 8:11)? How does the Spirit equip and empower us?

4. What kind of relationship did Jesus have with Lazarus, Mary, and Martha? Why did Jesus weep on the way to Lazarus's tomb? What impact did the raising of Lazarus have on those who witnessed that event? How did this same event affect the religious leaders? How can you apply this narrative to your own life?

PRAYER OF RESPONSE
Based on John 11:25–26; Ezekiel 37:1–14; Romans 8:6

Lord Jesus,
you are the resurrection and the life.
Like the valley of dry bones,
you breathe life into your people,
filling us with the breath of your Spirit.
Help us to set our minds,
not on the flesh, which is death,
but on the Spirit, who is life and peace.
In the name of Jesus we pray. Amen.

Palm Sunday

LECTIONARY READINGS

Psalm 118:1–2, 19–29

Matthew 21:1–11

DEVOTION

I love Palm Sunday. I love the transition that it provides as we begin to set our hearts and minds on Holy Week and Easter, the high points of the Christian year. There are only two readings for this Sunday, the account of the triumphal entry from Matthew's Gospel and a portion of Psalm 118.

A few things stand out as we reflect on Matthew's account of Jesus entering Jerusalem with his disciples. First of all, we consider the significance of the place from which they set out—Bethany. This village was home to a few of Jesus' close friends and companions: Mary, Martha, and Lazarus. It is a couple of miles from Jerusalem and is oriented on the eastern slope of the Mount of Olives (also a significant place in Jesus' life and ministry).

From there, Jesus sends out two disciples to a village ahead of them to locate a colt that has never been ridden. He gives them detailed instructions that turn out just as he said they would. Here, Jesus' sovereignty over all situations and circumstances is made evident. This display of foreknowledge would have served to further the disciples' belief that Jesus was the Messiah. We, too, can trust him and know that in him all things hold together (Col 1:17).

As he and the disciples began to draw near to Jerusalem, the crowd was stirred and began to roll out the red carpet for Jesus. Matthew writes,

> A very large crowd spread their cloaks on the road, and others cut branches from the trees and spread them on the road. The crowds that went ahead of him and that followed were shouting,
>
>> "Hosanna to the Son of David!
>> Blessed is the one who comes in the name of the Lord!
>> Hosanna in the highest heaven!" (Matt 21:8–9)

Many people in the crowd likely believed that Jesus was riding in to conquer Rome. There would have been those in the crowd that had been awaiting a messiah that would save them from their oppressors. For them, this entry was to regain power and control from Roman authorities. Jesus, however, had something very different in mind. Luke gives us a detail that serves as a window into Jesus' emotional state in this moment. He writes,

> As he came near and saw the city, he wept over it, saying, "If you, even you, had only recognized on this day the things that make for peace! But now they are hidden from your eyes." (Luke 19:41–42)

As the people were shouting and singing, Jesus was weeping over the city of Jerusalem for the people did not realize the nature of his mission. Jesus was not riding in to conquer Rome; he was riding in to die and bring atonement and salvation to those in sin and death. He would conquer, but not in the way the crowds expected. Jesus' mission was to defeat sin and death, not a political power.

So often, we come to Jesus with expectations just like those of the crowd on Palm Sunday. We come to Jesus with a plan and an agenda for him to fulfill, but Jesus is not interested in satisfying our misguided desires. When our prayers do not seem to be answered, it could be that Jesus is simply waiting for us to realize that his ways are not our ways. Usually, his unanswered prayers are a mercy, a gift. God does not give us all that we want, but all that we truly need.

The people laying down branches before Jesus did not need a new earthly king who would take over the city; they needed a heavenly Savior who would take over their hearts and lives. Unfortunately, they did not realize this deeper need. May God open our eyes to our need of him each and every day.

The song that the people were shouting that day was from Psalm 118:

> Blessed is the one who comes in the name of the Lord.
> We bless you from the house of the Lord. (Ps 118:26)

The psalms were Israel's hymnbook, the source of expression for all occasions: joy, sorrow, lament, praise, and celebration. On this day long ago, they were singing a song of celebration to their Messiah. Luke gives us another detail concerning this occasion and the fact that their song was warranted. He writes,

> Some of the Pharisees in the crowd said to him, "Teacher, order your disciples to stop." He answered, "I tell you, if these were silent, the stones would shout out." (Luke 19:39–40)

Though, in their hearts, the people may have had wrong motives that day long ago, with their lips they were offering appropriate praise to the King of kings. On this Palm Sunday, may we sing and celebrate the reality that Jesus is King. May we ponder how he rode into Jerusalem long ago to save his people and cry out, "Blessed is the one who comes in the name of the Lord."

QUESTIONS FOR REFLECTION

1. How does Jesus fail to meet your misguided wants and expectations? What might be a better approach when it comes to your expectations of Jesus?

2. Jesus' sovereignty was clearly on display as the two disciples located the colt. What does this tell you about Jesus' care over the details of your own life?

3. What is on your heart this year as you enter Holy Week? If you were to sing a song to the Lord, what form of expression would it be—joy, sorrow, celebration, lament, adoration?

PRAYER OF RESPONSE
Based on Matthew 21:5, 11

Lord Jesus,
we praise you as our Prophet,
who speaks and who is
the Word of life for hungry souls.
We worship you as our Priest,
who rode into Jerusalem to offer
and to be the atoning sacrifice for our sins.
We adore you as our King,
who came to save us and protect us as your own. Amen.

Maundy Thursday

LECTIONARY READINGS

Exodus 12:1–14

Psalm 116:1–2, 12–19

1 Corinthians 11:23–26

John 13:1–17, 31b–35

DEVOTION

Maundy Thursday is a special day of remembrance in the Christian year. In the readings for this day, we recall the institution of the Passover meal in Exodus 12. We read of how Jesus, during the Passover meal, instituted the Lord's Supper, which is recorded in the second reading from 1 Corinthians 11. Psalm 116 speaks of the "cup of salvation," which was part of the Passover meal. Finally, the Gospel reading from John 13 recalls Jesus washing the disciples' feet, a living lesson on how we are to love and serve others. Thus, the themes of God's rescue, the sacrament of the Lord's Supper, and love and service are threads in the readings for this day.

In the first reading from Exodus 12, we read of the Lord's instructions to Moses and Aaron regarding the Passover meal, a meal that Israel would celebrate each year to remember how the Lord rescued them from slavery in Egypt. We read,

> This day shall be a day of remembrance for you. You shall celebrate it as a festival to the Lord; throughout your generations you shall observe it as a perpetual ordinance. (Exod 12:14)

In his grace, God has given his people festivals, ways to actively remember his mighty acts and deeds. The first Passover meal was the means of Israel's exodus from Egypt. As a part of the instructions, each household was to eat a roasted lamb (without blemish) and smear some of its blood on their house as a sign for the Lord to "pass over" that household. We read,

> The blood shall be a sign for you on the houses where you live: when I see the blood, I will pass over you, and no plague shall destroy you when I strike the land of Egypt. (Exod 12:13)

I imagine that these instructions may have sounded odd to the people of Israel, but in obeying the Lord their God, they would be saved from the final plague on Egypt. Jesus instituted the Lord's Supper with his disciples on the evening that he was betrayed and arrested. Like the people of God from old, every time we eat of this meal, we remember how Christ has rescued us. Israel was rescued from the bondage of slavery in Egypt; Christ has rescued us from the bondage of sin and death. Through the sacrament of the Lord's Supper (also known as communion or the Eucharist), we remember all that God has done for us; we are nourished for our spiritual journey; and we enjoy union with Christ through the Holy Spirit who indwells us.

Psalm 116, the psalm of response, speaks of the "cup of salvation," likely a reference to the drink offering from Leviticus 23:13. This drink offering was a sign of gratitude for the Lord's salvation and sustained provision. This cup also has associations with the Passover meal and, likely, the cup that Jesus holds up when he declares, "This cup is the new covenant in my blood. Do this, as often as you drink it, in remembrance of me" (1 Cor 11:25).

The psalmist expresses his gratitude to God, saying,

> I will offer to you a thanksgiving sacrifice
> and call on the name of the Lord.
> I will pay my vows to the Lord
> in the presence of all his people,
> in the courts of the house of the Lord,
> in your midst, O Jerusalem.
> Praise the Lord! (Ps 116:17–19)

The psalmist is obeying Israel's form of worship, established by God and is bringing his drink offering to the Lord. When we partake of the Lord's Supper, a regular facet of our corporate worship, we are expressing our gratitude to God and obeying his exhortation to partake of this meal in remembrance of him.

The second reading from 1 Corinthians 11 provides us with some apostolic commentary on the Lord's Supper, recounted in the synoptic Gospels (Matt 26:17–30; Mark 14:12-25; Luke 22:7–23). Paul writes,

> For I received from the Lord what I also handed on to you, that the Lord Jesus on the night when he was betrayed took a loaf of bread, and when he had given thanks, he broke it and said, "This is my body that is for you. Do this in remembrance of me." In the same way he took the cup also, after supper, saying, "This cup is the new covenant in my blood. Do this, as often as you drink it, in remembrance of me." For as often as you eat this bread and drink the cup, you proclaim the Lord's death until he comes. (1 Cor 11:23–26)

These words should sound familiar to anyone who attends church regularly and partakes of the Lord's Supper. These words are known as the "words of institution," which a minister of the Lord will declare as part of the table liturgy.

It is good to remember that the Lord's Supper has past, present, and future references for believers. This passage from 1 Corinthians highlights the past reference, a means of remembering Christ's death and salvation. The Gospel of John, thought to be full of sacramental overtones and themes, does not record the institution of the Lord's Supper like the synoptic Gospels; however, John offers us a meditation on the present reference for the Lord's Supper as he recalls Jesus referring to himself as "the bread of life" (John 6:35–40). This passage invites us to remember the present nourishment that Jesus offers us in the Lord's Supper. Finally, John gives us the future reference for the Lord's Supper in his vision from the island of Patmos. In the book of Revelation, John talks about the "marriage supper of the Lamb" (Rev 19:9), a meal that believers will celebrate after the final victory and restoration of all things.

It is good to remember all of these facets of the sacrament when we come to the table of the Lord. We remember Jesus' past work of salvation; we receive his present nourishment for our spiritual journey; and we anticipate the future marriage supper of the Lamb, a celebration after Jesus returns and ushers in the new heaven and the new earth.

Finally, in the Gospel reading from John 13, we find Jesus taking up the basin and the towel to wash the disciples' feet. Jesus is modeling love and service to the disciples (and to us). In this expression of servanthood,

Jesus also gives us a new commandment (or mandate, which is where Maundy Thursday derives its name). John writes,

> After he had washed their feet, had put on his robe, and had reclined again, he said to them, "Do you know what I have done to you? You call me Teacher and Lord, and you are right, for that is what I am. So if I, your Lord and Teacher, have washed your feet, you also ought to wash one another's feet. For I have set you an example, that you also should do as I have done to you." (John 13:12–15)

The washing of the disciples' feet demonstrated to them, and to us, how we are to love as Jesus loved; how we are to serve as Jesus served. The "new" part of this commandment to love is that we are to love others *as Jesus loves us*. The call to love is not new, but the call to love as Jesus loves us *is* a new facet of the greatest commandment (Matt 22:37–40).

Jesus' act of servanthood must have surprised the disciples. I can imagine how they felt as he went around, with a basin and a towel, and washed their dirty feet. As we find ourselves in the midst of Holy Week, may we remember all of these facets of our faith. May we see and understand the rich connections to Israel's deliverance as we celebrate at the table of the Lord; may we experience the past, present, and future realities in the Lord's Supper; and may we learn afresh what it means to love and serve others as Christ loves and serves us.

QUESTIONS FOR REFLECTION

1. Moses describes the origin of the Passover meal and how God delivered his people from Egypt. Is it encouraging to see the connections with the Passover meal and the sacrament of the Lord's Supper? Explain.

2. The psalmist describes his liturgical duties (the drink offering/cup of salvation) in Psalm 116:12–14, expressing thanksgiving for God's salvation and sustained provision. What are some ways that you express your gratitude to God for his salvation and sustained provision in your own life?

3. The apostle Paul provides commentary on the institution of the Lord's Supper for us in his Letter to the Corinthians. What facet of the sacrament does Paul highlight in this passage? What other facets does the apostle John highlight in his Gospel and in the book of Revelation? How do these references edify and encourage you as a believer and in your journey of faith?

4. John describes the way that Jesus took up the basin and the towel and washed the disciples' feet on the evening that he was betrayed and arrested. How does this act serve as an example to us? What was "the new commandment" that Jesus gave his disciples (and us) on this evening in redemptive history?

PRAYER OF RESPONSE
Based on John 13:3–5, 14–16

Lord Jesus,
help us to take up the basin and the towel,
and minister to those around us.
May we wash the feet of those you bring our way,
seeking not to elevate ourselves in this world,
but following your example to serve others.
We confess that we are often wrapped up in our own lives,
and selfishly seek fortune and fame, comfort and approval.
In those moments, remind us of your humble act,
remind us of the gospel, and bring us to our knees once again,
ready to offer our lives in love and service.
In the name of Jesus we pray. Amen.

Good Friday

LECTIONARY READINGS

    Isaiah 52:13—53:12

    Psalm 22

    Hebrews 4:14–16; 5:7–9

    John 18:1—19:42

DEVOTION

Good Friday is a day that invites us into a sober remembrance and meditation on the cross of Christ. Though we know the resurrection is coming, it is good for us to linger first in the suffering and death of Jesus. Just as the stars shine brightly against the darkness of the night sky, so the joy of Easter Sunday is more glorious after we have lamented over the agony of the cross.

    In the readings for Good Friday, we discover the poignant and detailed descriptions of the suffering servant in Isaiah. We hear the cries of lament in Psalm 22, and we picture the tears of our Savior in Hebrews 5. The Gospel reading from John describes the full scope of the passion of Christ, from arrest and betrayal to suffering and death. Good Friday is part of the Easter triduum, the climax of the Christian year, beginning with Maundy Thursday and culminating on Easter Sunday. As we mark and actively remember these significant events, may we draw ever closer to our Lord and Savior who suffered and died that we may have life.

    In the first reading from Isaiah 52 and 53, the prophet offers us a detailed description of the suffering servant, a prophecy that is fulfilled in Christ. The prophet proclaims,

> He was despised and rejected by others;
> a man of suffering and acquainted with infirmity,
> and as one from whom others hide their faces
> he was despised, and we held him of no account.
>
> Surely he has borne our infirmities
> and carried our diseases,
> yet we accounted him stricken,
> struck down by God, and afflicted.
> But he was wounded for our transgressions,
> crushed for our iniquities;
> upon him was the punishment that made us whole,
> and by his bruises we are healed. (Isa 53:3–5)

These are sobering words. In this passage, Isaiah holds nothing back in expressing the full weight of the servant's suffering and our sin and rejection. Though we were not historically present, in Adam, we all have rejected Christ. Only through the sovereign grace and mercy of God are we able to find life and healing in Jesus' name. Though we know him now by faith, we were first enemies of the cross (Rom 5:10).

As we meditate on the cross, Isaiah invites us to remember how the suffering servant was despised and rejected; how he suffered, bore our sin and infirmities; how he was wounded, crushed, and punished that we may be whole, that we may be healed.

Psalm 22 is an appropriate psalm of response to the first reading from Isaiah. Here, we find the psalmist crying out in utter despair:

> My God, my God, why have you forsaken me?
> Why are you so far from helping me,
> from the words of my groaning? (Ps 22:1)

The words are stark and desperate. Jesus cried out these very words while hanging on the cross. We simply cannot fathom all that Jesus experienced as he suffered on the cross: the agony, the weight of our sin, and the feeling of being separated and forsaken by the Father. Jesus' suffering is almost too hard for us even to bear remembering, but we must linger in these harsh realities. We remain in the agony of Good Friday that we may fully know the joy of Easter Sunday.

The second reading from the book of Hebrews offers us encouragement as we embrace Jesus' suffering as the path to empathy and invitation. The author of Hebrews writes,

> For we do not have a high priest who is unable to sympathize with our weaknesses, but we have one who in every respect has been tested as we are, yet without sin. Let us therefore approach the throne of grace with boldness, so that we may receive mercy and find grace to help in time of need. (Heb 4:15–16)

The great reality of Jesus' suffering is that, as our high priest, he is able to sympathize with us in all of our trials and difficulties. Though he never sinned, Jesus experienced all of the temptations and all of the harsh realities of life as he walked this earth. And because of his life, we are invited to come boldly to the throne of grace to find grace and mercy in times of need.

This passage begins to elucidate the meaning of "Good Friday." Why on earth would we call the day of Christ's suffering and death "good"? Hebrews 4 begins to make that reason known. Through his death, we have life. Because of his suffering, we have a sympathetic high priest, one who knows all of our needs.

The author of Hebrews continues to describe Jesus' suffering. He writes,

> In the days of his flesh, Jesus offered up prayers and supplications, with loud cries and tears, to the one who was able to save him from death, and he was heard because of his reverent submission. (Heb 5:7)

In this passage, the author of Hebrews is likely referring (at least) to Jesus' prayer and wrestling in Gethsemane. Jesus was in utter anguish, wrestling with doing the will of the Father. Luke tells us that the time was so intense that "his sweat became like great drops of blood falling down on the ground" (Luke 22:44). Though Jesus' anguish was intense, his humanity can encourage us when we go through very difficult times, times when we are weeping in grief and despair.

As we meditate on the cross, may we remember that Christ not only knows us, he understands us. He understands our tears, our pain, and our sorrows. He cried out and shed tears himself. On this Good Friday, may we know that Jesus is our great high priest who stands with arms wide open to receive his children, just as we are.

Finally, in the Gospel reading from John, we recount the whole story of arrest, betrayal, suffering, and death. John makes it clear that though the various characters in this narrative think that they are in control, God is sovereign over these events. In responding to Pontius Pilate, a Roman governor, John writes, "Jesus answered him, 'You would have no power over me unless it had been given you from above'" (John 19:11).

Peter acknowledges these spiritual dynamics in his sermon on the day of Pentecost. Speaking of Jesus, he declares, "This man, handed over to you according to the definite plan and foreknowledge of God, you crucified and killed by the hands of those outside the law. But God raised him up, having released him from the agony of death, because it was impossible for him to be held in its power" (Acts 2:23–24).

The events surrounding Jesus' trial and death were all part of God's sovereign plan. Though it is hard for us to fully comprehend, God has always brought beauty from ashes (Isa 61:3). He loves to redeem and restore. The cross of Christ is part of the Father's plan to redeem and restore humankind. As we meditate on the cross, we can know that the Father is in control of all of life's circumstances and that Christ holds all things together (Col 1:17). We can rest in the sovereignty of God, even when our circumstances appear bleak.

John records the final words and the death of Jesus. He writes,

> After this, when Jesus knew that all was now finished, he said (in order to fulfill the scripture), "I am thirsty." A jar full of sour wine was standing there. So they put a sponge full of the wine on a branch of hyssop and held it to his mouth. When Jesus had received the wine, he said, "It is finished." Then he bowed his head and gave up his spirit. (John 19:28–30)

Like many other aspects of the passion narrative, it is hard for us to comprehend the death of Jesus. These words are stark, yet hopeful: "It is finished." The "it" in this sentence carries so much redemptive meaning. From exodus to promised land; from exile to restoration; from oppression to salvation; God has been at work, fulfilling promises and redeeming his people. Finally, on the cross, our atonement was accomplished; our ransom paid; our sin was forgiven. "It is finished."

On this Good Friday, as we remember the cross, may we know the depth of the Father's steadfast love. May we know the one who would send his only Son to die a gruesome death on a criminal's cross so that we would find forgiveness; so that we would be reconciled; so that we would have everlasting life and union with Christ.

QUESTIONS FOR REFLECTION

1. Isaiah describes in profound detail the agony of the suffering servant. Do you see yourself in the rejection of Christ? Explain. How does Isaiah's prophecy inform and complement your understanding of the Gospel accounts of Jesus' betrayal, suffering, and death?

2. The psalmist cries out in utter despair in Psalm 22. Why do you think Jesus chose some of these very words (such as Ps 22:1) as he cried out in anguish on the cross? Do you find it hard to fully remember and recall Jesus' suffering and agony on the cross? Explain. Does the sober remembrance of Good Friday help you anticipate the joy and celebration of Easter Sunday?

3. The author of Hebrews describes the way in which Jesus, our high priest, is able to sympathize with all of our weaknesses. Do you find this encouraging? Do you think of Jesus as your high priest or is this a new concept to you? Explain. Do you find it comforting that Jesus had loud cries and tears during his days on earth? How does Jesus' sorrow bring comfort to you in your own times of weeping and grief?

4. John hints at the sovereignty of God throughout his passion narrative. Describe the various power dynamics at work in John's narrative. What do Jesus' final words, "It is finished," mean? During Holy Week, have you spent time in worship and gratitude for all that Jesus suffered for your sake? If not, consider taking some time and space to do that now.

PRAYER OF RESPONSE
Based on Isaiah 53:4–6, 10–11

Lord Jesus,
we praise you for you bore
our infirmities and carried our diseases;
even though we accounted you stricken,
struck down by God, and afflicted.
You were wounded for our transgressions,
crushed for our iniquities;
you suffered the punishment that made us whole,
and by your bruises we are healed.

We confess that we, like sheep, have gone astray;
we have all turned to our own way,
and the Lord laid on you the iniquity of us all.
Yet, through you the will of the Lord shall prosper;
for you are the righteous one,
and you have made many righteous, for you bore our iniquities. Amen.

Easter

LECTIONARY READINGS

Acts 10:34–43

Psalm 118:1–2, 14–24

Colossians 3:1–4

Matthew 28:1–10

DEVOTION

In the readings for Easter Sunday, we celebrate the joy of the resurrection. Matthew records the joy of the women who first came to the tomb. In the first reading from Acts 10, Peter preaches the message of the death and resurrection of Jesus to gentiles. In his Letter to the Colossians, the apostle Paul reminds us that if we know Christ by faith, we have been raised with him and are now hidden with Christ in God.

Throughout the fifty days of Easter, the first reading is from the book of Acts. Reading from the book of Acts places the power of the resurrection in the church. Luke, the author of Luke and Acts, records the sermon that Peter proclaimed to Cornelius (a gentile) and his household. In this message, Peter declares,

> We are witnesses to all that he did both in Judea and in Jerusalem. They put him to death by hanging him on a tree, but God raised him on the third day and allowed him to appear, not to all the people but to us who were chosen by God as witnesses and who ate and drank with him after he rose from the dead. (Acts 10:39–41)

Peter boldly and clearly proclaimed who Jesus is to Cornelius and those who were present that day. In his message, Peter described what Jesus did during his earthly ministry, offered details about his resurrection, and noted that the apostles had been ordained to carry this message. Though the passage for today does not include it, we know that all who heard Peter's message were filled with the Holy Spirit and were baptized. This was significant because it meant that Jesus had come to save, not only the Jews, but gentiles as well.

In Psalm 118 (the psalm of response), the psalmist sings,

> I thank you that you have answered me
> and have become my salvation.
> The stone that the builders rejected
> has become the chief cornerstone.
> This is the Lord's doing;
> it is marvelous in our eyes. (Ps 118:21–23)

Our salvation comes through the death and resurrection of Jesus Christ. He is the "stone" that the people rejected. He is now the "chief cornerstone." He is the foundation of our lives, the one in whom all things hold together (Col 1:17). Though the psalmist lived centuries before Christ, his words are fulfilled in the person of Jesus.

In the second reading from Colossians 3, the apostle Paul is urging us to set our minds on the realities of the risen and ascended Lord. He writes,

> So if you have been raised with Christ, seek the things that are above, where Christ is, seated at the right hand of God. Set your minds on the things that are above, not on the things that are on earth, for you have died, and your life is hidden with Christ in God. (Col 3:1–3)

If we have been raised to new life in Christ, our hearts and our minds should not be focused merely on earthly realities, but on heavenly things, "things that are above" (Col 3:1). Christ is at the right hand of God, advocating and interceding on behalf of his church, individually and corporately. Fixing our minds on him changes our priorities and the way we live. We learn to seek the greater things of God's kingdom. Moreover, our lives are now "hidden with Christ in God" (Col 3:3). We live in union with Christ; we abide in him and he in us (John 15:4).

The more we walk with Jesus, spending time with him in word, sacrament, and prayer, the more we desire the things of heaven. Life in Christ brings meaning and hope to our lives here on earth. We grow in love for others as we abide in Christ.

In the Gospel reading from Matthew 28, we read of the women who first came to the empty tomb. Matthew writes,

> After the Sabbath, as the first day of the week was dawning, Mary Magdalene and the other Mary went to see the tomb. And suddenly there was a great earthquake, for an angel of the Lord, descending from heaven, came and rolled back the stone and sat on it. His appearance was like lightning and his clothing white as snow. (Matt 28:1–3)

Matthew describes a remarkable scene. First, we know that the resurrection took place on the first day of the week (Sunday), after the Sabbath (Saturday). This is why Christians worship on Sunday, what has become known as "the Lord's day" (Rev 1:10). As the women came to the tomb, they did not find what they anticipated. They encountered an earthquake, apparently caused by the angel who came down from heaven and rolled back the stone that secured the tomb. The women were frightened.

The angel tried to comfort the women and explained to them that Jesus had been raised from the dead and that they were to tell the other disciples. Matthew writes,

> So they left the tomb quickly with fear and great joy and ran to tell his disciples. Suddenly Jesus met them and said, "Greetings!" And they came to him, took hold of his feet, and worshiped him. Then Jesus said to them, "Do not be afraid; go and tell my brothers and sisters to go to Galilee; there they will see me." (Matt 28:8–10)

The women were filled with both fear and joy. They had just witnessed an incredible event, but learned that Jesus was alive. Running to tell the other disciples, Jesus encounters and greets the women, who then fall down and worship him. It is remarkable that the first eyewitnesses to Jesus' resurrection were two women. The details of the account add to its reliability.

The day would be one of great joy as the disciples would also find out that Jesus was alive. Easter should be a time of great rejoicing for the church today. The resurrection is one of the greatest moments in all of history. It changed everything. No more is creation subject to death and decay. Through the power that began with the resurrection, all things will be made new. May we remember and celebrate with joy, like the women at the tomb, for our Savior is alive. May we set our hearts and minds on him.

QUESTIONS FOR REFLECTION

1. What is significant about Peter sharing the gospel with Cornelius? What effect did the word have on Cornelius and all who heard it? What is the application of this narrative for our lives today?

2. Jesus quotes Psalm 118:22–23 to the religious leaders (Matt 21:42–44). How does his life fulfill this passage? If Jesus is the "cornerstone," what does that mean for us today?

3. Why does Paul exhort us to set our minds on things above? What does it mean that our lives are "hidden with Christ in God"? How do you cultivate your union with Christ throughout the day and week?

4. Describe the events of the resurrection (as recorded by Matthew) in your own words. What aspects of the story stand out to you? Why were the women filled with both fear and joy? How has the reality of the resurrection changed all of creation? How has the reality of the resurrection changed your own life?

PRAYER OF RESPONSE
Based on Colossians 3:1–4

Risen and ascended Lord,
help us to seek the things that are above,
where you are seated at the right hand of the Father.
By your grace, may we set our minds
on things that are above, not on things that are on earth,
for we have died, and our life is now hidden in you.
You are our life, and when you are revealed,
may we also be revealed with you in glory.
In the name of Jesus we pray. Amen.

Second Sunday of Easter

LECTIONARY READINGS

Acts 2:14a, 22–32

Psalm 16

1 Peter 1:3–9

John 20:19–31

DEVOTION

This Sunday is the second Sunday of Easter, part of the season known as Eastertide or the Great Fifty Days. In the readings for this Sunday, we find Peter preaching a sermon on the resurrection of Jesus on the day of Pentecost. We also read from Peter's first letter and discover the living hope that is ours through the resurrection of Christ. In the Gospel reading, we find the disciples encountering Jesus on the Sunday of his resurrection; we then find Jesus interacting with Thomas, demonstrating that he is the Lord. Thus, the power and the reality of the resurrection are common themes for this Sunday.

In the first reading from Acts 2, Peter delivers his first sermon to the people who were gathered to celebrate the day of Pentecost. He proclaimed,

> Fellow Israelites, listen to what I have to say: Jesus of Nazareth, a man attested to you by God with deeds of power, wonders, and signs that God did through him among you, as you yourselves know—this man, handed over to you according to the definite plan and foreknowledge of God, you crucified and killed by the hands of those outside the law. But God raised him up, having

> released him from the agony of death, because it was impossible for him to be held in its power. (Acts 2:22–24)

In this sermon, Peter clearly interprets and explains what took place regarding the death and resurrection of Jesus. He then quotes a portion of Psalm 16, stating that David was speaking prophetically in this psalm regarding the resurrection of Christ (Acts 2:25–28).

Psalm 16 is the psalm of response for this Sunday. It is natural to use this psalm since Peter quoted from it in his sermon on the day of Pentecost. Peter's point was to show how Jesus is the one to whom this psalm is pointing. Ultimately, it is Jesus' voice declaring, "For you do not give me up to Sheol or let your faithful one see the Pit" (Ps 16:10).

Perhaps Peter knew to quote from Psalm 16 because, in his post-resurrection appearances, Jesus was teaching the disciples how everything written about him "in the law of Moses, the prophets, and the psalms must be fulfilled" (Luke 24:44). Jesus also promised that the Holy Spirit would remind the disciples of all that he had taught them (John 14:26). Thus, it is possible that the Holy Spirit reminded Peter of a lesson Jesus may have taught the disciples regarding his fulfillment of Psalm 16, a lesson that Peter then shared on the day of Pentecost. The Holy Spirit still speaks to us today, reminding us of the power and the truth of God's word.

In the second reading from 1 Peter 1, we are reminded of the "new birth" and the "living hope" that we have in the resurrection. Moreover, Peter describes the inheritance we have been given that is "imperishable, undefiled, and unfading, kept in heaven" for us (1 Pet 1:4). These promises come in the form of praise to God in the opening portion of his letter. These promises were meant to encourage the church that was under persecution in the first century. They are still edifying for us today. We know that this world is not our home; our true home and our true life is waiting for us in heaven.

Peter also describes the joy of believers who did not see Jesus with their own eyes, yet have placed their faith in him. He writes,

> Although you have not seen him, you love him, and even though you do not see him now, you believe in him and rejoice with an indescribable and glorious joy, for you are receiving the outcome of your faith, the salvation of your souls. (1 Pet 1:8–9)

These words describe our situation today. We love Jesus and believe in him though we have not seen him with our eyes. Moreover, Peter describes the "indescribable and glorious joy" of those who have received their salvation by faith. Knowing Jesus brings us a joy and a peace that is hard to describe or explain to others. Walking with Jesus and communing with him also strengthens us and satisfies our souls.

In the Gospel reading from John 20, Jesus appears to the disciples. He spoke to them and said, "Peace be with you" (John 20:19). He also breathed on them and said, "Receive the Holy Spirit. If you forgive the sins of any, they are forgiven them; if you retain the sins of any, they are retained" (John 20:22–23). These are significant words from Jesus. Mostly likely, Jesus' word of peace was meant to put them at ease and to comfort them. His word regarding the Spirit is a foretaste of the greater outpouring on the day of Pentecost. It is also significant that he gives the disciples the authority to declare the forgiveness of sins. This teaching informs the process of discipline within the church.

Jesus appears a week later when Thomas is present. He is able to show Thomas the mark of the nails in his hands and side. To this, Thomas replies, "My Lord and my God!" (John 20:28). He knew without a doubt that Jesus had risen from the dead and that he is Lord. Finally, John states the overall purpose of his Gospel. He writes,

> Now Jesus did many other signs in the presence of his disciples that are not written in this book. But these are written so that you may continue to believe that Jesus is the Messiah, the Son of God, and that through believing you may have life in his name. (John 20:30–31)

The Gospel of John can be outlined into two major sections: the book of signs (John 1–11) and the book of glory (John 12–21); the book of glory recounts Jesus' farewell discourse, death, and resurrection. John offers seven signs, written that we may "continue to believe" in Jesus and have "life in his name" (John 20:31). During this season of Eastertide, may we come to believe more and more in the reality that Jesus is the Messiah, the Son of God. May we also experience more and more each day what it means to have life in him.

QUESTIONS FOR REFLECTION

1. What is the message that Peter declared on the day of Pentecost? How did Peter know to point to Psalm 16 and to understand King David as speaking prophetically through this psalm? How does God still speak to us today?

2. Read Psalm 16:8 and describe what David is saying in your own words. Do you live in the strength and stability of the Lord or do you rely more on your own resources?

3. What are the various promises and realities that we have as believers as a result of the resurrection?

4. What words did Jesus speak to the disciples in the evening of the day of his resurrection? Why were these words significant? Why did Thomas reply "My Lord and my God!" when Jesus showed him the marks in his hands and side? What was John's purpose in writing his Gospel? What do the various "signs" in his Gospel reveal to us?

PRAYER OF RESPONSE
Based on 1 Peter 1:3–7

Faithful God,
we worship and adore you,
for by your great mercy you have given us
a new birth into a living hope
through the resurrection of Jesus Christ from the dead.
You have given us an inheritance that is
imperishable, undefiled, and unfading, kept in heaven for us,
who are being protected by your power through faith
for a salvation ready to be revealed in the last time.
In this we rejoice, even if now for a little while
we have had to suffer various trials,
so that the genuineness of our faith may be found to result
in praise and glory and honor when Jesus Christ is revealed. Amen.

Third Sunday of Easter

LECTIONARY READINGS

Acts 2:14a, 36–41

Psalm 116:1–4, 12–19

1 Peter 1:17–23

Luke 24:13–35

DEVOTION

In the readings for the third Sunday of Easter, we find Jesus walking along the road with two disciples on their way to Emmaus. After expounding the truth of the Scriptures with these disciples, he is invited to their home. The disciples were kept from recognizing Jesus until he broke the bread with them. We find Peter preaching on the day of Pentecost; about three-thousand people came to faith that day. In Peter's first epistle, we find how we are to live in this world as exiles, demonstrating mutual love for one another. Thus, the themes of encountering Jesus in the breaking of the bread, responding to him in faith, and living as his disciples are themes in the readings for this Sunday.

In the first reading from Acts 2, we hear the conclusion of Peter's sermon on the day of Pentecost. Peter declares that Jesus is both "Lord and Messiah" (Acts 2:36). Peter's message spoke powerfully to the people assembled that day. When they asked how they should respond, Peter told them that they should be baptized, declaring, "For the promise is for you, for your children, and for all who are far away, everyone whom the Lord our God calls to him" (Acts 2:39). Luke gives us the detail that "those who welcomed his message were baptized, and that day about three thousand persons were added" (Acts 2:41).

The gospel is able to convict us and transform us by the power of the Holy Spirit. Baptism, the sacrament that is our initiation into the faith, is the natural response for those coming to Christ for the first time. For those born into Christian homes, the sign of baptism brings covenant promises that parents believe by faith will become their child's one day. Ideally, baptized children will be nurtured at home by loving, Christian parents and in their local church by a loving community that regularly partakes of the means of grace.

Psalm 116 expresses the psalmist's thanksgiving and love for the Lord who saved his life. He writes,

> I love the Lord because he has heard
> my voice and my supplications.
> Because he inclined his ear to me,
> therefore I will call on him as long as I live.
> The snares of death encompassed me;
> the pangs of Sheol laid hold on me;
> I suffered distress and anguish.
> Then I called on the name of the Lord,
> "O Lord, I pray, save my life!" (Ps 116:1–4)

This psalm ties in with the first reading as a way of responding to the Lord's salvation. In Acts 2, the people responded to Peter's sermon by being baptized and coming into a relationship with the Lord. Like the psalmist, those baptized on the day of Pentecost were able to express their love to the Lord.

In the second reading, Peter describes the way we are to live as exiles in this world, those who have been rescued by the "precious blood of Christ" (1 Pet 1:19). Peter writes,

> Through him you have come to trust in God, who raised him from the dead and gave him glory, so that your trust and hope are in God.
>
> Now that you have purified your souls by your obedience to the truth so that you have genuine mutual affection, love one another deeply from the heart. You have been born anew, not of perishable but of imperishable seed, through the living and enduring word of God. (1 Pet 1:21–23)

Peter describes how we deepen our trust in God and have our trust and hope set on him. As we are purified and sanctified by the power of the Holy Spirit, we grow in our faith and dependence upon God. Furthermore, we grow in our love towards others. Mutual love should characterize the people of God. Rather than thinking only of ourselves, we desire to reach out and serve others.

In the Gospel reading from Luke 24, we encounter the narrative of two disciples on the road to Emmaus on the day of Christ's resurrection. Luke lets us know that the disciples were kept from recognizing Jesus. As Jesus began to walk with them, he opened the word and began to teach them. Luke writes,

> Then beginning with Moses and all the prophets, he interpreted to them the things about himself in all the scriptures. (Luke 24:27)

Jesus gave these two disciples an amazing lesson on his fulfillment of the Scriptures in the Old Testament. After this teaching, the disciples invited Jesus to their home. During a meal, the disciples recognized that their guest was Jesus. Luke writes,

> When he was at the table with them, he took bread, blessed and broke it, and gave it to them. Then their eyes were opened, and they recognized him, and he vanished from their sight. They said to each other, "Were not our hearts burning within us while he was talking to us on the road, while he was opening the scriptures to us?" (Luke 24:30–32)

It is interesting that Jesus was not recognized until the breaking of the bread. In addition, the disciples commented on how their hearts were burning as Jesus taught them on the road. This same rhythm of word and table takes place in our Sunday worship gatherings. We hear the word read and preached and then we encounter Jesus at the table through the sacrament of the Lord's Supper. Luke also shares how the disciples went back to Jerusalem to share their joy and their story.

During this season of Eastertide, may we encounter Jesus in word and sacrament and find ourselves growing in mutual love for one another. May we be bold to share the truth of the gospel and the joy of our own salvation with those who need to hear that Christ is risen.

QUESTIONS FOR REFLECTION

1. What was the message that Peter spoke on the day of Pentecost? What did he exhort the people to do? How did the people respond? What is the application for our lives?

2. What is the overall tone of Psalm 116? If you had to describe it in one word, what would it be? How should Ps 116 inform our response to the Lord?

3. How does Peter describe the Christian life? Why? What are the marks of the Christian life? Does genuine mutual love characterize your life?

4. How is Jesus playful with the disciples on the road to Emmaus? Why would he ask them "What things?" (Luke 24:19)? What is the two-fold rhythm of his journey with these two disciples? How does our own encounter with Jesus reflect this two-fold rhythm? What did the two disciples do once they recognized they had been with Jesus? Are you excited to share the truth and joy of the gospel with others who need to hear it?

PRAYER OF RESPONSE
Based on Acts 2:36–38; Luke 24:27, 30–35

Jesus,
our Lord and Messiah,
forgive us of our sins
and fill us with the Holy Spirit.
Like the disciples on the road to Emmaus,
may we enjoy communion with you
in the breaking of the bread
and in the reading of your holy word.
Open our eyes to your work of redemption
and grant us the joy of sharing
the good news that the Lord is risen!
In the name of Jesus we pray. Amen.

Fourth Sunday of Easter (Good Shepherd Sunday)

LECTIONARY READINGS

Acts 2:42–47

Psalm 23

1 Peter 2:19–25

John 10:1–10

DEVOTION

This Sunday is the fourth Sunday of Easter, also known as Good Shepherd Sunday. In the Gospel reading, Jesus refers to himself as the gate. He is the one who calls his sheep and they know his voice. In the first reading from Acts 2, we find that the early followers devoted themselves to the apostles' teaching and fellowship, to the breaking of bread and the prayers. In the second reading, Peter informs us that we will endure suffering on earth, but Jesus cares for us. He is the shepherd and guardian of our souls. Thus, the way that Jesus shepherds us is a theme throughout the readings for this Sunday.

In Acts 2, we find the early followers giving themselves to four basic aspects of the Christian life: word, fellowship, sacrament, and prayer. Luke writes,

> They devoted themselves to the apostles' teaching and fellowship, to the breaking of bread and the prayers. (Acts 2:42)

This verse gives us a window into the worship and discipleship of the early church. The believers looked after one another's needs. The church is still called to live in this way today. We are formed regularly through word and sacrament. In the context of small groups, we can enjoy rich fellowship and biblical community, and we can make sure people are being cared for and that the poor are being served and loved.

Psalm 23 is the psalm for this Sunday as it highlights the Lord as our Shepherd. The psalmist sings,

> The Lord is my shepherd; I shall not want.
> He makes me lie down in green pastures;
> he leads me beside still waters;
> he restores my soul. (Ps 23:1–3)

As our Good Shepherd, the Lord leads us to a place of refuge and contentment, and he restores our souls. The work of restoring our souls is an ongoing process because our souls always need tending. Regular sabbath and time with God are ways to restore our souls. Spending time in community and fellowship with others (as Luke describes in Acts 2) is another way of restoring our souls. We need our Good Shepherd to lead us and guide us, and we need biblical community, a place to know and be known by others.

In the second reading from 1 Peter 2, the apostle teaches on the reality of suffering. Peter writes,

> If you endure when you are beaten for doing wrong, what credit is that? But if you endure when you do good and suffer for it, this is a commendable thing before God. For to this you have been called, because Christ also suffered for you, leaving you an example, so that you should follow in his steps. (1 Pet 2:20–21)

Placing our faith and hope in Christ does not assure us of a life of comfort and ease. Though we have a Good Shepherd who leads us to green pastures and beside still waters, we are also led through trials and hardship. Jesus suffered while he lived and ministered on earth; thus, we are not spared from trials and hard seasons. Sometimes these seasons may be the very means that our Good Shepherd uses to draw us back to himself. Peter writes, "For you were going astray like sheep, but now you have returned to the shepherd and guardian of your souls" (1 Pet 2:25). In his sovereignty and mercy, God ordains and governs the circumstances of our lives to wake us up and put us on the right path. He loves us so much that he intervenes when we go astray and leads us back to the sheepfold, the church.

In the Gospel reading from John 10, Jesus declares one of the famous "I am" sayings. In John 10 he says, "I am the gate" (John 10:9). Jesus is the way into the kingdom. His sheep hear and know his voice. John writes,

> The gatekeeper opens the gate for him, and the sheep hear his voice. He calls his own sheep by name and leads them out. When he has brought out all his own, he goes ahead of them, and the sheep follow him because they know his voice. (John 10:3–4)

Jesus is our Good Shepherd and the way to eternal life. He calls us by name and leads us and guides us. He goes before us to protect us and keep us. Jesus is not like the thieves and bandits who come to steal and kill and destroy. Jesus came that we may "have life and have it abundantly" (John 10:10).

Following the voice of our Good Shepherd leads us to an abundant life; not a life without trial and hardship, but a life of peace and restoration. We are formed by what or who we worship. When we worship Jesus, we desire what he desires; we come to love what he loves; we find our souls are in the green pastures and still waters of peace and safety and abundant life. When we are walking closely with Jesus, we are not weighed down by sin, but our souls are clean and light. During this season of Eastertide, may we follow Jesus one day at a time, looking to him as the shepherd and guardian of our souls.

QUESTIONS FOR REFLECTION

1. Based on Acts 2:42, how would you describe the life of the early church? What motivated them to live and love in this way? Do word, fellowship, table, and prayer characterize your own spiritual life?

2. Do you think of the Lord as *the* Good Shepherd, or as *your* Good Shepherd? Explain. Share how Jesus has fulfilled some of the descriptions of Psalm 23 in your own life.

3. Peter says that we will suffer in this life. How can we be encouraged in this reality? How does Jesus provide an example of suffering? What does it mean that Jesus is the shepherd and guardian of your soul (1 Pet 2:25)?

4. What does Jesus mean when he says "I am the gate" (John 10:9)? What does he mean when he says "I came that they may have life, and have it abundantly" (John 10:10). Do you feel that you are living in abundance or scarcity today? Explain.

PRAYER OF RESPONSE
Based on Psalm 23:1–4; John 10:1–10

Lord Jesus,
we praise you for you are the Good Shepherd
who leads us beside still waters,
and who restores our souls.
Even when we walk through the darkest valley,
you are there with us to protect and comfort us.
Help us to follow you as you go before us,
and to know your voice as you call us by name.
By your grace, may we have life, and have it abundantly.
In the name of Jesus we pray. Amen.

Fifth Sunday of Easter

LECTIONARY READINGS

> Acts 7:55–60
> Psalm 31:1–5, 15–16
> 1 Peter 2:2–10
> John 14:1–14

DEVOTION

In the readings for the fifth Sunday of Easter, we find Jesus speaking to the disciples in the upper room on the night of his arrest and betrayal. He tells them that he is the way, the truth, and the life. He also tells them that he must go and prepare a place for them. In the first reading from Acts 7, we find Stephen, one of the first deacons and the first Christian martyr, seeing the ascended Jesus just before he was stoned. Peter teaches about the church, that we are a chosen race, a royal priesthood, and a holy nation. Thus, suffering and persecution, the reality of Jesus' ascension and of heaven, and the identity of the church are themes in the readings for this Sunday.

In the first reading from Acts 7, we find Stephen gazing into heaven and seeing the ascended Jesus. Regarding Stephen's vision, Luke writes, "But filled with the Holy Spirit, he gazed into heaven and saw the glory of God and Jesus standing at the right hand of God" (Acts 7:55).

This vision comes just *after* a convicting message that Stephen preached to the religious leaders and just *before* he is stoned by those leaders. Seeing Jesus, not sitting as the Scriptures usually describe but "standing" at the right hand of God, is thought to be the welcoming posture of Jesus before his faithful servant Stephen. Jesus was welcoming home the first Christian martyr.

Luke also gives us the detail that Stephen prayed for those who would murder him. He writes, "Then he knelt down and cried out in a loud voice, 'Lord, do not hold this sin against them.' When he had said this, he died" (Acts 7:60). This whole scene has echoes of Jesus' crucifixion. Stephen's prayer is very similar to Jesus' prayer from the cross, "Father, forgive them, for they do not know what they are doing" (Luke 23:34).

Because of the chiastic organization of Luke-Acts, many parallels can be found between the Gospel of Luke and the book of Acts. I believe Luke wants to reveal that what Jesus began to do on earth, he continues to do from heaven through the power of the Spirit working through his people.

Lastly, Luke gives us the detail that a young Saul was present at Stephen's stoning (Acts 7:58). This detail foreshadows the later conversion and ministry of Paul, who will become the primary character from Acts 13 until the end of the book.

Psalm 31 is the response to the first reading. It is the perfect complement to the peace and the vision that Stephen received at his stoning. The psalmist sings,

> Into your hand I commit my spirit;
> you have redeemed me, O Lord, faithful God.
>
> My times are in your hand;
> deliver me from the hand of my enemies and persecutors.
> Let your face shine upon your servant;
> save me in your steadfast love. (Ps 31:5, 15–16)

In Acts 7:59, Stephen prayed, "Lord Jesus, receive my spirit." The psalmist prays, "Into your hand I commit my spirit; for you have redeemed me, O Lord, faithful God" (Ps 31:5). Stephen asks the Lord to receive his spirit; the psalmist commits his spirit to the Lord. Both appear to be laying down their lives, submitting themselves before the Lord. For Stephen, this was a final gesture.

The psalmist also prays that the Lord would deliver him from his persecutors. Though Stephen was not spared death, the Lord did bring him comfort, and he was filled with the Spirit during his time of greatest need. In that sense, the Lord was near and extended grace to his servant.

Like Stephen, the Lord fills us with his Spirit in our times of need. Often, we may look back and wonder how we made it through a given season or circumstance, only to realize that God was sustaining us and giving us the grace to endure a difficult time. I believe we can also be assured that, like Stephen, Jesus welcomes his children home. As he told his disciples, he is preparing a place for us. When our time on earth is done, we will join our ascended Lord in the glorious realm of heaven.

In the second reading from 1 Peter 2, we are given the identity of the church. Peter writes,

> But you are a chosen people, a royal priesthood, a holy nation, God's own people, in order that you may proclaim the excellence of him who called you out of darkness into his marvelous light. (1 Pet 2:9)

We are God's children, called out of sin and darkness to proclaim the mighty deeds of God and to share the gospel with others. Part of the good news is that we have been chosen by God; we are his priests, his shepherds; and we are a holy nation, a people set apart.

All of this comes from God. Before we accepted Christ, God had already chosen us; though we may not feel like it, we are called to be his priests and shepherds. And though we are still sinners, we are saints, a holy people only because of the grace of Christ in our lives. We are holy only because of Christ's righteousness that has been imputed to us. May we live more and more into this amazing identity, corporately and individually.

In the Gospel reading, we find Jesus delivering a portion of the very personal upper room narrative. John 13–17 is a long discourse between Jesus and his disciples on the night that Jesus would be arrested and betrayed. In the narrative for this Sunday, we find Jesus telling his disciples about heaven:

> Do not let your hearts be troubled. Believe in God; believe also in me. In my Father's house there are many dwelling places. If it were not so, would I have told you that I go to prepare a place for you? And if I go and prepare a place for you, I will come again and will take you to myself, so that where I am, there you may be also. And you know the way to the place where I am going. (John 14:1–4)

Jesus is seeking to comfort his disciples, knowing all that is about to take place. He is reassuring them that though he must depart, they will be reunited. Thomas said to Jesus, "Lord, we do not know where you are going. How can we know the way?" (John 14:5). Jesus answered,

> I am the way and the truth and the life. No one comes to the Father except through me. If you know me, you will know my Father also. From now on you do know him and have seen him. (John 14:6–7)

Jesus is the way of salvation. He is also the perfect reflection of the Father's glory (Heb 1:3). This is what John means when he says that if we know Jesus, we know the Father and "have seen him." The narrative concludes with Jesus telling the disciples that his work will continue through them. He declares,

> Very truly, I tell you, the one who believes in me will also do the works that I do and, in fact, will do greater works than these, because I am going to the Father. I will do whatever you ask in my name, so that the Father may be glorified in the Son. If in my name you ask me for anything, I will do it. (John 14:12–14)

This statement is similar to what we learned earlier about Luke-Acts. Jesus continues to do from heaven what he began to do on earth. We will do the works that Jesus did because the Spirit of Jesus indwells us. He is able to do more than we ask or imagine. Paul describes this power in his Letter to the Ephesians:

> Now to him who by the power at work within us is able to accomplish abundantly far more than all we can ask or imagine, to him be glory in the church and in Christ Jesus to all generations, forever and ever. Amen. (Eph 3:20–21)

Jesus continues to work in this world through the power of the Spirit who indwells his people. During this season of Eastertide, may we be comforted in knowing that, as he did with Stephen, Jesus provides the grace we need in difficult times. May we also be encouraged that though Jesus is in heaven preparing a place for us, he is still mightily at work, building his kingdom on earth through us, his disciples.

QUESTIONS FOR REFLECTION

1. Who did Stephen see just before he was stoned by the religious leaders? How was he able to pray for the very people who would murder him? How are we able to navigate the difficult and trying circumstances of our own lives?

2. For what was the psalmist praying in Psalm 31? What are some of the parallels between Acts 7:55–60 and Psalm 31:1–5, 15–16? How has the Lord been a "rock of refuge," a "strong fortress" for you (Ps 31:2)?

3. What are the characteristics of the church that Peter describes? How do these designations play out in our lives individually and corporately as the church?

4. John 14 begins with Jesus saying, "Do not let your hearts be troubled" (John 14:1). Why would Jesus set the tone of his long discourse with these words? What does it mean that Jesus is the way, the truth, and the life? Do you believe that Jesus is preparing a place for his people? How does this inform your day-to-day life? What does Jesus mean that his people will do "greater works" than him and that he will do whatever we ask in his name (John 14:12–13)?

PRAYER OF RESPONSE
Based on John 14:1–6; Acts 7:55–56

Lord Jesus,
you are the way, the truth, and the light.
Help us to live with the hope
that you are preparing a place for us,
and that where you are, we will be also.
Like Stephen, would you fill us with the Spirit,
that we may we see your glory at the right hand of the Father,
and know your presence with us here on earth.
In the name of Jesus we pray. Amen.

Sixth Sunday of Easter

LECTIONARY READINGS

Acts 17:22–31
Psalm 66:8–20
1 Peter 3:13–22
John 14:15–21

DEVOTION

In the readings for the sixth Sunday of Easter, we hear Jesus speaking to the disciples in the upper room, promising the Holy Spirit, our Advocate. We hear Paul's message to the people of Athens, and we read Peter's letter to a church that was being persecuted. The Holy Spirit, baptism, persecution, and the sovereignty of our Creator God are themes in the readings for this Sunday.

In the first reading from Acts 17, we find the apostle Paul preaching to a gentile culture in Athens. He declares,

> Athenians, I see how extremely spiritual you are in every way. For as I went through the city and looked carefully at the objects of your worship, I found among them an altar with the inscription, "To an unknown god." What therefore you worship as unknown, this I proclaim to you. (Acts 17:22–23)

At this point in the book of Acts, the focus has shifted from Peter's ministry around Jerusalem to Paul's ministry throughout the wider, gentile world. Paul tailors his message to the context in Athens, quoting Greek poets and commenting on their pagan objects of worship (Acts 17:23). The need to adapt one's message to communicate effectively is demonstrated so well by Paul. Rather than speaking of Yahweh (a Jewish title for God), he refers more broadly to the "God who made the world and everything in it, he who is Lord of heaven and earth" (Acts 17:24).

People of different cultures can relate to the created world and have some concept of a power greater than themselves. Paul uses these references to enter into a spiritual conversation with the people of Athens. As we engage with our own culture, we should use images and references that will be meaningful to the people we are trying to reach with the gospel.

Psalm 66 is the psalm of response. Verse 16 forms a connection with the first reading by extending an invitation to all who would hear of the Lord's mighty deeds. The psalmist sings,

> Come and hear, all you who fear God,
> and I will tell what he has done for me. (Ps 66:16)

The psalmist invites his hearers to receive a personal testimony of God's mighty power. In the same way, the apostle Paul was inviting the Athenians to hear his testimony of the Creator God, the one who "commands all people everywhere to repent" (Acts 17:30). Paul and the psalmist simply shared about what the Lord had done in their personal lives and for the life of the world. They were not responsible for how the people who heard their message would respond. They simply shared their testimony. We are called to do the same. We are not responsible for how people will respond to the gospel. We are only called to go and share; we leave the outcome to God.

In the second reading from 1 Peter 3, we find the apostle talking openly about sharing our faith. He writes,

> Always be ready to make your defense to anyone who demands from you an accounting for the hope that is in you, yet do it with gentleness and respect. Maintain a good conscience so that, when you are maligned, those who abuse you for your good conduct in Christ may be put to shame. For it is better to suffer for doing good, if suffering should be God's will, than to suffer for doing evil. (1 Pet 3:15–17)

As we saw in Acts 17 and Psalm 66, we should be willing and ready to share with others about what Christ has done in our lives. Peter offers the caveat that we should do it "with gentleness and respect" (1 Pet 3:16). We should not share our faith with a sense of arrogance or superiority; we offer our testimony with gentle and humble hearts and trust that God is in control of the outcome. Moreover, we should not be surprised if people try to mock us or shame us for what we believe. This kind of suffering is better than suffering for doing evil. The latter kind of suffering, we often bring on ourselves.

Lastly, Peter alludes to Noah's ark, how it saved eight people, and how it points to our baptism. He writes,

> And baptism, which this prefigured, now saves you—not as a removal of dirt from the body but as an appeal to God for a good conscience, through the resurrection of Jesus Christ. (1 Pet 3:21)

The connection between the ark and baptism has a long history within the church. The word "nave" is derived from *navis*, which means "ship." This term was used to refer to the main body of the church building because the ship had been adopted as a symbol for the church. As a ship, the church protects those inside it from the waves and storms of the world.

In the Gospel reading from John 14, we find Jesus sharing with the disciples on the eve of his arrest and betrayal. He assures them that though he must leave, he will send the Holy Spirit to be with them. He says,

> If you love me, you will keep my commandments. And I will ask the Father, and he will give you another Advocate, to be with you forever. This is the Spirit of truth, whom the world cannot receive because it neither sees him nor knows him. You know him because he abides with you, and he will be in you. (John 14:15–17)

Though the disciples did not seem to grasp what Jesus was telling them at the time, the promise of the Holy Spirit would be fulfilled on the day of Pentecost (Acts 2:1–4). Jesus promised that the Spirit would be in us. The indwelling Spirit is the key to our union with Christ and to our sacramental practice. God abides in us through the power of the Holy Spirit who has taken up residence within his people.

Furthermore, Jesus tells us that he is our Advocate. He is like our defense attorney, reminding us of the truth of who we are. We need the advocacy of the Holy Spirit because we have an enemy who is constantly on the prowl, seeking to kill and destroy us (1 Pet 5:8). He tempts us and lies to us, but the Holy Spirit reminds us that we are children of God, no longer slaves to the world, the flesh, and the devil.

During this season of Eastertide, may we be ready to give an account for the hope that is within us. And may we not be surprised if we are mocked and persecuted for our testimony. May we also remember our baptism and the reality that we have been saved from the flood waters of sin and death. The church is our ship, our protection against the wind and the waves, the storms of this life. May we be quick to call on our Advocate, the Holy Spirit in our times of trial. He is always with us, reminding us of who we are and protecting us from the evil in this world.

QUESTIONS FOR REFLECTION

1. How did Paul contextualize the gospel during his time in Athens? How can we share the gospel in ways that will connect with our neighbors, friends, and others who do not know Christ? What are some common themes with which everyone can relate?

2. How does verse 16 sum up the whole of Psalm 66? What would be some of the highlights, the major themes you might share to convey what the Lord has done for you?

3. Peter encourages us to always be ready to share about the hope that is within us. Do you think of your testimony as the "hope" within you? Explain. Peter also talks about suffering for doing good and for doing evil. How are we to understand suffering in this life? How is baptism connected to Noah, the ark, and the flood?

4. Who did Jesus promise he would send to us? What is the role of the Holy Spirit in our lives? What does it mean that the Holy Spirit abides in us? How does this affect your everyday life?

PRAYER OF RESPONSE
Based on John 14:15–21

Risen Lord Jesus,
we praise you and thank you
that you have not left us as orphans,
but have given us the promised Holy Spirit,
our Advocate and Comforter;
the one who leads us into righteousness and truth.
We long to keep your commandments,
though we confess we often follow our own way.
By your grace and by your power within us,
help us to love you and live in a manner
that brings honor and glory to your name.
In the name of Jesus we pray. Amen

Ascension of the Lord

LECTIONARY READINGS

Acts 1:1–11
Psalm 47
Ephesians 1:15–23
Luke 24:44–53

DEVOTION

The ascension of Christ, though a vital aspect of our faith, is often neglected as something to celebrate in worship. We give much attention to Christ's birth, death, resurrection, and even his second coming. His ascension, however, is overlooked even though it is the center of Luke-Acts and the fulcrum of redemptive history. In the following passages we will see the importance and implications of this event for the church and for our personal lives.

In the first reading from Acts 1, we pick up where the Gospel of Luke ended. Luke tells us that in his first book (Luke) he wrote about "all that Jesus began to do and teach until the day when he was taken up to heaven" (Acts 1:1-2). He is implying that in his second book (Acts), he will write about what Jesus is continuing to do from heaven through the Holy Spirit working through the people of God.

First, however, he talks about how Jesus appeared to the apostles and "presented himself alive to them by many convincing proofs, appearing to them during forty days and speaking about the kingdom of God" (Acts 1:3). We remember how Jesus ate a piece of fish in front of them (Luke 24:41-43) and how he showed Thomas the scars on his hands and on his side (John 20:27). It was crucial for them to be eyewitnesses of his resurrection. There could be no mistaking that they spoke with and interacted with Jesus in his resurrected body.

Jesus then gave them their mandate, which is also the basic outline of the book of Acts:

> But you will receive power when the Holy Spirit has come upon you, and you will be my witnesses in Jerusalem, in all Judea and Samaria, and to the ends of the earth. (Acts 1:8)

The narrative of Acts follows this progression as we see the gospel going forth from Jerusalem, to Samaria, and to the "ends of the earth" (Acts 2:37–42; 8:14–17; 10:1–2, 44–48; 15:12; 28:11–16). From the various accounts of Peter, Philip, Paul, and his companions, we see Jews and gentiles being baptized and receiving the gift of the Holy Spirit. It was a remarkable time in redemptive history as these first conversions were taking place all along the Mediterranean.

After they received their commission from the Lord, Jesus ascended before their very eyes. Luke writes, "When he had said this, as they were watching, he was lifted up, and a cloud took him out of their sight" (Acts 1:9). We know that Jesus did not rocket up into the sky, but he did ascend to some height before entering the realm of heaven. From the various biblical accounts, it appears that heaven is not so much up in the sky somewhere, but a realm that is probably much closer than we realize.

I have heard people comment, often after a powerful time of worship, that the "veil between heaven and earth seemed very thin." What they mean in this description is that for a moment, it was as if heaven was opened just a bit and we could almost sense the presence of the Lord in a palpable way. It is hard to describe, but I have felt this way at times.

An interesting narrative in the life of the prophet Elisha gives us a window into the presence of heavenly realities:

> When an attendant of the man of God rose early in the morning and went out, an army with horses and chariots was all around the city. His servant said, "Alas, master! What shall we do?" He replied, "Do not be afraid, for there are more with us than there are with them." Then Elisha prayed, "O Lord, please open his eyes that he may see." So the Lord opened the eyes of the servant, and he saw; the mountain was full of horses and chariots of fire all around Elisha. (2 Kgs 6:15–17)

Elisha's servant was able to see the army of heaven. Likewise, the author of Hebrews encourages us with this vision of the heavenly realities:

> But you have come to Mount Zion and to the city of the living God, the heavenly Jerusalem, and to innumerable angels in festal gathering, and to the assembly of the firstborn who are enrolled in heaven, and to God the judge of all, and to the spirits of the righteous made perfect, and to Jesus, the mediator of a new covenant, and to the sprinkled blood that speaks a better word than the blood of Abel. (Heb 12:22–24)

In some mysterious way, as we gather for worship we are not just one local body; we are joined with the heavenly host as we gather together. The point is, Jesus did not ascend into space; he returned to his Father in heaven, a realm that is closer than we may realize. From there, he now rules and reigns over all.

Luke ends this narrative with the appearance of two men in white robes, possibly the same two beings at the empty tomb (Luke 24:1–5). He writes,

> While he was going and they were gazing up toward heaven, suddenly two men in white robes stood by them. They said, "Men of Galilee, why do you stand looking up toward heaven? This Jesus, who has been taken up from you into heaven, will come in the same way as you saw him go into heaven." (Acts 1:10–11)

We are given the interesting detail that Jesus will return to earth in the same way that he departed. We do not know when that day will be, but we live now in anticipation of his second coming.

The psalm of response, Psalm 47, speaks of how the Lord has "subdued peoples under us and nations under our feet" (Ps 47:3). As it pertains to Christ's ascension, the psalmist writes prophetically,

> God has gone up with a shout,
> the Lord with the sound of a trumpet.
> Sing praises to God, sing praises;
> sing praises to our King, sing praises.
> For God is the king of all the earth;
> sing praises with a psalm. (Ps 47:5–7)

Indeed, Jesus has "gone up with a shout." He was taken up to heaven. We live now in response to this reality and sing our praises unto our Lord, the "king of all the earth" (Ps 47: 7).

The second reading is mostly a prayer from the apostle Paul to the believers in Ephesus. Paul prays that the

> God of our Lord Jesus Christ, the Father of glory, may give you a spirit of wisdom and revelation as you come to know him, so that, with the eyes of your heart enlightened, you may perceive what is the hope to which he has called you, what are the riches of his glorious inheritance among the saints, and what is the immeasurable greatness of his power for us who believe, according to the working of his great power. (Eph 1:17–19)

Paul prays that the eyes of our hearts would be enlightened that may we know three things: the hope to which he has called us, the riches of his glorious inheritance among the saints, and the immeasurable greatness of his power for us who believe.

We, too, should pray regularly for these promises to be realities in our lives today: this hope, these riches, and this power. When we experience hardship and disappointment, when we grieve, we do not do so without a knowledge of our eternal hope. When we think we are missing out or that we lack something that we feel we need, we can remind ourselves of the riches of the inheritance that we share with our fellow believers as sons and daughters of God. We are children of the King, heirs of all that his. We are not lacking in anything!

Finally, when we are fearful or feel inadequate for a given task, we can remember the power that is ours through the Holy Spirit. "What is the nature of this power?" one may ask. Paul tells us that "God put this power to work in Christ when he raised him from the dead and seated him at his right hand in the heavenly places" (Eph 1:20). The same power that raised Jesus from the dead and seated him in the heavenly places is ours. May we more regularly be aware of this great power that is ours through the Holy Spirit. We can call on him and ask him for an answer. We can ask him for clarity, for strength, for wisdom, whatever our need. He is for us. May we learn to rely more on him and less on our own resources.

The Gospel reading is from Luke 24. Here we read how Jesus opened the minds of the disciples as he did the two men on the road to Emmaus. Their hearts were burning as Jesus spent time expounding on the Scriptures and his fulfillment of them. Surely Jesus referred back to the law of Moses, the prophets, and the psalms and showed the disciples how he fulfilled these portions of Scripture. We can imagine, for example, Jesus saying to them, "Here, in Psalm 16, David was not referring to himself. He was a prophet, and he knew God had promised that one of his own descendants would sit on his throne. David was looking into the future and speaking of my resurrection."

Of course, this is speculation, but it is a plausible scenario. We know that on the day of Pentecost, as Peter stood up to preach and explain what was taking place, he quoted from the prophet Joel (Joel 2:28–32) and two psalms of David (Ps 16:7–11; 110:1). It is likely that the Holy Spirit reminded Peter of these texts (as in Acts 11:16) and of Jesus' interpretation of them as described in Luke 24:45.

This passage is, of course, similar to Jesus' commission in Acts 1. He tells the disciples that "repentance and forgiveness of sins is to be proclaimed in his name to all nations, beginning from Jerusalem" (Luke 24:47). He also tells them that they will receive what the Father promised, the Holy Spirit. The ascension narrative in Luke is told in this manner:

> Then he led them out as far as Bethany, and, lifting up his hands, he blessed them. While he was blessing them, he withdrew from them and was carried up into heaven. And they worshiped him and returned to Jerusalem with great joy, and they were continually in the temple blessing God. (Luke 24:50–53)

Luke ends his Gospel with the disciples full of joy and worship, "continually in the temple blessing God." We should live in this same way: full of joy and worship and the Holy Spirit, continually blessing God and loving others as we anticipate his return.

QUESTIONS FOR REFLECTION

1. Has the full scope and present implications of Jesus' ascension gripped your heart and imagination, or is it an overlooked and neglected aspect of his life and present ministry? Explain.

2. Like the psalmist, do you find yourself singing praises to God, the King of all the earth, the one who has "gone up with a shout" (Ps 47:5)? Do you find yourself praying and singing to the ascended Jesus? In other words, do you picture Jesus in this way or do you only have a vague idea of his current ministry and presence?

3. Are you encouraged by the gospel promises that Paul lays out for us in his prayer to the Ephesian believers? Do you remind yourself of the hope, the riches, and the power we have as children of God? Explain.

4. Jesus opened the eyes of the disciples so that they could understand the Scriptures (Luke 24:44–45). How does Jesus still do this for us today? How does he open the Bible to us so that we can understand his fulfillment of the Old Testament as well as his life and ministry in the New Testament? Do you experience the joy of the Lord like Luke describes (Luke 24:52–53)?

PRAYER OF RESPONSE
Based on Ephesians 1:17–21

Father God,
we pray that you would give us
a spirit of wisdom and revelation as we come to know Christ,
so that, with the eyes of our heart enlightened,
we may know the hope to which you have called us,
the riches of Christ's glorious inheritance among the saints,
and the immeasurable greatness of Christ's power for us who believe.
We thank you that you put this power to work in Christ
when you raised him from the dead and seated him
at your right hand in the heavenly places, far above all rule and authority
and power and dominion, and above every name that is named,
not only in this age, but also in the age to come. Amen.

Seventh Sunday of Easter

LECTIONARY READINGS

Acts 1:6–14

Psalm 68:1–10, 32–35

1 Peter 4:12–14; 5:6–11

John 17:1–11

DEVOTION

In the readings for the seventh Sunday of Easter, we read of Jesus' ascension to heaven in Acts 1. We also find the disciples returning to Jerusalem where, joined with a number of women and Jesus' brothers, they devoted themselves to prayer. Psalm 68 encourages us to sing praise to the one who "rides upon the clouds," echoing the imagery of Christ's ascension (Acts 1:9). In the second reading from 1 Peter, we are encouraged to rejoice as we share in Christ's sufferings and to be alert with regard to the enemy's schemes. In the Gospel reading from John 17, we find Jesus praying for his disciples in the last section of his final discourse. Thus, the ascension of Christ and a life of prayer are common threads in the readings for this Sunday.

In the first reading from Acts 1, we engage the story of Christ's ascension to heaven. Luke writes,

> When he had said this, as they were watching, he was lifted up, and a cloud took him out of their sight. While he was going and they were gazing up toward heaven, suddenly two men in white robes stood by them. They said, "Men of Galilee, why do you stand looking up toward heaven? This Jesus, who has been taken

up from you into heaven, will come in the same way as you saw him go into heaven." (Acts 1:9–11)

Though the event and reality of the ascension is a vital aspect of our faith and the center of Luke's two-volume work (Luke-Acts), it is not as widely celebrated in the church as Christmas and Easter, unfortunately. The ascension brings us to the present ministry of Jesus and helps elucidate the present ministry of the Holy Spirit and the present realm of heaven.

Part of Jesus' present ministry as our ascended Lord is intercessory prayer for his church. Prayer is what we find the disciples doing just after they returned to Jerusalem, following the bodily ascension of Jesus. Referring to the eleven disciples, Luke writes, "All these were constantly devoting themselves to prayer, together with certain women, including Mary the mother of Jesus, as well as his brothers" (Acts 1:14).

There are many reasons why the disciples were devoted to prayer. They no longer had Jesus with them, physically, so they likely felt a sense of urgency and need. They were probably a bit anxious as well, not knowing exactly what to expect in terms of the arrival of the promised Holy Spirit and when Jesus was to return. They also knew that they were to be Jesus' witnesses to the world (Acts 1:8), a daunting kingdom mission for this small band of disciples. This alone would encourage much prayer.

In many respects, things are still the same for us today. We pray because we do not know when Christ will return; thus, there is a sense of urgency and anticipation. In addition, we have the same mission as those early disciples: to be Christ's witnesses to the world. We should be in much prayer over our role in sharing the gospel with those around us.

Psalm 68 is the psalm of response to this first reading. Here, the psalmist offers words of praise and adoration with language that includes echoes of the ascension. The psalmist sings,

> Sing to God; sing praises to his name;
> lift up a song to him who rides upon the clouds—
> his name is the Lord—
> be exultant before him.

> Sing to God, O kingdoms of the earth;
> sing praises to the Lord,
> O rider in the heavens, the ancient heavens;
> listen, he sends out his voice, his mighty voice.

> Ascribe power to God,
> whose majesty is over Israel
> and whose power is in the skies.
> Awesome is God in his sanctuary,
> the God of Israel;
> he gives power and strength to his people.
> Blessed be God! (Ps 68:4, 32–35)

The psalmist speaks of him "who rides upon the clouds" and of "the rider in the heavens," "whose power is in the skies." The account of the ascension in Luke and in Acts describes Jesus as being lifted upon a cloud (Acts 1:9) and of being "carried up into heaven" (Luke 24:51). Luke is most likely recalling descriptions from an interview with an eyewitness (possibly Peter). The disciples were likely in awe and wonder as Jesus was taken to heaven on a cloud. The language of Psalm 68 correlates with the power and majesty of our ascended Christ.

During this season of Eastertide, as we remember the event of the ascension, may we be filled with awe and wonder at the power of Jesus, the one who sits at the right hand of the Father in heaven.

The second reading from 1 Peter invites us to rejoice even in the midst of trials. Peter writes,

> But rejoice insofar as you are sharing Christ's sufferings, so that you may also be glad and shout for joy when his glory is revealed. If you are reviled for the name of Christ, you are blessed, because the spirit of glory, which is the Spirit of God, is resting on you. (1 Pet 4:13–14)

In the original context, Peter was likely writing to early Christians who were facing various levels of trial and persecution. These words, then and now, go against natural intuition and proclivities. We do not naturally want to rejoice when we face hardship and persecution, but that is what Peter is encouraging us to do. In God's economy, we share in the sufferings of Christ and, thus, our union with him when we face trials of various kinds. We rejoice because we will also share in his glory. This is exactly what Jesus taught in his Sermon on the Mount:

> Blessed are you when people revile you and persecute you and utter all kinds of evil against you falsely on my account. Rejoice and be glad, for your reward is great in heaven, for in the same way they persecuted the prophets who were before you. (Matt 5:11–12)

In addition to its correlation with Jesus' teaching, Peter's exhortation to rejoice in the midst of trials is one of many examples of the fulfillment of the role of the Holy Spirit in our lives. Jesus teaches, "But the Advocate, the Holy Spirit, whom the Father will send in my name, will teach you everything and remind you of all that I have said to you" (John 14:26). We find this dynamic in the life of Peter here in his epistle (and in Acts 11:16) and in our own lives as well. The Holy Spirit will remind us of the truth of God's word.

We rejoice in times of trial and persecution because we have a heavenly, eternal perspective on the events of our earthly life. Moreover, we know the Spirit of God rests upon us during these times of trial (1 Pet 4:14). Peter is encouraging us to keep these realities in mind.

Peter also exhorts the people of God to be aware of and resist the evil one. He writes,

> Discipline yourselves; keep alert. Like a roaring lion your adversary the devil prowls around, looking for someone to devour. Resist him, steadfast in your faith, for you know that your brothers and sisters in all the world are undergoing the same kinds of suffering. (1 Pet 5:8–9)

Too often, we forget about the reality of spiritual forces in this world. We forget that we have a real enemy whose desire is to devour and destroy the followers of Christ. Peter urges us to remain "steadfast" in our faith as we live in unity with brothers and sisters around the world. It is encouraging to know that we are not alone but are undergoing the same trials and temptations with others who are part of the global church. May we be in earnest prayer for ourselves and for others as we experience spiritual warfare, and may we remain steadfast in our faith, not giving in to whims and falling away from the truth and from our convictions.

Finally, in the Gospel reading from John 17, we find Jesus praying for the disciples. He prays,

> All mine are yours, and yours are mine, and I have been glorified in them. And now I am no longer in the world, but they are in the world, and I am coming to you. Holy Father, protect them in your name that you have given me, so that they may be one, as we are one. (John 17:10–11)

Jesus prays that his disciples would be protected and that they would be one. Jesus' prayer for these early disciples is likely his heavenly prayer now for all who know him by faith. We should be encouraged, knowing that our ascended Jesus, the one who "always lives to make intercession" for us, is praying for our protection and for our unity as the people of God (Heb 7:25).

During this season of Eastertide, actively remembering the ascension of Jesus, may we be encouraged to pray, even as our ascended Lord is praying for us. May we be aware of and resist the enemy. And may we remain steadfast in our faith, even as we undergo trials and hardship because we know there is a heavenly reward waiting for us.

QUESTIONS FOR REFLECTION

1. Luke recalls the event of the ascension in Acts 1. Do you reflect upon the ascension as you do the incarnation, death, and resurrection of Jesus? Explain. What are the implications of Jesus' ascension for us today? Luke gives us the disciples' account of Jesus' departure from earth. Where might one find a description of his heavenly arrival? Hint: read Psalm 24:7–10.

2. Psalm 68 encourages us to praise the one who "rides upon the clouds" and "whose power is in the skies." Do you find yourself praising Jesus as your ascended Lord, the one who was taken to heaven? Explain.

3. Why does Peter encourage us to rejoice in the midst of trials and sufferings? The Lord reminded Peter of Jesus' words on various occasions (see Acts 11:16). Should we expect this same dynamic in our own lives (see John 14:26)? Peter reminds us to be aware of and to resist the enemy. Why does he encourage us in this way? Do you find yourself praying in light of the reality of spiritual warfare? Explain.

4. Jesus prays for his disciples in John 17. For what is he praying? Do you think Jesus is interceding for us even now, praying for our protection and unity? See Hebrews 7:25.

PRAYER OF RESPONSE
Based on Acts 1:8–9, 14; John 17:1–11; 1 Peter 4:12–13

Ascended Lord Jesus,
we praise you for you have given us eternal life
and have made yourself known to us.
We ask for your protection,
that we, your people, may be one as you are one.
Help us not to be surprised when we face various trials,
but to rejoice, knowing that we are sharing in your sufferings.
By your grace, may we regularly devote ourselves to prayer,
seeking your strength and power as we live as witnesses
in this world to the grace and glory of the gospel.
In the name of Jesus we pray. Amen.

Day of Pentecost

LECTIONARY READINGS

Acts 2:1–21

Psalm 104:24–34, 35b

1 Corinthians 12:3b–13

John 20:19–23

DEVOTION

On the day of Pentecost, we celebrate the many roles of the third person of the Trinity, the Holy Spirit. Too often, we may have a caricature of the Holy Spirit that is shaped by questionable practices rather than by the word of God. The readings for this Sunday will help to give us a biblical understanding of the Spirit's many functions in birthing the church and empowering us with gifts.

In the first reading from Acts 2, on the day of Pentecost, the Holy Spirit (as promised) filled the early disciples and they began to speak in other languages. There was a larger crowd (greater than three thousand people) and each person heard of God's "deeds of power" in their own native tongue. It is hard to miss the miraculous nature of this event. Luke records the crowd's response in this way:

> All were amazed and perplexed, saying to one another, "What does this mean?" But others sneered and said, "They are filled with new wine." (Acts 2:12–13)

Peter then stood up and began to preach and explain to the crowd what was happening among them. He refuted the claim that they were drunk and then quoted from the prophet Joel, saying,

Indeed, these are not drunk, as you suppose, for it is only nine o'clock in the morning. No, this is what was spoken through the prophet Joel:

> "In the last days it will be, God declares,
> that I will pour out my Spirit upon all flesh,
> and your sons and your daughters shall prophesy,
> and your young men shall see visions,
> and your old men shall dream dreams.
> Even upon my slaves, both men and women,
> in those days I will pour out my Spirit,
> and they shall prophesy." (Acts 2:15–18)

Peter pointed the crowd back to this passage to give them insights on the miraculous events they witnessed. Though it is not a part of our reading for today, Peter went on to preach the gospel about Jesus Christ and around three thousand people were added to the church that day. Clearly, the power of the Spirit was at work, leading people into truth and bringing them to a place of faith and repentance before the Lord.

In the psalm of response, the psalmist sings,

> When you hide your face, they are dismayed;
> when you take away their breath, they die
> and return to their dust.
> When you send forth your spirit, they are created,
> and you renew the face of the ground. (Ps 104:29–30)

Here, we see the psalmist acknowledging the role of the Spirit in creation. The Spirit is the power that not only creates all things, but sustains all things. If the Spirit removes his life-giving spirit, creatures will die and "return to their dust." The psalms are full of "Holy Spirit" language. It was his breath and life at work, knitting us together within the womb (Ps 139:13–14). The Holy Spirit plays a prominent role in David's prayer of confession, after he repented of his adulterous affair with Bathsheba. David prays,

> Create in me a clean heart, O God,
> and put a new and right spirit within me.
> Do not cast me away from your presence,
> and do not take your holy spirit from me.
> Restore to me the joy of your salvation,
> and sustain in me a willing spirit. (Ps 51:10–12)

Here, we see David pleading for various petitions related to the Spirit. Truly, we can agree with the psalmist: "O Lord, how manifold are your works! In wisdom you have made them all; the earth is full of your creatures" (Ps 104:24). May we worship the Spirit for his powerful work in creating and sustaining our very lives as well as the beauty of the creation all around us.

In the second reading from 1 Corinthians 12, Paul demonstrates both the unity and the diversity of the body of Christ. He writes,

> Now there are varieties of gifts but the same Spirit, and there are varieties of services but the same Lord, and there are varieties of activities, but it is the same God who activates all of them in everyone. To each is given the manifestation of the Spirit for the common good. (1 Cor 12:4–7)

Though we have the same Lord, we are given different gifts to edify and build up the body of Christ. Some are given the gift of wisdom; some, the gift of faith; others, the gift of healing. All of these various gifts come from the Holy Spirit and are meant to equip and empower God's people for mutual edification.

We can see this unity and diversity exemplified within a given local church. In any given church, some are called and gifted to lead in song; others are called to teach; others are particularly gifted in caring and listening; others are eager to serve through deeds of mercy. The diversity of gifts is what allows a church to love and care for one another and the community in which it is located.

In the Gospel reading from John 20, Jesus meets with the disciples on the evening of his resurrection. He breathes on them and commissions them for ministry. John writes,

> Jesus said to them again, "Peace be with you. As the Father has sent me, so I send you." When he had said this, he breathed on them and said to them, "Receive the Holy Spirit. If you forgive the sins of any, they are forgiven them; if you retain the sins of any, they are retained." (John 20:21–23)

Jesus calms the disciples by offering his peace; he empowers them by breathing the Holy Spirit into them; and he commissions them by giving them the authority to declare that one is forgiven or not forgiven. The receiving of the Holy Spirit in John 20 precedes the disciples being filled with the Spirit on the day of Pentecost in Acts 2. This commission to the disciples, the authority to declare one's sins as forgiven or retained, is the basis for the exercise of church discipline through its officers in some denominations.

On this Pentecost Sunday, may we be grateful for the person and work of the Holy Spirit. The Holy Spirit not only breathed creation into existence, but breathed the church into existence on the day of Pentecost. And the Holy Spirit continues to gift, equip, and empower God's people for the work of ministry and service to one another and to the world. May we praise our good God for his many blessings and for the advocacy of the Holy Spirit in our lives and for the world.

QUESTIONS FOR REFLECTION

1. Why is the day of Pentecost so significant in the life of the church? Why do we recognize it as a festival within the Christian year like Christmas and Easter?

2. What are some of the roles of the Holy Spirit as evidenced in Ps 104? How does the Spirit sustain God's creation? How does the Spirit work in our lives today?

3. How do unity and diversity characterize the body of Christ? What are some of the gifts that Paul lists in 1 Corinthians 12? What are some of your spiritual gifts? How do you use your gifts for the edification of the church?

4. Why would Jesus need to speak a word of peace to the disciples in John 20? What did he commission them to do? Why would Jesus give church leaders the authority to declare that one is forgiven of sins? How might this commissioning play out in a given local church?

PRAYER OF RESPONSE
Based on Acts 2:1–21; John 20:19–23

Lord Jesus,
we thank you for sending the Holy Spirit in power
to your church on the day of Pentecost.
Continue to fill us and renew us in your ways.
Grant us your peace and help us
to experience the Spirit's work in our lives
by not harboring bitterness and resentment,
but by forgiving those who have wronged us and hurt us.
In the name of the Father, Son, and Holy Spirit, we pray. Amen.

Season after Pentecost

Trinity Sunday

LECTIONARY READINGS

Genesis 1:1—2:4a

Psalm 8

2 Corinthians 13:11–13

Matthew 28:16–20

DEVOTION

Trinity Sunday, the first Sunday after Pentecost, is the one Sunday that recognizes a doctrine (the triune nature of our God) rather than an event. Trinity Sunday marks the beginning of the long season after Pentecost. In the readings for this Sunday, we find the triune God creating the world from nothing. We find the apostle Paul closing his Letter to the Corinthians with a trinitarian blessing. In the Gospel of Matthew, Jesus commissions the eleven to go and make disciples and to baptize them in the name of the Father, Son, and Holy Spirit. Thus, the doctrine of the Trinity is celebrated in a variety of ways in the readings for this Sunday.

In the first reading from Genesis 1, the triune God creates the world from nothing. There is a "wind" from God that swept over the waters (Gen 1:2), most likely an allusion to the Spirit. Most significantly, a first-person plural pronoun is used in Genesis 1:26, as humankind is created. Scripture records,

> Then God said, "Let us make humans in our image, according to our likeness, and let them have dominion over the fish of the sea and over the birds of the air and over the cattle and over all

the wild animals of the earth and over every creeping thing that creeps upon the earth." (Gen 1:26)

The use of the pronoun "us" is thought to be a reference to the Father, Son, and Holy Spirit. We are made in the image of God, and it is his breath that gives us life.

Psalm 8 is the psalm of response. The psalmist expresses his wonder and awe as he contemplates God's creation. He writes,

> When I look at your heavens, the work of your fingers,
> the moon and the stars that you have established;
> what are humans that you are mindful of them,
> mortals that you care for them? (Ps 8:3–4)

The psalmist is utterly amazed at the beauty and splendor of creation. And as he stands in awe of God's creation, he wonders how God can still remain in such an intimate relationship with humankind. The Lord has ordered and still governs the cosmos, yet he cares for his people. This truth is astounding. The maker of heaven and earth initiated a relationship with his people. He established a covenantal relationship with us. He is our Father, our brother, and our advocate.

The Father cares for us; Christ, our brother intercedes for us; and the Holy Spirit equips us and empowers us to edify one another and to serve and love our world. Our triune God did not create the world and then distance himself from it. He remains intimately involved in the lives of his people and in governing and sustaining his creation.

In the second reading from 2 Corinthians 13, the apostle Paul closes his letter to the Corinthian believers with a trinitarian blessing. He writes, "The grace of the Lord Jesus Christ, the love of God, and the communion of the Holy Spirit be with all of you" (2 Cor 13:13). Paul both encouraged and admonished the Corinthians over the course of two different letters. In closing, however, he offers them a strong word of blessing by reminding them of the grace of Christ, the love of God, and the communion of the Holy Spirit.

We, too, are encouraged to live in this trinitarian blessing. We need to be reminded of the grace of Christ which comes from his present intercession on our behalf and his invitation to draw near to his throne to find help and mercy in our time of need. We are strengthened by the love of God, our heavenly Father, who shepherds us and cares for us in countless ways. And we join in the fellowship and communion of the

Holy Spirit who indwells us. We know his presence with us, corporately and individually (1 Cor 3:16; 6:19).

Finally, in the Gospel reading from Matthew 28, we find Jesus commissioning the disciples after his resurrection. Jesus declares,

> Go therefore and make disciples of all nations, baptizing them in the name of the Father and of the Son and of the Holy Spirit and teaching them to obey everything that I have commanded you. And remember, I am with you always, to the end of the age. (Matt 28:19–20)

Jesus offers a strong trinitarian commission as he exhorts the eleven to make disciples and to baptize them in the name of the Father, Son, and Holy Spirit. We are created physically by the power of our triune God, and we are reborn through the work of the triune God. Our initiation into faith is through the work of the Father, Son, and Holy Spirit. Even as we remember Jesus' baptism, we will recall the presence of the Father as he spoke to the Son, "This is my Son, the Beloved, with whom I am well pleased" (Matt 3:17); and we recall the presence of the Spirit, "descending like a dove and alighting on him" (Matt 3:16).

Through our baptism, we become sons and daughters of God and the Spirit comes to dwell within us as we are made alive by the blood of Christ. As we celebrate Trinity Sunday, may we remember all of the various ways our triune God ministers to us and sustains his creation.

QUESTIONS FOR REFLECTION

1. How do we know that the members of the Trinity were present at creation? How does this knowledge inform our understanding of the various roles of the Father, Son, and Holy Spirit?

2. How would you describe the tone of Psalm 8? What is the cause for the psalmist's awe and wonder? Do you stand in awe of God's creation? Are you even more amazed that our creator God has initiated such an intimate relationship with us? Explain.

3. Why would it be important for Paul to close his letter with such a strong trinitarian blessing? How should this blessing encourage us?

4. Matthew 28:19–20 is known as the "Great Commission." Why would Jesus make a point to acknowledge the Trinity in this commission? How does this inform the way we evangelize today?

PRAYER OF RESPONSE
Based on Genesis 1:1–28; Matthew 28:19;
2 Corinthians 13:11–13

Triune God,
we praise you for your work of creation.
We delight in all that you have made
and seek to fulfill the command you have given us
to be fruitful and multiply, to fill the earth and subdue it.
By your grace, may we live in peace with one another,
and carry out the Great Commission to make disciples of all nations.
In all that we do, may the grace of the Lord Jesus Christ,
the love of God, and the communion of the Holy Spirit be with us. Amen.

Proper 3[1]

Sunday between May 24 and May 28 inclusive

LECTIONARY READINGS

Isaiah 49:8–16a

Psalm 131

1 Corinthians 4:1–5

Matthew 6:24–34

DEVOTION

In the readings for this Sunday, Jesus comforts his people with a message about the love and care of the Father in the Gospel reading from Matthew 6. In the first reading from Isaiah 49, God's love for his people is understood as greater than the love of a mother towards her nursing child. Psalm 131 builds on this theme of nurturing love through the psalmist's expression of contentment in God being like that of a weaned child. In the second reading from 1 Corinthians 4, the apostle Paul teaches on the judgment of God, exposing the purposes of each of our hearts. Thus, the love and care as well as the judgment of God are common themes in the readings for this Sunday.

In the first reading from Isaiah 49, the prophet brings hope and encouragement to the people of God who are in exile. He promises that his covenant will remain true as the people return to and reestablish the land (Isa 49:8). Moreover, the Lord describes his role as shepherd in leading the people out of darkness and exile. He writes,

---

1. The readings for the eighth Sunday after Epiphany match those for Proper 3. As a result the devotion, questions for reflection, and prayer of response also match.

> They shall feed along the ways;
> on all the bare heights shall be their pasture;
> they shall not hunger or thirst,
> neither scorching wind nor sun shall strike them down,
> for he who has pity on them will lead them
> and by springs of water will guide them.
> And I will turn all my mountains into a road,
> and my highways shall be raised up. (Isa 49:9–11)

God will guide his people home and will make sure their journey is successful, providing food, protection, and a safe path. Though the prophet is speaking of a future return from Babylonian exile, he is also revealing how the Lord continues to lead and guide his people throughout the centuries as the Good Shepherd. God is still faithful to restore his people.

The prophet also describes the profound, divine love that God has for his people. Isaiah proclaims,

> But Zion said, "The Lord has forsaken me;
> my Lord has forgotten me."
> Can a woman forget her nursing child
> or show no compassion for the child of her womb?
> Even these might forget,
> yet I will not forget you.
> See, I have inscribed you on the palms of my hands;
> your walls are continually before me. (Isa 49:14–16)

Isaiah responds to the people's doubts about God's love by revealing how God's love surpasses even that of mother for her nursing child. Such language offers us a window into the profound love that God has for us, his children. Moreover, through the prophet, God encourages us with the language that we are inscribed "on the palms" of his hands. We are ever before him and he cares for us more than we often realize. Such tender expressions from God's word reveal the depth and consistency of his love for his people.

Psalm 131 is an appropriate response to the first reading from Isaiah 49. Here, David speaks of his contentment in the Lord. He does not occupy himself with things too great for him to understand, but simply finds rest in the tender love of God. David sings,

> But I have calmed and quieted my soul,
> like a weaned child with its mother;
> my soul is like the weaned child that is with me. (Ps 131:2)

An unweaned child will often cry for food and nourishment and is satisfied only when his or her cravings have been met. A weaned child has learned to trust in and rest in the mother who has proven that she will take care of her child's needs. A weaned child has a deeper sense of his mother's love. As those who first learned to trust God for our "felt needs," we also learn to trust him during times of trial and suffering. This is the kind of trust that David is expressing. He has learned to rest and be content in the love of his Good Shepherd, the one who is with him through all of life's circumstances.

Learning to trust the Lord is a journey for all of those who have put their faith in God. We must rest in the one who gives us, not all that we want, but all that we truly need. Moreover, we learn that we can trust in the Lord's steadfast love, his covenant faithfulness towards his children. Though we walk through valleys, God is with us in all things. Our souls can rest in his divine love and care.

In the second reading from 1 Corinthians 4, the apostle Paul reveals the role of God as judge. He writes,

> Therefore do not pronounce judgment before the time, before the Lord comes, who will bring to light the things now hidden in darkness and will disclose the purposes of the heart. Then each one will receive commendation from God. (1 Cor 4:5)

In the context of this passage, Paul is expressing what a "very small thing" (1 Cor 4:3) it is to be judged by humans. As an apostle, Paul was defending his role as a leader in the church; however, in the midst of his defense, he encourages the Corinthians to be concerned about the Lord's judgment of each of us. Only God can expose the true nature of our hearts.

This reading complements the previous expressions of God's nurturing love and care as our Good Shepherd with the reality that he is also our judge, the one who brings "to light the things now hidden in darkness" (1 Cor 4:5). For those who have placed their hope in the Lord, we should not feel worried or anxious about this reality; though our hearts will be exposed, we will not be condemned. In God's economy, bringing truth to light brings relief to those who know him as Lord (Ps 32:1-5).

Finally, in the Gospel reading from Matthew 6, we hear the comforting words of Jesus who reminds us not to worry, but to rest in God's constant love and care for his children. Jesus declares,

> But if God so clothes the grass of the field, which is alive today and tomorrow is thrown into the oven, will he not much more clothe you—you of little faith? Therefore do not worry, saying, "What will we eat?" or "What will we drink?" or "What will we wear?" For it is the gentiles who seek all these things, and indeed your heavenly Father knows that you need all these things. But seek first the kingdom of God and his righteousness, and all these things will be given to you as well. (Matt 6:30–33)

Jesus encourages us with the Father's sovereign care of his creation. As Isaiah encouraged the people of God in his day by expressing that God's love and care is greater than that of a mother; here, Jesus expresses God's care for his people as greater than his care of the birds of the air and the lilies and grass of the field. If God feeds and clothes them, how much more will he feed and clothe us, his beloved children? Jesus even describes how we lack faith when we fail to trust in God's steadfast love for us.

Jesus' deeper point, however, is that the Father not only provides for our physical needs; he provides for our spiritual needs as well. More than food and shelter, the Lord provides the righteousness we need that can only be found in Christ. We find true contentment and rest from worry and anxiety when we seek the kingdom of God. Jesus' exhortation is similar to that of the apostle Paul to the Colossians. Paul writes,

> So if you have been raised with Christ, seek the things that are above, where Christ is, seated at the right hand of God. Set your minds on the things that are above, not on the things that are on earth, for you have died, and your life is hidden with Christ in God. (Col 3:1–3)

We must remember our baptismal identity as sons and daughters of God. With this knowledge, we are able to put earthly concerns in their proper perspective. We do not need to worry about physical needs when we trust the goodness of our loving God. He knows what we need. He is our Good Shepherd who guides us, loves us, protects us, and provides for us. His love for us is greater than a mother's love for her child. This is the good news of the gospel.

During this season after Pentecost, may we rest in the nurturing love and care of our heavenly Father, the one who has given us his one and only Son to make us righteous.

QUESTIONS FOR REFLECTION

1. The prophet Isaiah reveals the guidance and protection of God (Isa 49:9–11). How does God guide and protect you today? Isaiah also reveals that God's love for his people is greater than the love of a mother for her child. How does this image encourage you?

2. In Psalm 131, David describes his contentment in God. Put the imagery of David's soul being like that of a weaned child in your own words. Is your soul at rest in this way? Explain.

3. In his Letter to the Corinthians, Paul reminds the people that God is the judge who will expose the true nature of our hearts. Does this bring you comfort or fear? Explain. How is God's love both tender (greater than the love of a mother for her child) and just (bringing to light things that are now hidden)?

4. In Matthew 6, Jesus teaches us about God's sovereign care for his creation and for his beloved children. Knowing how much he loves us, why do we still doubt that he will care for us and provide for our needs? What is our greatest need? How has God provided for that? Do you find rest and contentment by setting your heart and mind on the kingdom of God and on things that are above? Explain.

PRAYER OF RESPONSE
Based on Matthew 6:25–34

Lord Jesus,
our hearts long for rest.
Help us not to worry about our life,
what we will eat or what we will drink,
or about our bodies, what we will wear.
We know that you care for all of your creation,
providing food and nourishment for all living things.
When we become anxious and fearful, by your grace,
help us to trust in your provision for each new day.
May we strive first for your kingdom and your righteousness,
knowing that all of these earthly concerns will be given to us as well.
In the name of Jesus we pray. Amen.

Proper 4[1]

Sunday between May 29 and June 4 inclusive

LECTIONARY READINGS

Deuteronomy 11:18–21, 26–28

Psalm 31:1–5, 19–24

Romans 1:16–17; 3:22b–31

Matthew 7:21–29

DEVOTION

In the readings for this Sunday, we hear the final words of Jesus' Sermon on the Mount in Matthew 7 as he offers sobering words about the day of judgment and exhorts us to live out what we hear. In the first reading from Deuteronomy 11, we hear the words of Moses on the plains of Moab, instructing the people to teach the next generation about the faith and to obey God's commands. In Psalm 31, the psalmist looks to God as his rock. In the second reading from the book of Romans, the apostle Paul teaches us that we are justified by faith and not by works. Thus, the themes of hearing and doing the word, of living by faith and obedience are common threads in the readings for this Sunday.

In the first reading from Deuteronomy 11, Moses is instructing the people of God and renewing God's covenant with them before they cross the Jordan River and enter the promised land. He declares,

> You shall put these words of mine in your heart and soul, and you shall bind them as a sign on your hand and fix them as an

---

1. The readings for the ninth Sunday after Epiphany match those for Proper 4. As a result the devotion, questions for reflection, and prayer of response also match.

> emblem on your forehead. Teach them to your children, talking about them when you are at home and when you are away, when you lie down and when you rise up. (Deut 11:18–19)

Moses gave the people of God this same instruction in Deuteronomy 6. Evidently, it is so important that he is repeating himself for emphasis. Moreover, Moses is exhorting the people of God to make God's word a part of their heart and soul. These commandments are not meant to be mere information, but words that shape who we are and inform how we live our lives. Through Moses, the Lord tells the people of the blessing for living according to God's word and the curse for disobeying God's word.

We should take these words to heart. Like the Israelites long ago, we are to pass on God's story to our children and to future generations. We should talk about all that God has done in the Bible and in our own lives when we are at home and when we are away, when we lie down and when we rise. The story of God should permeate our homes. Having spiritual conversations should be a normal and natural rhythm of our lives. God blesses us in countless ways when we live genuine, humble lives of faith and obedience.

In Psalm 31, the psalm of response, David sings of the Lord as his rock, saying,

> Be a rock of refuge for me,
> a strong fortress to save me.
>
> You are indeed my rock and my fortress;
> for your name's sake lead me and guide me;
> take me out of the net that is hidden for me,
> for you are my refuge. (Ps 31:2b–4)

The imagery and stability of a rock will be discussed in the Gospel reading from Matthew 7. Here, David describes the Lord as his "rock of refuge." He knows his God is faithful and unchanging, and that he can trust the Lord for guidance and protection.

Moreover, David places his hope and trust in the steadfast love of the Lord. He sings,

> Blessed be the Lord,
> for he has wondrously shown his steadfast love to me
> when I was beset as a city under siege.
> I had said in my alarm,
> "I am driven far from your sight."

> But you heard my supplications
> when I cried out to you for help. (Ps 31:21–22)

David knew that the Lord would protect him, even as he felt "beset as a city under siege." The Lord heard David's prayers and cries for help.

We can look to the Lord as our rock of refuge still today. He keeps his covenant with his children and is faithful even when we are unfaithful. As our rock of refuge, we cling to him by faith and rely on the Holy Spirit to lead us and guide us in the way we should go. The Lord is our advocate who protects us and reveals his steadfast love in countless ways. Like David, our lives are lived by faith and in humble reliance upon the Lord.

In the second reading from the book of Romans, the apostle Paul teaches about the power of the gospel. He writes,

> For I am not ashamed of the gospel; it is God's saving power for everyone who believes, for the Jew first and also for the Greek. For in it the righteousness of God is revealed through faith for faith, as it is written, "The one who is righteous will live by faith." (Rom 1:16–17)

Here, we find that the gospel is "God's saving power" and that it contains instructions for living "by faith." Those who are righteous live by faith. It is vital that we understand this truth: "The one who is righteous will live by faith" (Rom 1:17). As we will see in the Gospel reading from Matthew 7, many people do good things, even things that appear to be of the Spirit (prophesying, casting out demons, performing deeds of power). These actions alone, however, do not mean that a person truly knows the Lord. This is a sobering reality, but one that we need to hear. All is in vain if we are not saved by faith, to live by faith.

Paul further writes, "For we hold that a person is justified by faith apart from works prescribed by the law" (Rom 3:28). We are declared right before God, not by works, but by faith. As Moses stressed to the people of God in Deuteronomy 11, we do not take in the word for knowledge alone or merit before God, but as a means of informing our heart and soul. As we teach our children and the future generations about faith and the story of God, our hope is that one day, by the power of God's grace, they will make this faith their own.

Finally, in the Gospel reading from Matthew 7, Jesus finishes his Sermon on the Mount by offering a sobering message about the day of the Lord. He declares,

> Not everyone who says to me, "Lord, Lord," will enter the kingdom of heaven, but only the one who does the will of my Father in heaven. On that day many will say to me, "Lord, Lord, did we not prophesy in your name, and cast out demons in your name, and do many mighty works in your name?" Then I will declare to them, "I never knew you; go away from me, you who behave lawlessly." (Matt 7:21–23)

As he brings his sermon to a close, Jesus speaks candidly about those who thought they were doing things in his name, but were never actually saved by faith in him. This message should not cause us to doubt our salvation; we have the inner witness of the Spirit with our spirit that we are sons and daughters of God (Rom 8:16). It should cause us to be more discerning, however, and to realize that not everyone who has the outward signs of faith is truly a child of God. In other words, not everyone who preaches, teaches, sings, attends church on Sunday, or goes to a small group during the week is a true believer.

Jesus also teaches about those who are both hearers and doers of the word versus those who are hearers only. Regarding the hearers and doers, he declares,

> Everyone, then, who hears these words of mine and acts on them will be like a wise man who built his house on rock. The rain fell, the floods came, and the winds blew and beat on that house, but it did not fall because it had been founded on rock. (Matt 7:24–25)

As Moses and the apostle Paul taught, the word is not for knowledge alone. The word should be in our hearts and souls, informing our lives, and empowering us to live by faith. Like David, Jesus is exhorting us to know God as our rock of refuge. Those who live in such a way are wise. Those who are wise are able to persevere through trials and the various circumstances of life because their faith and hope are in Christ.

Those who are foolish, Jesus taught, build their houses on sand. The word of God has not changed their hearts and souls; it is not the foundation and source of their faith. Ultimately, those who are foolish put their faith and hope in themselves.

During this season after Pentecost, may we live by faith in Christ. Like Paul, may we not be ashamed of the gospel for it is God's saving power for those who believe. May the wisdom of God be evident to the world as we live in humble obedience to the Lord.

QUESTIONS FOR REFLECTION

1. In Deuteronomy 11, Moses teaches the people of God to put the word of God in their hearts and souls and to teach this word to their children and future generations. What does it mean to put God's word in your heart and in your soul? How do you teach your child or children about the story of God?

2. In Psalm 13, David describes the Lord as his "rock of refuge." How would you express this metaphor in your own words? How is God your rock of refuge? How do you experience the steadfast love of the Lord in your life? Do you cry out to the Lord in prayer for help? Describe.

3. In his Letter to the Romans, Paul teaches about the power of the gospel. How would you articulate the gospel in your own words? What does this statement mean: "The one who is righteous will live by faith" (Rom 1:17)? What does living by faith look like in your own life?

4. In Matthew 7, Jesus teaches us about the day of the Lord and of being hearers and doers of the word. Is it sobering to you that not everyone who appears to be a Christian is one? Explain. How can we have assurance of our own faith? What does the message about building one's house on rock versus sand mean? Why is it foolish to build one's house on sand?

PRAYER OF RESPONSE
Based on Deuteronomy 11:18–21; Matthew 7:24–27

Lord Jesus,
help us to put your word in our heart and soul,
feasting on it in such a way that it would nourish us and fill us.
May we be diligent to teach our children about your mighty deeds,
talking about them when we are at home and when we are away,
when we lie down and when we rise.
By your grace, let the truth of the gospel
bring abundant blessing upon our lives.
Forgive us when we foolishly neglect your word and commandments,
finding ourselves vulnerable to temptation;
lacking in faith, hope, and love;
and quenching our fellowship with the Holy Spirit.

Our desire is to be like a wise man who built his house on a rock,
able to withstand the storms and trials of this life,
and drawing ever closer to you.
In the name of Jesus we pray. Amen.

Proper 5

Sunday between June 5 and June 11 inclusive

LECTIONARY READINGS

>   Hosea 5:15—6:6
>   Psalm 50:7–15
>   Romans 4:13–25
>   Matthew 9:9–13, 18–26

DEVOTION

In the readings for this Sunday, the prophet Hosea speaks of the healing that comes from the Lord when his people are repentant. The apostle Paul writes to the church at Rome about the faith of Abraham. In the Gospel reading from Matthew 9, we find Jesus calling Matthew to be a disciple. We also find Jesus eating with tax collectors and sinners, healing a woman, and raising a girl from the dead. Thus, faith and repentance are common themes in the readings for this Sunday.

In the first reading from Hosea, we hear the poetic repentance of God's people. The prophet proclaims,

> Come, let us return to the Lord,
> for it is he who has torn, and he will heal us;
> he has struck down, and he will bind us up.
> After two days he will revive us;
> on the third day he will raise us up,
> that we may live before him. (Hos 6:1–2)

The people of God recognize their idolatry and seek to return to the Lord, knowing that the Lord is able to heal and restore them. The prophet also speaks for the Lord who expresses the fickle faith of his people, declaring,

> What shall I do with you, O Ephraim?
> What shall I do with you, O Judah?
> Your love is like a morning cloud,
> like the dew that goes away early. (Hos 6:4)

The faith of God's people is short-lived, "like the dew that goes away early" (Hos 6:4). It comes and goes; it is not stable and steadfast. The Lord desires "steadfast love and not sacrifice, the knowledge of God rather than burnt offerings" (Hos 6:6). Too often, our faith is fickle and our worship is routine. God desires for us to be firm and steadfast in our love, our faith, and our worship. Our life should reflect a genuine relationship, not just rituals that we observe or words that we say.

Psalm 50 echoes this same sentiment as a psalm of response. The people were continually bringing their sacrifices before the Lord, but something was missing. They were simply going through the motions of worship. The psalmist sings,

> Offer to God a sacrifice of thanksgiving,
> and pay your vows to the Most High.
> Call on me in the day of trouble;
> I will deliver you, and you shall glorify me. (Ps 50:14–15)

The psalmist is encouraging the people to express their thanksgiving and their adoration to God, letting their lips reflect their gratitude and love. Moreover, the psalmist, speaking for God, invites his people to call on him when they are in need. He promises to deliver and restore them and they will worship and glorify him in response.

The Lord knows that often it is when we are in trouble, when we are in need, that we call on him. A genuine cry for help is desired over an empty ritual. God did not *need* the people's sacrifices. He owns "the cattle on a thousand hills" (Ps 50:10). Rather, he loves a broken and contrite heart; he loves to restore those who realize their need of him.

In the second reading from Romans 4, Paul teaches on the faith of Abraham. He declares that Abraham believed in the promise of God centuries before the law of God was established through Moses. And

Abraham's faith was "reckoned to him as righteousness" (Rom 4:22). Paul then writes,

> Now the words, "it was reckoned to him," were written not for his sake alone but for ours also. It will be reckoned to us who believe in him who raised Jesus our Lord from the dead, who was handed over for our trespasses and was raised for our justification. (Rom 4:23–25)

Paul is making the connection between Abraham and believers today. We are counted as righteous because of our faith in the resurrection of Jesus. We are not saved by the law, but by believing that Jesus was raised from the dead for our salvation. Some believe that we are saved by our works. Paul makes it clear that this is not so and that the salvation of God is all of grace.

In the Gospel reading from Matthew 9, we find Jesus calling Matthew to be his disciple. Soon after, Jesus is eating among tax collectors and sinners. Matthew writes,

> And as he sat at dinner in the house, many tax collectors and sinners came and were sitting with Jesus and his disciples. When the Pharisees saw this, they said to his disciples, "Why does your teacher eat with tax collectors and sinners?" But when he heard this, he said, "Those who are well have no need of a physician, but those who are sick. Go and learn what this means, 'I desire mercy, not sacrifice.' For I have not come to call the righteous but sinners." (Matt 9:10–13)

In this narrative, we find Jesus quoting from Hosea 6:6 (part of the first reading) when he says, "I desire mercy, not sacrifice" (Matt 9:13). This whole narrative is full of people who have a need and express their faith in Jesus to heal them. During the meal, Jesus is sought by a leader whose daughter had died and by a woman who has suffered from a chronic ailment. Out of their desperate need, both the leader and the woman put their faith in Jesus' power to heal. The woman was healed of her ailment and the leader's daughter was raised from the dead.

These narratives underscore the themes of the first reading from Hosea, the psalm of response (Ps 50), and the second reading from Romans 4: God loves to come to us when we humbly acknowledge our need (rather than bring him empty worship rituals) and express our faith in him.

Our barrier is often believing that we do not need God; we trust in our own resources rather than the Lord. Thus, our lives can be filled with spiritual practices that are void of genuine faith because we are not desperate for God at some level. When we come to God out of desperation, like the people Jesus healed in Matthew 9, beautiful things often follow. God desires mercy, not sacrifice. He did not come for those who believe they have it all together, the "righteous." He came for sinners, those who know they need a physician.

During this season after Pentecost, may we learn to acknowledge our desperate need for Jesus. May we not see ourselves as "well," but as those who are sick and in need of the healing and restoration of our Lord. We do not have to feel the need to perform for God or "fake it" as though our empty works will earn us favor. We only need to come to him in faith, seeking mercy in our time of need.

QUESTIONS FOR REFLECTION

1. What was the problem with the people in Hosea's day? How was their worship distorted? What lessons can we learn from this passage?

2. Why is Psalm 50 such an appropriate psalm of response to the first reading? The psalmist tells us that God owns the cattle on a thousand hills. How should that truth inform our worship practices? What kind of offering does the Lord desire from us?

3. How does Paul distinguish the promise from the law? Did the promise come before or after the law? Why is this important? How is our faith, like that of Abraham, reckoned to us as righteousness? What is the object of our faith (Rom 4:24)?

4. Jesus teaches that those who are well have no need of a physician, but those who are sick do. Jesus also quoted from Hosea 6:6, saying, "I desire mercy, not sacrifice." How does the rest of the Gospel narrative unpack those statements? What can we learn from the leader whose daughter was dead and from the woman who suffered a chronic ailment?

PRAYER OF RESPONSE
Based on Matthew 9:12–13; Hosea 6:1, 6

Lord Jesus,
help us to understand your words,
"Those who are well have no need of a physician,
but those we are sick."
May we see ourselves from your perspective,
and may we be humble and honest about our condition,
for we are desperate for you.
By your grace, help us not to become self-righteous,
for you desire steadfast love, not sacrifice;
genuine fellowship with you, not empty rituals.
Let us return to you, O Lord.
In the name of Jesus we pray. Amen.

Proper 6

Sunday between June 12 and June 18 inclusive

LECTIONARY READINGS

Exodus 19:2–8a

Psalm 100

Romans 5:1–8

Matthew 9:35—10:23

DEVOTION

In the readings for this Sunday, we find Jesus sending the disciples to share the gospel in word and deed. In the first reading from Exodus 19, we find the Lord, through Moses, commissioning the people of Israel to be a kingdom of priests and a holy nation. The apostle Paul teaches about the peace we have with God and of our justification. Thus, sharing our faith, being ambassadors of Christ to this world, and living at peace with God are themes in the readings for this Sunday.

In the first reading from Exodus 19, the people of Israel are camped near Mount Sinai. Moses goes up the mountain to speak with God and receives the words he is to speak to the nation of Israel. This is the message the Lord told Moses to give to the people:

> You have seen what I did to the Egyptians and how I bore you on eagles' wings and brought you to myself. Now, therefore, if you obey my voice and keep my covenant, you shall be my treasured possession out of all the peoples. Indeed, the whole earth is mine, but you shall be for me a priestly kingdom and a holy nation. (Exod 19:4–6)

This passage was chosen to parallel the Gospel reading in which Jesus commissions the disciples to share the gospel in word and deed. The people of Israel were chosen by God to be priests, mediators between God and the world, and a light to the nations. Though time after time, they failed to obey God and often chose to go their own way, the Lord had set them apart as a holy nation. And despite their rebellion, the nations were witnesses to the power of God at work through his people. The Egyptians saw the power of God as the Lord miraculously rescued his people from slavery and brought them safely across the Red Sea.

As Christians, we are called to be priests as well. The apostle Peter, using language very similar to that of Exodus 19, reminds us of our calling and status. He writes,

> But you are a chosen people, a royal priesthood, a holy nation, God's own people, in order that you may proclaim the excellence of him who called you out of darkness into his marvelous light. (1 Pet 2:9)

As the nation of Israel was to be a light to the world, so we are to be ambassadors for Christ. Our lives should demonstrate to the world the power of the gospel, that those who once lived in darkness have been called into the marvelous light of God.

In Psalm 100, we find the response to the first reading. The psalmist exhorts the whole earth to worship the Lord. The psalmist sings,

> Make a joyful noise to the Lord, all the earth.
> Serve the Lord with gladness;
> come into his presence with singing.
>
> Know that the Lord is God.
> It is he that made us, and we are his;
> we are his people and the sheep of his pasture. (Ps 100:1–3)

The people of Israel were to be a light to the world, bringing the nations into a knowledge of God. This psalm has a missional thrust to it, inviting everyone to know the Lord as creator and redeemer. As Christians, we also share the good news of the gospel so that others will come to know the Lord as creator and redeemer.

The whole point of "missions" is to claim more and more worshipers of God. The exhortation to "make a joyful noise to the Lord, all the earth" has missional implications. As ambassadors of Christ, it is our calling to share the gospel in word and deed; we are instruments used by God to bring others into the kingdom. In this way, all the nations of the earth are able to make a joyful noise, worship the Lord, and know that the Lord is God.

In the second reading from Romans 5, the apostle Paul teaches about our peace with God and on the doctrine of justification, how we are legally declared God's own. He writes,

> Therefore, since we are justified by faith, we have peace with God through our Lord Jesus Christ, through whom we have obtained access to this grace in which we stand, and we boast in our hope of sharing the glory of God. (Rom 5:1–2)

The gospel teaches us that we are able to have peace with God, that we have been justified by faith. God legally declares us righteous because of the saving and atoning work of Christ. This is a profound truth for us who believe. It means that we have access to God through Christ and are able to approach the throne of grace at any time (Heb 10:19–22). It also means that our consciences are clean; Christ's once-for-all sacrifice has purified us and has atoned for our sins (past, present, and future).

Moreover, Paul exhorts us to boast in our sufferings, "knowing that affliction produces endurance, and endurance produces character, and character produces hope, and hope does not put us to shame, because God's love has been poured into our hearts through the Holy Spirit that has been given to us" (Rom 5:3–5). In God's economy, suffering and affliction are seen as agents of sanctification. Through suffering, God shapes us into the people he desires us to be.

The love of God has been poured into our hearts through the Holy Spirit, and that love produces godly character within us. Though we do not often see it this way, trials and hardship are agents of spiritual transformation in our lives. Through them, we become more and more like Christ and are filled with hope in the process.

In the Gospel reading from Matthew 10, we find the disciples being called out to share the good news of the kingdom in both word and deed. Jesus instructs them,

> As you go, proclaim the good news, "The kingdom of heaven has come near." Cure the sick; raise the dead; cleanse those with a skin disease; cast out demons. (Matt 10:7–8)

Jesus exhorts the disciples to proclaim a message and to bring healing to the people they encounter. He offers them practical counsel on how they should enter and exit a given town. He also encourages them not to worry about what they will say, "for what you are to say will be given to you at that time, for it is not you who speak, but the Spirit of your Father speaking through you" (Matt 10:19–20).

Like the disciples, Jesus calls us to go into the world, to proclaim the message of the kingdom, and to be agents of transformation to those in need. As we engage with our own culture, we should also be "wise as serpents and innocent as doves" (Matt 10:16). This calling takes us out of our comfort zones and into the messiness of this broken world. As we referenced earlier, however, how can the nations of the earth worship the Lord and know him as the one, true God if we do not go into all the world with the message of the gospel?

Too often we can settle into a spiritual complacency, being satisfied with our own salvation and possibly the salvation of our children, losing sight of the fact that "the harvest is plentiful, but the laborers are few" (Matt 9:37). Like Jesus, we should have compassion on our neighbors and the people in our community, seeing them not just as sinners in need of grace, but as people who are "like sheep without a shepherd" (Matt 9:36).

During this season after Pentecost, may we be reminded that we are a royal priesthood and a holy nation. We are the church, the people of God, and we are to be on mission where we live. May we share the light and love of Christ with those around us so that all the nations of the earth will make a joyful noise unto the Lord.

QUESTIONS FOR REFLECTION

1. What does it mean that God declared Israel to be "a kingdom of priests and a holy nation." What implications did this have on them as a people? Did they succeed or fail in this calling?

2. How do worship and mission intersect in Psalm 100? What is the ultimate goal of missions, taking the gospel to the nations?

3. What is profound about Paul's message in Romans 5? What does it mean that we have been justified by faith and that we have peace with God? What are the implications for our lives?

4. Jesus sent the disciples out to share the gospel in word and deed. Where do we find his call to us to do the same? The disciples experienced obstacles in their gospel journey. What are the obstacles we often face in sharing the gospel with others today? How can we be encouraged and not worried about what we will say? How does Jesus speak into our anxiety regarding evangelism?

PRAYER OF RESPONSE
Based on Matthew 10:5–7, 16, 19–20

Lord Jesus,
in the same way that you sent the disciples
to proclaim the good news
that the kingdom of heaven has come near;
so empower us and fill us with faith
to share this same message
with our neighbors and loved ones who do not yet know you.
As we go, help us to be wise as serpents and innocent as doves.
May we not worry about how we are to speak or what we are to say;
for what we are to say will be given to us at that time;
for it is not we who speak, but the Spirit speaking through us.
In the name of Jesus we pray. Amen.

Proper 7

Sunday between June 19 and June 25 inclusive

LECTIONARY READINGS

Jeremiah 20:7–13

Psalm 69:7–18

Romans 6:1b–11

Matthew 10:24–39

DEVOTION

In the readings for this Sunday, we find Jesus describing both the value of being known by the Father and the cost of being a disciple. In the first reading from Jeremiah 20, we find the prophet being mocked for proclaiming the word of the Lord. In the second reading from Romans 6, the apostle Paul describes the union we have with Christ; we have died to sin and have been made alive to God in Christ. Thus, union with Christ and the cost of discipleship are themes in the readings for this Sunday.

In the first reading from Jeremiah 20, the prophet is lamenting his situation and the way he is mocked by his own people. He writes:

> O Lord, you have enticed me,
> and I was enticed;
> you have overpowered me,
> and you have prevailed.
> I have become a laughingstock all day long;
> everyone mocks me.
> For whenever I speak, I must cry out;

> I must shout, "Violence and destruction!"
> For the word of the Lord has become for me
> a reproach and derision all day long. (Jer 20:7–8)

Jeremiah finds himself warning the people of God to return to the Lord, but they will not listen. Jeremiah learns what it is like to suffer for the Lord. He understands the trials and tribulations of following the call of God on your life. And though Jeremiah tries to resist, he learns that he has something "like a burning fire" in his bones (Jer 20:9). He has to preach and proclaim the word of the Lord.

We can relate to Jeremiah's lamentation. We, too, are called to live and follow God under hard circumstances at times. The Christian life is not without trials and hardship. As believers, we need to be comfortable with seasons of lamentation, suffering, and perhaps even persecution. However, like Jeremiah, we can be encouraged that if God is calling us into these seasons, he will give us the grace to sustain us. And he will put a burning fire in our bones, a grace that compels us to share the gospel in word and deed to those who need it.

In Psalm 69, the psalmist echoes Jeremiah's lamentation as he describes his situation. The psalmist sings,

> It is for your sake that I have borne reproach,
> that shame has covered my face.
> I have become a stranger to my kindred,
> an alien to my mother's children.
>
> It is zeal for your house that has consumed me;
> the insults of those who insult you have fallen on me.
> When I humbled my soul with fasting,
> they insulted me for doing so.
> When I made sackcloth my clothing,
> I became a byword to them.
> I am the subject of gossip for those who sit in the gate,
> and the drunkards make songs about me. (Ps 69:7–12)

Like Jeremiah, the psalmist has become the source of mockery by his own people. Zeal for the ways of God has caused the psalmist to be shunned by his friends and family. He is the source of gossip to those around him. Yet, he places his hope and trust in the steadfast love of the Lord. In his desperate situation, the psalmist prays,

> Answer me, O Lord, for your steadfast love is good;
> according to your abundant mercy, turn to me.
> Do not hide your face from your servant,
> for I am in distress—make haste to answer me.
> Draw near to me; redeem me;
> set me free because of my enemies. (Ps 69:16–18)

Desperate situations reveal who we really trust. The psalmist has clearly placed his hope of redemption and rescue in the Lord. When we walk through desperate circumstances, do we place our hope in the Lord or in our own resources and abilities? Crying out to the Lord for help and for his abundant mercy is the most natural posture for a child of God. If we know we are part of God's family, we do not have to feel alone; we can turn to God, who is good and who draws near to the broken and contrite of heart (Ps 51:17).

In the second reading from Romans 6, the apostle Paul describes our union with Christ. He writes,

> For if we have been united with him in a death like his, we will certainly be united with him in a resurrection like his. We know that our old self was crucified with him so that the body of sin might be destroyed, so we might no longer be enslaved to sin. For whoever has died is freed from sin. But if we died with Christ, we believe that we will also live with him. (Rom 6:5–8)

Paul is describing a profound mystery, that because Christ died, we have died; because Christ lives, we too have been made alive. We are "united" with Christ in both his death and his resurrection. Moreover, Paul teaches in his letter to the Colossians that our lives are "hidden with Christ in God" (Col 3:3). In a real but mysterious way, our lives are united, hidden, and connected with Christ. The Christian life is not meant to be a mere "moral" life, but one lived in intimate union with Christ.

Often in Paul's letters, he describes the nature of "putting off" the old self and "putting on" the new life in Christ. Here in his letter to the Romans, he describes this way of life. He describes how we are no longer slaves to sin because we have been made alive to God in Christ. We are free to live for Christ.

These teachings should inform our day-to-day lives. The Christian life is not about doing good deeds so that we can go to heaven; the Christian life is about a profound and intimate union with Christ. Because we have died to sin, we are made alive to God. Moreover, our lives are to be characterized by gratitude for what Christ has done (Col 3:16–17) and empowerment from the Spirit who lives within us (Eph 1:19–20).

In the Gospel reading from Matthew 10, the theme of suffering and being mocked for our faith is articulated by Jesus himself. He declares,

> Do not think that I have come to bring peace to the earth; I have not come to bring peace but a sword.
>
> For I have come to set a man against his father,
> and a daughter against her mother,
> and a daughter-in-law against her mother-in-law,
> and one's foes will be members of one's own household. (Matt 10:34–36)

The words of Jesus are not always peace and comfort. Sometimes, his words bring conviction; other times, he speaks about realities of which we need to be aware. In all that he says, we can be assured that his words are divine; they are the very words of God, so we are called to listen and respond.

Jesus is not teaching us that love for our family is not important. The rest of the Bible teaches on the value and importance of the household. Jesus is, however, discussing the importance of ultimate authority and loyalty. As Christians, we cannot place anyone or anything above Christ. He is the King of kings and Lord of lords. It is to his name that we bow our knees.

The reality is that when we place Christ first in our lives, every other relationship can function properly. We cannot be a godly child, sibling, spouse, or parent unless we have first yielded and surrendered our lives to Christ. And in those various relationships, we may find resistance to our own faith. We may find ourselves sharing the gospel with a loved one. We do not know how those conversations will be received, but we trust that God is at work, and we leave the outcome to him.

One other facet of this narrative that we must acknowledge is the sovereign love the Father has for those who are part of his family. Jesus teaches,

> Are not two sparrows sold for a penny? Yet not one of them will fall to the ground apart from your Father. And even the hairs of your head are all counted. So do not be afraid; you are of more value than many sparrows. (Matt 10:29–31)

In this passage, the depth of the Father's divine concern and care for his children is revealed. As Christians, we can rest in knowing that God watches over every detail of our lives. We are more valuable to him than any other creature of all of his creation. Indeed, we were created in his own image (Gen 1:26). Whatever trial or circumstance we face, God is there with us and nothing can separate us from the love of God in Christ Jesus our Lord (Rom 8:38–39).

During this season after Pentecost, though we may have seasons of trial and hardship, may we know the love of our Father, and may we be bold in sharing his love with those we love the most.

QUESTIONS FOR REFLECTION

1. Though Jeremiah felt mocked by his own people, he could not squelch the fire in his bones for preaching the word of the Lord. How does this Old Testament passage (Jer 20:7–13) inform our lives today? Do we have a healthy place for lamentation in our own faith journeys?

2. The psalmist also expressed the trials and hardships associated with following the Lord. For the psalmist, it was "zeal" for the Lord's house that was the source of insults and mockery. Has your faith ever been the cause of mockery and insults from others? Describe. What was the remedy and balm for the psalmist during his hardships and trials? Is honest prayer a source of healing and comfort for you during hard seasons? Explain.

3. Paul describes our union with Christ. Is this concept new for you? How would you describe it in your own words? Do you think of the Christian life as a list of rules to follow or as a close, intimate relationship with Jesus to be cultivated and enjoyed? What do you think Paul has in mind when he says we are to consider ourselves "dead to sin and alive to God in Christ Jesus" (Rom 6:11)?

4. Jesus speaks both tender and hard words in Matthew 10:24-39. Does it bring you comfort knowing that God the Father is intimately involved in all of the details of your life (e.g., he knows the number of hairs on your head, Matt 10:30)? Explain. What do you think Jesus meant when he said, "I have not come to bring peace but a sword" (Matt 10:34)? How does following Christ affect our relationships with others?

PRAYER OF RESPONSE
Based on Psalm 69:16–18; Matthew 10:30

Answer us, O Lord,
for your steadfast love is good;
according to your abundant mercy, turn to us.
Do not hide your face from your people,
for we are in distress—make haste to answer us.
Draw near to us, redeem us,
set us free from our difficulties.
Because you know us intimately,
help us not to be afraid, but to find rest in you.
In the name of Jesus we pray. Amen.

Proper 8

Sunday between June 26 and July 2 inclusive

LECTIONARY READINGS

Jeremiah 28:5–9

Psalm 89:1–4, 15–18

Romans 6:12–23

Matthew 10:40–42

DEVOTION

In the readings for this week, we find Jesus teaching on hospitality. If those who followed Christ were accepted and welcomed, then Christ was accepted and welcomed as well. The first reading from Jeremiah 28 also speaks of a prophet's acceptance and welcome based on if his predictions were founded as being true. In the second reading from Romans 6, the apostle Paul describes how we are not under law but grace. Thus, identifying with Jesus, showing hospitality, and living as instruments of righteousness are common themes in the readings for this Sunday.

In the first reading, the prophet Jeremiah questions the prophecy of Hananiah regarding the exile of God's people. Hananiah gave a more optimistic prophecy than those of earlier times. Jeremiah teaches,

> The prophets who preceded you and me from ancient times prophesied war, famine, and pestilence against many countries and great kingdoms. As for the prophet who prophesies peace, when the word of that prophet comes true, then it will be known that the Lord has truly sent the prophet. (Jer 28:8–9)

Jeremiah is alluding to the requirement of a prophet from the book of Deuteronomy which states, "If a prophet speaks in the name of the Lord but the thing does not take place or prove true, it is a word that the Lord has not spoken" (Deut 18:22).

Jeremiah is challenging Hananiah's prophecy that the people of God would return from exile within two years. Ultimately, it was revealed that Hananiah was giving false prophecy, and he died because of his sin and rebellion against the Lord. Jeremiah was a true prophet though he was often rejected and mocked by the people of God (Jer 20:7).

Hananiah spoke words that he knew would be received well by the people even though they were lies. The same happens in our context today. Many people preach messages that are appealing to masses, but they are not based on the word of God. Speaking what is true of God's word is not always easy to absorb, but its purpose is to convict us and refine us. It is important that we share God's word honestly and truthfully with those around us, not teaching what we think people want to hear.

Psalm 89 is the psalm of response to the first reading. The psalmist sings of proclaiming God's faithfulness and of walking in truth and honesty before the Lord. He declares,

> I will sing of your steadfast love, O Lord, forever;
> with my mouth I will proclaim your faithfulness to all generations.
>
> Happy are the people who know the festal shout,
> who walk, O Lord, in the light of your countenance;
> they exult in your name all day long
> and extol your righteousness. (Ps 89:1, 15–16)

Walking in the light of God's countenance reveals favor with God as well as integrity and openness before him. The one who walks with God is not trying to hide his or her sin, but is living honestly before the Lord. Hananiah was not living with truth and integrity; Jeremiah was walking in truth before the Lord. Those who live in this kind of open and transparent manner delight in being in God's presence, and they love his righteousness.

When we try to hide our sin from the Lord, we are unable to walk in close fellowship with him. We do not long for his righteousness, but find ourselves in bondage to our own sinful and selfish ways. The psalmist knew the freedom of delighting in the Lord and walking in his ways.

In the second reading from Romans 6, the apostle Paul speaks of two forms of slavery. We are either slaves to sin and death or slaves to righteousness, sanctification, and eternal life. He writes,

> When you were slaves of sin, you were free in regard to righteousness. So what fruit did you then gain from the things of which you now are ashamed? The end of those things is death. But now that you have been freed from sin and enslaved to God, the fruit you have leads to sanctification, and the end is eternal life. For the wages of sin is death, but the free gift of God is eternal life in Christ Jesus our Lord. (Rom 6:20–23)

As Jeremiah 28 and Psalm 89 revealed, we are either walking in truth or in darkness; we are either following God or rebelling against him. According to Paul, we are either slaves to sin or slaves to righteousness. Paul is exhorting the people of God to walk according to their new identity and way of life. As followers of Christ, we are no longer under the power of sin; thus, we are called to walk in righteousness. Paul also points out that just because we are under grace, we are not to go on sinning. Because of our new identity in Christ, we are called to live as those who are being sanctified.

In the Gospel reading from Matthew 10, Jesus tells his disciples that those who welcome them also welcome him. He also describes how those who receive prophets and honor the righteous will receive the benefits and rewards of such acceptance. Jesus' words encourage us to follow the teachings of Christ and to welcome other believers. Having community with other believers is vital to our spiritual growth. Moreover, offering "a cup of cold water" (Matt 10:42) to one of Christ's followers is commended as an honorable form of love.

So often our love of God is displayed when we give simple, but loving gifts to friends and neighbors. Such giving and receiving highlights the nature of God's kingdom. During this season after Pentecost, may way learn how to walk closely and honestly with God, while demonstrating love and hospitality to those around us.

QUESTIONS FOR REFLECTION

1. Why did Jeremiah question Hananiah's prophecy? Who was right in the end? Do we still have false prophets today? Explain.

2. Reread Psalm 89:15. What does it mean to walk in the light of God's countenance? Does this characterize your everyday life? Explain.

3. What two paths does the apostle Paul describe in Romans 6:12–23? To what does each path lead? Read Romans 6:22. What is the advantage and destination of the path of righteousness? How would you describe your own sanctification right now?

4. Who do we ultimately welcome when we show hospitality to others? What does it mean to offer someone "a cup of cold water" (Matt 10:42)? What are the benefits we receive from such hospitality?

PRAYER OF RESPONSE
Based on Psalm 89:15–18; Matthew 10:40–42

Sovereign Lord,
we are blessed when we walk
in the light of your countenance.
You are the glory of our strength,
our shield and our protection.
Help us to live lives of generosity and hospitality,
showing kindness to those we encounter,
and offering a cup of cold water to those in need.
In the name of Jesus we pray. Amen.

Proper 9

Sunday between July 3 and July 9 inclusive

LECTIONARY READINGS

> Zechariah 9:9–12
>
> Psalm 145:8–14
>
> Romans 7:15–25a
>
> Matthew 11:16–19, 25–30

DEVOTION

In the readings for this Sunday, we find the prophet Zechariah pronouncing the coming of a future king, one who will come riding on a donkey and bringing peace. The apostle Paul describes our ongoing struggle with sin. In the Gospel reading from Matthew 11, Jesus thanks the Father for revealing the ways of the kingdom not to the wise and intelligent, but to infants. Jesus also invites us to come to him to find rest for our souls. Thus, the nature of Jesus' kingship and our struggle with sin are themes in the readings for this week.

In the first reading from Zechariah 9, the prophet describes a coming king who will bring peace to the nations. He proclaims,

> Rejoice greatly, O daughter Zion!
> Shout aloud, O daughter Jerusalem!
> See, your king comes to you;
> triumphant and victorious is he,
> humble and riding on a donkey,
> on a colt, the foal of a donkey. (Zech 9:9)

This passage is often read on Palm Sunday. Jesus' entry into Jerusalem on a donkey is the prophetic fulfillment of Zechariah 9. Jesus is our humble king who will ultimately bring peace to the nations. He is not like the earthly kings and rulers who are tainted by a hunger for personal power and prestige. Jesus came to serve; he road into Jerusalem to die. Because our King is unlike all other kings, we should not be surprised that his kingdom is also unlike any earthly kingdom.

The message of Scripture can sound foreign to us at times because as it describes the nature of the kingdom, it describes the values of peace, love, justice, unity, humility, and servanthood. These values are often at odds with the values of the world. We are called to obey King Jesus and to let his life shape and inform our own.

As the psalm of response, Psalm 145 speaks of God's kingdom. The psalmist sings,

> All your works shall give thanks to you, O Lord,
> and all your faithful shall bless you.
> They shall speak of the glory of your kingdom
> and tell of your power,
> to make known to all people your mighty deeds
> and the glorious splendor of your kingdom. (Ps 145:10-12)

As already mentioned, God's kingdom should reflect his own character. Thus, Psalm 145 begins and ends with descriptions of God himself. He is "gracious and merciful, slow to anger and abounding in steadfast love," and he is "good to all, and his compassion is over all that he has made" (Ps 145:8-9). Furthermore, he "upholds all who are falling and raises up all who are bowed down" (Ps 145:14).

God, our King, is full of compassion, love, faithfulness, and mercy. He restores the broken and heals the weak. He is not a God who remains distant from his creation, but is concerned with all of the various details of our lives.

In the second reading from Romans 7, the apostle Paul describes our ongoing struggle with sin and the way it deceives and entangles us. He writes,

> For I do not do the good I want, but the evil I do not want is what I do. Now if I do what I do not want, it is no longer I who do it but sin that dwells within me. (Rom 7:19-20)

Though we are being sanctified and transformed by the Spirit, we will never reach perfection as believers. We will always struggle with sin and the temptations of the flesh. We battle daily with the world, the flesh, and the devil. All three spiritual forces are at work against us.

It is important to recognize this spiritual reality so that we do not become complacent or naive in our walk with the Lord. Paul tells us, "work on your own salvation with fear and trembling, for it is God who is at work in you, enabling you both to will and to work for his good pleasure" (Phil 2:12–13). We are called to cooperate with God in our sanctification, which is a life-long process.

In the Gospel reading from Matthew 11, we find Jesus thanking the Father that the ways of the kingdom have not been revealed to the wise and intelligent religious leaders, but to "infants" (Matt 11:25), those we would not expect to understand this message.

Often, our pride and arrogance can keep us from truly understanding and living out the principles of the kingdom. Having much knowledge about God does not qualify one as a follower of Christ. In God's economy, those who are broken, humble, and contrite of heart are typically those who follow and obey Jesus. In God's upside-down kingdom, outsiders become insiders, and insiders become outsiders. Jesus calls us to show hospitality and love to those who are often overlooked in our own cultural contexts.

Finally, Jesus invites us to come to him to find rest for our souls. He proclaims,

> Come to me, all you who are weary and are carrying heavy burdens, and I will give you rest. Take my yoke upon you, and learn from me, for I am gentle and humble in heart, and you will find rest for your souls. For my yoke is easy, and my burden is light. (Matt 11:28–30)

During this season after Pentecost, may we know the nature of our King and his kingdom. He invites us to find rest for our souls as we struggle with sin. Moreover, he calls us to a life of compassion and service that we might demonstrate the love of Christ to our broken world.

QUESTIONS FOR REFLECTION

1. What event in Jesus' life fulfills the prophecy in Zechariah 9? Describe Jesus' kingship. How does his kingship contrast with the kings of this world?

2. Describe the nature of God's kingdom from Psalm 145. What words and phrases stand out to you? Why?

3. How does Paul describe our daily struggle with sin? How are we to find victory in our battle with sin?

4. To whom did Jesus reveal the ways of his kingdom? Do you regularly go to Jesus to find rest for you soul? Describe.

PRAYER OF RESPONSE
Based on Psalm 145:8–9, 13–14; Matthew 11:28–29

Lord Jesus,
we praise you for you are gracious and merciful,
slow to anger and abounding in steadfast love.
You are good to all,
and your compassion is over all that you have made.
You are faithful in all your words,
and gracious in all your deeds.
You uphold all who are falling,
and raise up all who are bowed down.
You invite all who are weary
and are carrying heavy burdens, to come to you.
For you are gentle and humble in heart,
and, in you, we will find rest for our souls.
In the name of Jesus we pray. Amen.

Proper 10

Sunday between July 10 and July 16 inclusive

LECTIONARY READINGS

Isaiah 55:10–13

Psalm 65

Romans 8:1–11

Matthew 13:1–9, 18–23

DEVOTION

In the readings for this Sunday, we find Jesus telling a parable about the sower and the seed. The prophet Isaiah compares the way in which God waters the earth and brings forth renewal with the way his word brings forth fruit within his people. The apostle Paul describes how the Spirit brings life within a believer. Thus, the fruit of God's word and the life of the Spirit are themes in the readings for this week.

In the first reading from Isaiah 55, the prophet describes the renewing power of God's word. Speaking for the Lord, he declares,

> For as the rain and the snow come down from heaven
> and do not return there until they have watered the earth,
> making it bring forth and sprout,
> giving seed to the sower and bread to the eater,
> so shall my word be that goes out from my mouth;
> it shall not return to me empty,
> but it shall accomplish that which I purpose
> and succeed in the thing for which I sent it. (Isa 55:10–11)

As God tends to the physical well-being of the earth, he also tends to the spiritual life of his people. His word brings life to his people and accomplishes its purpose. Regularly feeding our souls with the word of God is a vital part of the Christian life. We practice this kind of spiritual nourishment both in the home and in the congregation. As Christians, we let the word dwell in us richly in corporate worship as the body of Christ and in the home through personal and family devotions.

Psalm 65 is the response to the first reading. Here, the psalmist sings poetically of God's care for the earth and his people. The psalmist sings,

> You visit the earth and water it;
> you greatly enrich it;
> the river of God is full of water;
> you provide the people with grain,
> for so you have prepared it.
> You water its furrows abundantly,
> settling its ridges,
> softening it with showers,
> and blessing its growth. (Ps 65:9–10)

The message implied in Psalm 65 is spoken about clearly in Jesus' Sermon on the Mount. He teaches,

> And why do you worry about clothing? Consider the lilies of the field, how they grow; they neither toil nor spin, yet I tell you, even Solomon in all his glory was not clothed like one of these. But if God so clothes the grass of the field, which is alive today and tomorrow is thrown into the oven, will he not much more clothe you—you of little faith? (Matt 6:28–30)

Our God, who clothes the fields and waters the earth, will take care of his people. He will provide for our physical as well as our spiritual needs.

In the second reading from Romans 8, the apostle Paul continues his teaching on life in the flesh and life in the Spirit. Following the desires of the flesh leads to sin and death, but following the Spirit leads to life and peace. Moreover, the Spirit who lives within us is the same Spirit who raised Jesus from the dead. It is this indwelling Spirit who empowers us to live as Christ's followers. Paul writes,

> If the Spirit of him who raised Jesus from the dead dwells in you, he who raised Christ Jesus from the dead will give life to

your mortal bodies also through his Spirit that dwells in you. (Rom 8:11)

When we think about living the Christian life, we have to remember that the same Spirit who raised Jesus from the dead lives within us. The Spirit is the one who empowers us and equips us to face the various challenges and circumstances in our lives. The Spirit is the one who helps us to pray (Rom 8:26), gives us gifts for mutual edification (1 Cor 12:7), leads us in all truth (John 16:13), brings Scripture to mind (John 14:26), and brings forth fruit in our lives (Gal 5:22-23). Our advocate, the Spirit, provides for our needs.

In the Gospel reading from Matthew 13, Jesus tells a parable about a sower and seed. The main takeaway from his parable comes from the explanation of the parable that Jesus gives to the closer circle of disciples. In his explanation he describes how much of the seed fell upon unhealthy soil. Some of the seed, however, fell upon fertile soil. Regarding this soil, Jesus teaches,

> But as for what was sown on good soil, this is the one who hears the word and understands it, who indeed bears fruit and yields in one case a hundredfold, in another sixty, and in another thirty. (Matt 13:23)

For some, God's word is heard, but is snatched away by the enemy. For others, the word is received, but does not take root and, thus, when trials come, it withers away. For a third group, the word is received, but the desire for wealth and the cares of this world choke it out and it never takes root.

For those whose hearts are "good soil," God's word bears much fruit. Jesus' parable causes us to ask about the condition of our heart and soul. During this season after Pentecost, may we evaluate the spiritual practices throughout our day and week that allow us to receive God's word. May the Spirit bear fruit in our lives as we allow opportunities for God to sow the seed of his word in our hearts.

QUESTIONS FOR REFLECTION

1. What are the life applications for us regarding the imagery in Isaiah 55:10–11? How is engaging God's word similar to the way in which God waters the earth?

2. The psalmist poetically describes the various ways in which God cares for his creation. What lessons can we take away from this description of physical care?

3. The apostle Paul teaches about life in the flesh and life in the Spirit. Describe these two ways of living. How are we empowered to live the Christian life? Explain.

4. Jesus taught a parable about four different kinds of soil in which the seed fell. How would you describe the "soil" of your heart? Is it like the path, the rocky soil, the thorns, or the good soil? Explain.

PRAYER OF RESPONSE
Based on Isaiah 55:10–11; Matthew 13:8

Sovereign God,
we thank you that your word is like the rain
and the snow that come down from heaven,
watering the earth, making it bring forth and sprout,
giving seed to the sower and bread to the eater.
May our hearts be good soil so that
as the seed of your word is sown in us,
it would accomplish its purpose,
bearing much fruit in the lives of your people.
In the name of Jesus we pray. Amen.

Proper 11

Sunday between July 17 and July 23 inclusive

LECTIONARY READINGS

Isaiah 44:6–8

Psalm 86:11–17

Romans 8:12–25

Matthew 13:24–30, 36–43

DEVOTION

In the readings for this Sunday, we find Jesus telling a parable about the wheat and the weeds. The prophet Isaiah speaks for the Lord as being the alpha and the omega, the first and the last. The apostle Paul teaches about life in the Spirit as children of God, waiting with creation for the Lord's return. Thus, judgment, life in the Spirit, and the return of Christ are common themes in the readings for this week.

In the first reading from Isaiah 44, the prophet speaks for the Lord who is the one powerful God. He proclaims,

> Thus says the Lord, the King of Israel,
> and his Redeemer, the Lord of hosts:
> I am the first, and I am the last;
> besides me there is no god.
> Who is like me? Let them proclaim it;
> let them declare and set it forth before me. (Isa 44:6–7)

There is no one like our God. He is the beginning and the end, the first and the last. From the Ten Commandments, we know we are to have no other God but the Lord. Isaiah 44 complements this truth and makes it clear that all other gods are idols. We are to worship God alone. Yet, even in the midst of such strong language regarding God's preeminence, the Lord tells us not to fear or be afraid. Though God is the only true God, he is loving and compassionate toward his people.

Psalm 86 is the response to the first reading, a song about our undivided worship. The psalmist sings,

> Teach me your way, O Lord,
> that I may walk in your truth;
> give me an undivided heart to revere your name.
> I give thanks to you, O Lord my God, with my whole heart,
> and I will glorify your name forever. (Ps 86:11–12)

Since God is the only true God, we are called to worship him with an undivided heart. He is jealous for our love and devotion; we are not to have any gods before him. When our hearts are divided, we lose the peace and serenity, the intimacy and closeness of walking in step with Lord. When our hearts are undivided, we have nothing to fear.

When we turn to idols, putting something created before the Creator, we lose our peace and our joy for our souls were not meant to worship anyone but the Lord. Without God we become anxious and fearful, trying to live and navigate this life on our own.

In the second reading from Romans 8, the apostle Paul teaches on life in the Spirit as children of God. He writes,

> For all who are led by the Spirit of God are children of God. For you did not receive a spirit of slavery to fall back into fear, but you received a spirit of adoption. (Rom 8:14–15)

Like Isaiah 44 and Psalm 86 have already described, there is only one God and he is the only God we are to worship; we are to have no other gods besides him. When we worship idols such as power, money, comfort, or fame, we put something before God and become slaves to fear, as Paul describes. Idolatry creates divided hearts and fills us with fear and anxiety because we lose the intimacy and humble confidence of walking with the Lord. It is not that God turns his back on us; we turn our backs on God and try to live in our own power.

Living in this way is like living as orphans. How foolish we are! We are sons and daughters of the King, and we have the Spirit within us to lead us and guide us. God calls us to live in the Spirit as his children, to have undivided hearts, and to enjoy an intimate relationship with him.

Paul also teaches about Christ's return and the eager anticipation that we, like creation, should have for this glorious day. The return of Christ helps us to keep our current trials and tribulations in perspective. We can endure our current sufferings because we know our hope is in the new heaven and the new earth. With creation, we long for this day and wait patiently for Christ's return.

In the Gospel reading from Matthew 13, Jesus tells a parable about the wheat and the weeds. He explains the parable to his disciples, teaching,

> The one who sows the good seed is the Son of Man; the field is the world, and the good seed are the children of the kingdom; the weeds are the children of the evil one, and the enemy who sowed them is the devil; the harvest is the end of the age, and the reapers are angels. (Matt 13:37–39)

The world contains good seed and bad seed; those who know Christ and those who do not. Some, even though they may attend church and may appear to be Christians, are not truly believers in Christ. Sometimes the terms the "visible church" and the "invisible church" are used to describe the nature of the kingdom. The visible church is made up of believers and non-believers, the wheat and the weeds. We cannot always discern, however, who is a true believer and who is not a true believer. Jesus' parable reveals that it is not our job to judge who is and who is not a believer. God is the only judge, and he will separate the believers from the non-believers, the wheat from the weeds, at the end of the age.

As we live and move in this world, we cannot always discern who is a fellow believer. We have the Spirit within us to bear witness with our own spirit that we are a son or daughter of God, but we cannot judge for others. In this season after Pentecost, may we learn to live in the Spirit and await Jesus' return with hope and with anticipation. May we love our fellow church members with the love of Christ and leave judgment of one's salvation to the Lord.

QUESTIONS FOR REFLECTION

1. How would Isaiah's words about the Lord's preeminence encourage the people of God? How does knowing that God is the first and the last bring perspective to you and your own life today?

2. What does the psalmist mean by the phrase "give me an undivided heart" (Ps 86:11)? How would you describe your own heart? What are some of the idols in your life that compete with the one, true God? Why do you turn to them?

3. What is our status according to Paul? How does the Spirit remind us of our status? Do you, like creation, long for the return of Christ? How does the hope of heaven give us perspective on our current situations?

4. Explain the parable of the good seed and the weeds. How is this parable relevant for us today?

PRAYER OF RESPONSE

Based on Psalm 86:11; Romans 8:14–17, 24–25; Matthew 13:37–38

Holy God,
teach us your way,
that we may walk in your truth;
give us undivided hearts to revere your name.
Remind us that we have been adopted by you;
that your Spirit bears witness with our spirit
that we are your children.
Help us to place our hope in what we do not see
and rest in knowing that we are children of the kingdom,
the good seed that you have sown.
In the name of Jesus we pray. Amen.

Proper 12

Sunday between July 24 and July 30 inclusive

LECTIONARY READINGS

1 Kings 3:5–12

Psalm 119:129–136

Romans 8:26–39

Matthew 13:31–33, 44–52

DEVOTION

In the readings for this Sunday, we find Jesus using parables to describe the kingdom of God. Solomon asks the Lord for wisdom to govern the people. The apostle Paul describes the present ministry of Christ and the Holy Spirit. Thus, the nature of the kingdom, the wisdom of God, and the present ministry of Christ and the Holy Spirit are themes in the readings for this Sunday.

In the first reading from 1 Kings 3, we listen to a conversation between God and King Solomon. Feeling young and inadequate to rule the nation of Israel, Solomon asks the Lord for wisdom. He prays,

> Your servant is in the midst of the people whom you have chosen, a great people so numerous they cannot be numbered or counted. Give your servant, therefore, an understanding mind to govern your people, able to discern between good and evil, for who can govern this great people of yours? (1 Kgs 3:8–9)

Solomon was taking over as king after his father, David. He felt very overwhelmed and unable to lead and govern the people of God.

The Lord had come to Solomon and asked what he should give to him. Solomon asked for wisdom. He did not ask for long life, or riches, or for the life of his enemies. These might be the things on our minds for which to ask God. We want to make a name for ourselves, make a lot of money, and have no enemies. Given the choice, we might not think to ask God for wisdom.

Knowing how to discern right from wrong and the will of the Lord is an important characteristic. We should desire it more in our lives so that we might be able to better discern how to be a good parent, spouse, friend, or family member. We certainly find a desire for wisdom and godly guidance in other places in Scripture (Exod 33:12–14; Acts 6:1–6; 15:1–21)

Psalm 119, the psalm of response, expresses God's guidance and protection; The psalmist sings,

> Your decrees are wonderful;
> therefore my soul keeps them.
> The unfolding of your words gives light;
> it imparts understanding to the simple. (Ps 119:129–30)

Here, we find the psalmist elevating God's word, including his decrees and his commands, which give us direction and light for our journey. God's word gives us healthy boundaries in which to walk. The wise person delights in God's commands and understands the way in which the word feeds our soul and grants us peace in the midst of hard circumstances. Like Solomon and the psalmist, we should long for the light of God's word and seek the healthy boundaries his commandments provide for us.

In the second reading from Romans 8, the apostle Paul teaches on the ministry of the Spirit, giving us "groanings too deep for words" (Rom 8:26). In addition, Paul gives us the strong promise that God goes before us and works and redeems all of the aspects of our lives for his good. He is the one in control, and it is his will that is accomplished through the lives of his people. He will conform us into the image of Christ.

Moreover, we can rest in the present ministry of Christ, who is at the right hand of the Father interceding for his chosen ones. We do not need to fear because God is for us. He fights for us and advocates for us, even in ways of which we are unaware. We have been raised to new life and live in the power of Christ and the Holy Spirit. These promises are true and keep us steady when we feel weak or when we falter.

Lastly, because God is for us, nothing can separate us from the love of God in Christ. Paul closes this section with a climax of promises regarding our standing before him. Paul writes,

> No, in all these things we are more than victorious through him who loved us. For I am convinced that neither death, nor life, nor angels, nor rulers, nor things present, nor things to come, nor powers, nor height, nor depth, nor anything else in all creation will be able to separate us from the love of God in Christ Jesus our Lord. (Rom 8:37-39)

These gospel promises should strengthen and steady us wherever we find ourselves on our faith journey. Whether we are too grieved to pray, too fearful to take the next step, too anxious to think clearly, or too lonely to feel God's love, these promises reveal to us that God is at work in our lives. He provides the sighs; he provides the strength and grace; he is the rock in whom we can trust, whose love for us was demonstrated on the cross. Nothing can separate us from his love, and no one can condemn us because God is for us. We may not always be able to discern these realities, but, by faith, we believe them to be true.

In the Gospel reading from Matthew 13, Jesus offers several parables to describe the nature of the kingdom. Each of them speaks to a characteristic of the kingdom. For example, one parable describes the kingdom as something seemingly small but which blossoms into something big and flourishing (Matt 13:31-32). Two other parables describe the kingdom as something which brings such joy that you give everything for it (Matt 13:44-46).

Jesus offers a parable about the power of yeast, saying, "The kingdom of heaven is like yeast that a woman took and mixed in with three measures of flour until all of it was leavened" (Matt 13:33). In this parable, we find how the kingdom, though undetectable at times, has the power to influence individuals, families, and societies. Jesus' parables teach us much about the nature of the kingdom and the force it exerts on our lives, creation, and the various sphere of society.

We would be wise to listen to these parables and ask God to help us bring his kingdom to our lives, our families, and our city and culture. Empowered by Christ and the Holy Spirit, may we be used, like leaven in the dough, to bring gospel renewal and transformation where we live.

QUESTIONS FOR REFLECTION

1. Why did Solomon ask the Lord for wisdom? What were the circumstances in Solomon's life that motivated him to ask for wisdom? How would you respond if the Lord asked, "What should I give you?" Explain your answer.

2. The psalmist prayed, "Keep my steps steady according to your promise, and never let iniquity have dominion over me" (Ps 119:133). What do you think this means and why would the psalmist pray in this way? Do you ever pray that the Lord would keep your steps steady? Explain.

3. What are some of the gospel promises that Paul articulates in Romans 8:26-39? Which particular promise stands out to you personally? Why? What is the overall tone of this passage? Who keeps us steady and allows us to persevere in our faith journey—us or God? Explain.

4. What is the meaning behind the various parables Jesus shares? Is the kingdom of God of great worth to you? Would you be willing to give all you have to obtain it?

PRAYER OF RESPONSE

Based on Psalm 119:132–133; 1 Kings 3:9; Romans 8:26–27; Matthew 13:31–33, 44–46

Holy God,
turn to us and be gracious to us.
Keep our steps steady according to your promise,
and never let iniquity have dominion over us.
Give us understanding minds and
help us to discern between good and evil.
May your Spirit intercede for us
with sighs too deep for words.
Fill us with the joy and power of the kingdom,
making disciples of all nations
and finding our greatest treasure in you.
In the name of Jesus we pray. Amen.

Proper 13

Sunday between July 31 and August 6 inclusive

LECTIONARY READINGS

Isaiah 55:1–5

Psalm 145:8–9, 14–21

Romans 9:1–5

Matthew 14:13–21

DEVOTION

In the readings for this Sunday, Jesus feeds the five thousand, revealing his power and his compassion. The prophet Isaiah speaks of the food that only God can provide, food that truly satisfies the hunger of our souls. The apostle Paul teaches on the place of the Jewish people in God's plan of salvation. Thus, spiritual food and nourishment and salvation for God's people are common themes in the readings for this Sunday.

In the first reading from Isaiah 55, the prophet speaks beautifully and poetically, inviting those who are hungry and thirsty to partake of the food that satisfies the soul. Isaiah declares,

> Hear, everyone who thirsts;
> come to the waters;
> and you who have no money,
> come, buy and eat!
> Come, buy wine and milk
> without money and without price.
> Why do you spend your money for that which is not bread

> and your earnings for that which does not satisfy?
> Listen carefully to me, and eat what is good,
> and delight yourselves in rich food.
> Incline your ear, and come to me;
> listen, so that you may live. (Isa 55:1–3)

We are prone to forget God's goodness and covenantal love. Isaiah reminds us that all we truly need comes from the Lord. He alone provides the food that nourishes our souls. Too often, however, we turn to things that do not satisfy, making an idol of something that can only bring temporary satisfaction. Time spent in relationship with God (word, prayer, worship) brings a satisfaction of an eternal quality.

Psalm 145 provides the response to the first reading. The psalmist sings,

> The Lord upholds all who are falling
> and raises up all who are bowed down.
> The eyes of all look to you,
> and you give them their food in due season.
> You open your hand,
> satisfying the desire of every living thing. (Ps 145:14–16)

Like the prophet Isaiah, the psalmist recognizes that the Lord takes care of and provides for all of his creation. In his compassion, God provides for our physical and spiritual needs. In his sovereign care, he feeds all of his creation, and he nourishes the souls of his people, made in his image.

In the second reading from Romans 9, the apostle Paul begins the portion of his letter that addresses the place of Israel in God's plan of salvation. Paul openly expresses his grief over his own people. He recognizes that not all of Israel are truly God's people. However, he acknowledges their place in redemptive history. Paul writes,

> They are Israelites, and to them belong the adoption, the glory, the covenants, the giving of the law, the worship, and the promises; to them belong the patriarchs, and from them, according to the flesh, comes the Christ, who is over all, God blessed forever. Amen. (Rom 9:4–5)

Chapters 9–11 of Romans can be confusing at times. The overall message is that, though God has a special place for the Jews in his plan of salvation, not every Jew is part of the eternal kingdom. In the passage for this week, Paul articulates all of the practices and covenants that God established with Israel throughout the centuries. He names the law, the covenants, worship, promises, and the patriarchs.

Most importantly, Paul acknowledges that Jesus was born a Jew. We should feel gratitude in knowing that we have been grafted into this spiritual family and are now partakers of the covenant promises first given to Abraham and later to the nation of Israel. Israel is part of our spiritual family and heritage.

Finally, in the Gospel reading from Matthew 14, Jesus miraculously feeds more than five thousand people in the desert. This miracle should remind us of how God provided for the people of Israel as they wandered in the desert. Matthew wants to show us the connection between Moses, Jesus, and the people of God. In the wilderness, Moses and the people of God were fed manna from heaven. In Matthew 14, Jesus feeds the people and demonstrates his role as the Son of God, providing nourishment for his people.

Several of the readings for this Sunday focus on physical and spiritual nourishment. In our corporate worship gatherings, we are fed regularly by word and sacrament. Also, in our homes and small group gatherings, we are fed by God's word and in prayer and fellowship with one another. During this season after Pentecost, may these various means of grace provide food for our journey of faith.

QUESTIONS FOR REFLECTION

1. Speaking for the Lord, the prophet Isaiah invites us to feast on the good things of God. Why are we often reluctant to accept this invitation, turning to lesser things to satisfy us? Do the lesser things ever truly nourish us? Explain.

2. In Psalm 145, the psalmist speaks of God's compassion and provision for all of his creation. Do you thank and praise God for his provision in your life? Describe.

3. In his letter to the church at Rome, Paul begins to explain God's relationship with Israel. Read Deuteronomy 7:7–11. Why did God initiate a close relationship with Israel? What are aspects of Israel's heritage and legacy (Rom 9:4–5)? In what way are the Israelites our spiritual ancestors (Rom 11:22–24)?

4. Just before sharing the miracle of the feeding of the five thousand, Matthew gives us the detail that Jesus withdrew to be alone. Why did he come back to the crowds and feed them? What does this tell us about Jesus and his relationship with us today? Jesus fed the crowds with physical food. How does he feed us spiritually?

PRAYER OF RESPONSE

Based on Isaiah 55:1–2; Psalm 145:8–9, 15–16; Matthew 14:13–21

Lord Jesus,
we praise you for the abundance of your grace and mercy,
for you are slow to anger and abounding in steadfast love.
You invite us to feast freely on all that you provide,
for you are good to all,
and your compassion is over all that you have made.
The eyes of all look to you,
and you give us our food in due season.
You open your hand, satisfying the desire of every living thing.
As you fed the multitudes long ago
with only five loaves and two fish,
so satisfy the hunger in our souls today
with the nourishment of your word and Spirit.
In the name of Jesus we pray. Amen.

Proper 14

Sunday between August 7 and August 13 inclusive

LECTIONARY READINGS

1 Kings 19:9–18
Psalm 85:8–13
Romans 10:5–15
Matthew 14:22–33

DEVOTION

In the readings for this Sunday, Jesus walks on the water to the disciples and calms the stormy seas. The prophet Elijah hears God in the silence at Mount Horeb. The apostle Paul teaches about the need to confess our faith with our lips and to believe in our hearts that Jesus was raised from the dead. Thus, personal faith and experiencing the power and the silence of God are common themes in the readings for this week.

In the first reading from 1 Kings 19, the prophet Elijah experiences God not in the mighty wind, or the earthquake, or the fire, but in the silence. Elijah has fled to Mount Horeb (Mount Sinai) after having won a battle against King Ahab and the prophets of Baal. He flees to Mount Horeb, where he appears somewhat depressed (even though he has just experienced an amazing spiritual victory), feeling that he is alone in his faith in God. It is while Elijah is in this emotional state that God appears to him. The author writes,

> Now there was a great wind, so strong that it was splitting mountains and breaking rocks in pieces before the Lord, but the Lord was not in the wind, and after the wind an earthquake, but

the Lord was not in the earthquake, and after the earthquake a fire, but the Lord was not in the fire, and after the fire a sound of sheer silence. When Elijah heard it, he wrapped his face in his mantle and went out and stood at the entrance of the cave. Then there came a voice to him that said, "What are you doing here, Elijah?" (1 Kgs 19:11–13)

It may be puzzling to us why Elijah has such a mood swing. The prophet goes from being an instrument of God's power to fleeing for his life and wallowing in self-pity. Though we may not fully understand Elijah's emotional state, we can find comfort in knowing that God meets us wherever we are. God comes to Elijah and engages him more than once, asking, "What are you doing here, Elijah?" Does God not know the answer to this question? Of course, he does. The God of the universe is drawing near to Elijah and questioning him to reveal the state of his heart.

God does the same with us. He is not shaken by our mood swings. God is not puzzled by our zeal and spiritual fervor displayed in one moment and our doubt and frustration in another moment. He knows us better than we know ourselves. The God of the Bible is not distant or aloof. He engages his people in personal and powerful ways throughout Scripture.

In addition, the contrast between God's power displayed on Mount Sinai (Exod 19:16-25) before Moses and the people and his silence manifested with Elijah is profound and compelling. We should not be surprised that God is able to reveal himself to us in any way that he chooses. He may choose to reveal himself through powerful demonstrations; however, he may choose to reveal himself in the simple, ordinary means of grace (word, prayer, sacrament, song) and even in silence. Ultimately, our sovereign Lord knows what we need and is able to communicate in a way that ministers to our present need.

Psalm 85, as the psalm of response, continues with the theme of God's communication with his people. The psalmist sings,

> Let me hear what God the Lord will speak,
> for he will speak peace to his people,
> to his faithful, to those who turn to him in their hearts.
> Surely his salvation is at hand for those who fear him,
> that his glory may dwell in our land. (Ps 85:8–9)

As previously noted, our God is personal; he is not distant or aloof. Through the ministry of his word and the Holy Spirit, God continues to speak to his people, bringing comfort, conviction, illumination, love, mercy, tenderness, reassurance, exhortation, and clarity. He loves his people and delights in dwelling with us. We should not be surprised that God speaks to us. He is our Good Shepherd and his sheep know his voice (John 10:4).

In the second reading from Romans 10, the apostle Paul teaches on our confession of faith and salvation. He writes,

> For one believes with the heart, leading to righteousness, and one confesses with the mouth, leading to salvation. The scripture says, "No one who believes in him will be put to shame." For there is no distinction between Jew and Greek; the same Lord is Lord of all and is generous to all who call on him. For "everyone who calls on the name of the Lord shall be saved." (Rom 10:10–13)

One's ethnic background does not determine one's salvation. What does matter, is the object of one's faith. Salvation is for those who confess Jesus as Lord. Some people may have been raised in a Christian culture or a Christian home, but each person must make their own profession of faith. This does not mean that everyone must have a "radical" personal testimony; however, it does mean that everyone must settle the lordship questions within one's own heart and mind. Do you believe that Jesus is Lord and have you placed your hope and trust in him alone for your salvation? These are the ultimate questions that everyone must answer.

Finally, in the Gospel reading from Matthew 14, Jesus appears to the disciples as they are in a boat in the midst of a storm. Jesus walks on the water to them. After a dialogue with Peter, Jesus ends up saving Peter and getting in the boat with the rest of the disciples. When he joins them in the boat, the storm is calmed. Matthew gives us the detail that the disciples "worshiped him, saying, 'Truly you are the Son of God'" (Matt 14:33).

The calming of the storm had a profound effect on the disciples. Interestingly, as Jesus approached the boat, Peter called out, requesting an invitation from Jesus for Peter to join him on the water. So, Jesus summoned him, and Peter was able to walk on the water at first; however, he became frightened by the storm and began to sink into the sea.

Jesus rescued him and they all got into the boat. That is when the storm subsided according to Matthew.

The whole narrative has so many interesting facets. We can be amazed by Peter's faith, but can also relate to his fear. We can understand the disciples' awe at Jesus' display of power over the created order. As we ponder this narrative, we can also reflect on the first reading from 1 Kings 19 regarding God speaking to Elijah through the silence. Again, in this Gospel narrative, we see Jesus displaying his power in the midst of frightening events and in the midst of stillness and quiet. Jesus is Lord. He can speak to the wind and the waves, and they obey him. He also speaks intimately to his people, and we obey.

During this season after Pentecost, may we know that Jesus is Lord. He is the Creator who governs the wind and the waves, and he is the intimate Redeemer who rescues us from our fear, pride, and self-absorption. God desires to have a relationship with his people, to speak to us and reveal himself to us in a variety of ways. Though our hearts often deceive us, God is greater than our hearts (1 John 3:20). As he did with Elijah and the disciples, God knows just how to minister to us in our time of need.

QUESTIONS FOR REFLECTION

1. Why do you think Elijah felt fearful and alone? Why do you think God chose to reveal himself to Elijah through silence? How does God minister to us in our time of need?

2. The psalmist says that God speaks peace to his people (Ps 85:8). Do you have an issue or circumstance in your life today in which you need God to speak peace? Explain.

3. Paul writes about confessing with our lips and believing in our hearts that Jesus is Lord and was raised from the dead. Have you settled your relationship with the Lord? Have you confessed him as Lord and placed your faith in him? If you know the Lord as your Savior, have you shared the gospel with someone in your life recently? Describe.

4. Jesus calmed the storm and the disciples worshiped him. Have you experienced the wonder and awe of God recently in your own life? Have you had a recent opportunity to worship the Lord in a meaningful way for who he is? Describe.

PRAYER OF RESPONSE
Based on 1 Kings 19:9–18; Matthew 14:22–33

Lord Jesus,
we know you are powerful,
able to stir up great winds, earthquakes, and fires.
Yet, you often choose to speak to us,
as you spoke to Elijah,
through silence and with a still, small voice.
Like the disciples, may we see your power
to calm the storms in our lives.
Help us to put our faith in you
and worship you in all circumstances;
knowing deeply and trusting wholly
that you are the Son of God.
In the name of Jesus we pray. Amen.

Proper 15

Sunday between August 14 and August 20 inclusive

LECTIONARY READINGS

Isaiah 56:1, 6–8

Psalm 67

Romans 11:1–2a, 29–32

Matthew 15:10–28

DEVOTION

In the readings for this Sunday, Jesus clarifies what truly defiles someone, making a distinction between what goes into the body and what comes out of the body. Jesus also interacts with a Canaanite woman who demonstrates great faith. The prophet Isaiah speaks of foreigners coming to the Lord and of God's house being a house of prayer. The apostle Paul continues his teaching on Jews and gentiles, highlighting that both receive the mercy of God. Thus, God's love and mercy to insiders and outsiders is a common theme in the readings for this Sunday.

In the first reading from Isaiah 56, the prophet speaks of outsiders coming to the Lord. He declares,

> And the foreigners who join themselves to the Lord,
> to minister to him, to love the name of the Lord,
> and to be his servants,
> all who keep the Sabbath and do not profane it,
> and hold fast my covenant—
> these I will bring to my holy mountain

and make them joyful in my house of prayer;
their burnt offerings and their sacrifices
will be accepted on my altar,
for my house shall be called a house of prayer
for all peoples. (Isa 56:6–7)

Isaiah reveals God's love for all peoples, all who worship him and seek to follow and obey him. The temple had a space, the court of the gentiles, where foreigners could pray and worship the Lord. During the time of Jesus, this space was taken over for buying and selling (Matt 21:12-13). Jesus was full of righteous anger and overturned the tables, quoting from Isa 56, saying, "My house will be called a house of prayer" (Matt 21:13).

It can be hard for us to show love and concern for the outsiders among us: the people in our neighborhood, workplace, or school who do not know Jesus. We can become so consumed with providing for our own needs that we neglect the call of being a light to the nations. The Lord will gather people from every tribe and tongue, and he uses us to proclaim the gospel to those who do not know him. Isaiah 56 is a reminder that God loves all people and desires that those who want to know him more would not be unnecessarily hindered from doing so. Our churches and our homes should be places where outsiders can come to know and love the Lord Jesus.

Psalm 67 is an appropriate psalm of response. Here, the psalmist exhorts all the nations to praise and worship the Lord. He sings,

> May God be gracious to us and bless us
> and make his face to shine upon us,
> that your way may be known upon earth,
> your saving power among all nations.
> Let the peoples praise you, O God;
> let all the peoples praise you.
>
> Let the nations be glad and sing for joy,
> for you judge the peoples with equity
> and guide the nations upon earth. (Ps 67:1–4)

The psalmist sings of an outward witness to nations. His desire is that God's blessing on his people would be a light to the world, a manifestation of God's saving power. Moreover, his exhortation is that the nations and people of the world would sing the praise of God in harmony together. This desire echoes the desire of the first reading from Isa 56 that foreigners would come to know the Lord.

The psalmist also notes that it is the Lord who guides the nations. In our autonomy, we often forget God, thinking he is not at work in the events of the world. God, however, is sovereign and immanent. He governs all things in his creation, including the nations of the earth. All global leaders will one day submit to the one, true King of kings. Psalm 67 reminds us that God is the one who will ultimately judge the nations and extend justice to all who have been treated unjustly.

In the second reading from Romans 11, the apostle Paul teaches that both Jew and gentile need the mercy of God. He writes,

> Just as you were once disobedient to God but have now received mercy because of their disobedience, so also they have now been disobedient in order that, by the mercy shown to you, they also may now receive mercy. For God has imprisoned all in disobedience so that he may be merciful to all. (Rom 11:30–32)

Jews and gentiles are no different in the fact that both need the mercy of God. It is not one's race or ethnicity that brings salvation, only God has the power to save. In our own day, there are those who may think that just because they belong to a Christian home or attend church regularly, they are saved. Outward factors do not save us; only the grace of God brings salvation.

In the Gospel reading from Matthew 15, Jesus speaks about what defiles a person. He uses a parable to teach them of the inner reality of righteousness. Jesus declares,

> Do you not see that whatever goes into the mouth enters the stomach and goes out into the sewer? But what comes out of the mouth proceeds from the heart, and this is what defiles. For out of the heart come evil intentions, murder, adultery, sexual immorality, theft, false witness, slander. These are what defile a person, but to eat with unwashed hands does not defile. (Matt 15:17–20)

Jesus is making a point about the Jewish purity laws and eating with unwashed hands. These outwardly religious acts do not make a person righteous or unrighteous. Jesus points to the heart, the inner spiritual reality of a person. After teaching on righteousness being a matter of the heart and not outward acts, Matthew shares the narrative of a Canaanite woman (an outsider) who demonstrates great faith

(Matt 15:28). This narrative reinforces Jesus' teaching on empty religious actions and also complements Paul's teaching from Romans 11. Our righteousness is about the condition of our heart, not our religious actions or ethnicity. The Canaanite woman, though an outsider, seemed to demonstrate greater faith than the religious leaders.

During this season after Pentecost, may we live in light of Jesus' teaching, examining our hearts and our motives. May we learn to speak with kindness and show love toward outsiders. May we not be preoccupied with external matters and outward appearances, but seek to love the Lord and those around us.

QUESTIONS FOR REFLECTION

1. Why is it hard for us to love outsiders? What is meant by the phrase "my house shall be called a house of prayer for all peoples" (Isa 56:7)? Are churches today houses of prayer? Explain.

2. Psalm 67 speaks of the nations singing for joy. What are some of the various ways that God works through us to extend his salvation to others?

3. According to Paul, what do Jews and gentiles have in common? Does race or ethnicity save a person? What is meant by the terms the "visible" and "invisible" church? What is the distinction and how is it relevant to Romans 11:1–2, 29–32?

4. What lesson was Jesus teaching in Matthew 15:10–20? Why do we often get hung up on outward acts and appearances rather than tending to the inner reality and condition of our heart? In the second half of the Gospel reading from Matthew 15, Jesus has an interesting conversation with a Canaanite woman. What lesson do we learn from this narrative? Do you view certain people as outsiders? Why? How do you think Jesus would view those same people?

PRAYER OF RESPONSE
Based on Psalm 67:1–3; Isaiah 56:6–7; Matthew 15:10–20

Lord Jesus,
we know that one day all the nations
of the earth will praise you,
people from every tribe and tongue
will bow before your throne.
Help us to be a light to those around us,
declaring your mighty deeds and saving power;
for you desire that your house would be
a house of prayer for all peoples.
And by your grace, would you cleanse our hearts,
so that the words of our mouth would not
slander, curse, or ridicule, but edify, encourage,
and bless you, our neighbors, our family members, and friends.
In the name of Jesus we pray. Amen.

Proper 16

Sunday between August 21 and August 27 inclusive

LECTIONARY READINGS

Isaiah 51:1–6

Psalm 138

Romans 12:1–8

Matthew 16:13–20

DEVOTION

In the readings for this week, Jesus declares that he will build his church upon Peter's confession. Isaiah speaks poetically of God's people as having descended from the rock and quarry of their spiritual ancestors, Abraham and Sarah. The apostle Paul teaches about the edification of the church through the exercise of spiritual gifts. Thus, the church, the people of God, is a common theme throughout the readings for this Sunday.

In the first reading from Isaiah 51, the prophet speaks poetically about the spiritual heritage of Israel, the people of God. Isaiah declares,

> Listen to me, you who pursue righteousness,
> you who seek the Lord.
> Look to the rock from which you were hewn
> and to the quarry from which you were dug.
> Look to Abraham your father
> and to Sarah, who bore you,
> for he was but one when I called him,
> but I blessed him and made him many. (Isa 51:1–2)

Isaiah is speaking a comforting and encouraging word to the people, reminding them of their spiritual heritage and of how they have been blessed by God. Abraham and Sarah are the "rock" from which the Lord has grown them into a vast nation. They can look back on all that the Lord has done for them and be strengthened in their faith, knowing that he will continue to work in their lives.

We are called to do the same. Paul tells us that we have been grafted into the vine as gentiles, having become part of the covenantal heritage that began with Abraham (Rom 11:11–18). We can look back and be encouraged by our own spiritual heritage as the church. Abraham, Moses, David, Sarah, and Mary are our spiritual ancestors. We all look to the same Lord and Savior.

Isaiah also speaks of the restorative work of God. He proclaims,

> For the Lord will comfort Zion;
> he will comfort all her waste places
> and will make her wilderness like Eden,
> her desert like the garden of the Lord;
> joy and gladness will be found in her,
> thanksgiving and the voice of song. (Isa 51:3)

Our God is the one who brings life to dry, barren places. He is the one who brings joy, gladness, and songs of thanksgiving where there was sorrow and despair. Like the people of old, we often journey through the desert, only to be refreshed by the grace of God. Though we face trials and hardship, the Lord's steadfast love sustains us on our journey of faith.

Psalm 138 is the psalm of response. We find the psalmist singing of God's rescue and power in his life. He declares,

> Though I walk in the midst of trouble,
> you preserve me against the wrath of my enemies;
> you stretch out your hand,
> and your right hand delivers me. (Ps 138:7)

The psalmist is aware of God's presence and power to save and shield him from his enemies. He acknowledges the Lord's deliverance in his life. We, too, can offer our praise for the rescue that God provides through the salvation of Christ as well as his sustaining grace as we encounter opposition in life.

Like the psalmist, we may find ourselves in the midst of "trouble," seeking the Lord and receiving a way of escape. Often, it is through the counsel and care of others that God works in our lives. He providentially puts people in our lives to speak encouragement or to provide for physical or emotional needs. We also receive the advocacy and empowerment of Christ and the Holy Spirit who provide grace in our time of need (Heb 4:16; Rom 8:26).

In the second reading from Romans 12, the apostle Paul teaches on how our very lives, not animals, are now the spiritual sacrifice that we are to offer. He writes,

> I appeal to you therefore, brothers and sisters, on the basis of God's mercy, to present your bodies as a living sacrifice, holy and acceptable to God, which is your reasonable act of worship. (Rom 12:1)

Paul is describing a change in the way we are to worship. In the Old Testament, God prescribed various sacrifices that the Israelites were to offer (Lev 1–7). We no longer bring these sacrifices to God; rather, we offer our very bodies and our lives to the Lord in response to the final sacrifice that Christ made on our behalf. Since we have been cleansed by Christ's sacrifice on the cross, our response is to offer our lives to him as an act of worship.

In addition, we exercise the gifts we have been given to build up and edify the body of Christ. Paul writes,

> We have gifts that differ according to the grace given to us: prophecy, in proportion to faith; ministry, in ministering; the teacher, in teaching; the encourager, in encouragement; the giver, in sincerity; the leader, in diligence; the compassionate, in cheerfulness. (Rom 12:6–8)

These various gifts edify and strengthen us. Some of us are called to teach; others are called to encourage; and others are to show compassion. Whatever our gift may be, we are called to exercise it faithfully in service to the body of Christ. We need one another. We need the local church, the place where we can be blessed and be a blessing to others. So much of our culture today emphasizes individualism; the church of Christ highlights our interdependence.

In the Gospel reading from Matthew 16, Jesus asks the disciples, "But who do you say that I am?" (Matt 16:15). Always the first one to speak, Peter declares, "You are the Messiah, the Son of the living God" (Matt 16:16). Jesus responds by acknowledging that Peter did not come up with this truth on his own; it was revealed by divine means. Jesus also declares, "And I tell you, you are Peter, and on this rock I will build my church, and the gates of Hades will not prevail against it" (Matt 16:18).

Though various interpretations have been offered over the centuries, the most likely meaning is that Jesus will build his church upon Peter's confession, the confession that Jesus is the Messiah. Jesus is the true cornerstone and foundation of the church, not Peter. And with Jesus as the head of the church, no power can prevail against it. Nothing can destroy the church. Though she has been persecuted, mocked, and beaten, the church will prevail. Christ will sustain his bride until he returns.

This truth is comforting as we reflect on the status of the church today. In many ways, it may seem that the church is weak, too often plagued by the same sinful lifestyles and failures as the world. We are being sanctified and refined, however, and one day we will be presented to God, spotless and without blemish because of the blood of Christ (Eph 5:25–27).

During this season after Pentecost, may we consider ourselves part of a covenantal heritage, stretching back to Abraham and Sarah. We are part of the church, the bride of Christ, and we shall persevere until Christ's return. Until that day, may we exercise our gifts faithfully, seeking to build up and edify one another in love, for the glory of God and in service of his kingdom.

QUESTIONS FOR REFLECTION

1. Reread Isaiah 51:1–2. What is the imagery that Isaiah uses to speak about our spiritual ancestry? Who does he name and how do these people connect with us today?

2. The psalmist speaks of God's deliverance in the midst of trouble. How does God provide rescue for us today? How has God shown himself faithful in your own life during times of trouble, trial, or hardship?

3. What does Paul mean by the phrase, "present your bodies as a living sacrifice, holy and acceptable to God, which is your reasonable act of worship" (Rom 12:1)? What are your spiritual gifts? Do you exercise your gifts to edify the body of Christ? Describe.

4. Why did Jesus ask the disciples, "But who do you say I am?" (Matt 16:15). Didn't they already know the answer to this question? Reread Matthew 16:16–18. Upon what or whom will Christ build his church? Explain.

PRAYER OF RESPONSE
Based on Matthew 16:16; Isaiah 51:1–6

Lord Jesus,
we believe that you are the Messiah,
the Son of the living God.
Help us to pursue your righteousness
and to seek you in all things.
Thank you for the many ways you comfort us,
and bring refreshment to the parched places of our lives.
May your people be full of joy and gladness;
may songs of thanksgiving be on our lips.
Encourage us to be messengers of the good news
of your salvation to all the nations of the earth.
Your salvation is forever, and your deliverance will never end.
In the name of Jesus we pray. Amen.

Proper 17

Sunday between August 28 and September 3 inclusive

LECTIONARY READINGS

>   Jeremiah 15:15–21
>
>   Psalm 26:1–8
>
>   Romans 12:9–21
>
>   Matthew 16:21–28

DEVOTION

In the readings for this Sunday, Jeremiah experiences suffering because of his unpopular message. Jesus teaches that in order to be his disciple, one must take up one's cross and follow him. The apostle Paul teaches on how to love and serve others through the radical call of the gospel. Thus, taking up our cross, experiencing rejection, and loving and serving others are themes in the readings for this week.

In the first reading from Jeremiah 15, we encounter the emotional state of the prophet as he wrestles with God and questions why he has to suffer so much for proclaiming the message given to him. He declares,

>   Your words were found, and I ate them,
>   and your words became to me a joy
>   and the delight of my heart,
>   for I am called by your name,
>   O Lord, God of hosts.
>   I did not sit in the company of merrymakers,
>   nor did I rejoice;

> under the weight of your hand I sat alone,
> for you had filled me with indignation.
> Why is my pain unceasing,
> my wound incurable,
> refusing to be healed?
> Truly, you are to me like a deceitful brook,
> like waters that fail. (Jer 15:16–18)

Jeremiah is expressing the fact that he delivered God's message, but has suffered rejection and ridicule because of it. Jeremiah did not speak what the people wanted to hear, but only the words that God gave him. He wonders, however, why he has to suffer for obeying his call.

In the book of Job, God does not give Job answers for his suffering, but he does give him a powerful sense of his authority and presence. In a similar way, God answers Jeremiah by stating that, through it all, "I am with you" (Jer 15:20). And God acts in a similar way with us. As we face trials and hardships; as we may suffer for our faith, God promises that he will never leave us or forsake us (Heb 13:5). God is our advocate, and though we do not always understand the circumstances we must endure, we know that God is present with us.

Psalm 26 is the psalm of response. Like Jeremiah, the psalmist expresses his integrity and how he has followed the Lord. He sings,

> Vindicate me, O Lord,
> for I have walked in my integrity,
> and I have trusted in the Lord without wavering.
> Prove me, O Lord, and try me;
> test my heart and mind.
> For your steadfast love is before my eyes,
> and I walk in faithfulness to you. (Ps 26:1–3)

Like Jeremiah, the psalmist has chosen to walk with and trust the Lord. He has not chosen to follow wicked and evil people (Ps 26:4–5), but has remained steady in his relationship with the Lord. The psalmist also expresses his love of God's house and God's glorious presence (Ps 26:8).

The psalmist and Jeremiah both express their devotion to the Lord, choosing not to go along with the wicked and idolatrous ways of the people around them. We, too, are called to be in the world, but not of the world. We are called to be salt and light to the people in our lives: our neighbors, friends, and family members (Matt 5:13–16). And like the psalmist and Jeremiah, we should have a hunger for the presence of the Lord. When we walk through hard times, or when we feel we are surrounded by worldly influences, having a sense of God's abiding presence will sustain us.

In the second reading from Romans 12, the apostle Paul teaches on how we are to live from the beauty of the gospel. He lays out how we are to love and serve others with the love of Christ, being salt and light in this world. When we read this text, we can almost hear the echoes of Jesus' Sermon on the Mount. Much of how Jesus exhorted us to live is expressed in Paul's admonition as well. Paul writes,

> Bless those who persecute you; bless and do not curse them. Rejoice with those who rejoice; weep with those who weep. Live in harmony with one another; do not be arrogant, but associate with the lowly; do not claim to be wiser than you are. (Rom 12:14–16)

Paul is calling us to take the high road of the gospel and love those who do not love us. He calls us not to think too highly of ourselves, but to serve those of lesser means. Paul closes his exhortation by stating, "Do not be overcome by evil, but overcome evil with good" (Rom 12:21). This statement is a beautiful summary of all that Paul has written.

As followers of Christ, living in a fallen world, we are called to live according to kingdom values. These values are often in stark contrast and opposition to the values that our culture endorses. As ambassadors for Christ, we are called to overcome evil with good. When God sanctifies us, he does not just remove sinful behaviors, he replaces unhealthy patterns with healthy ones. He slowly removes our selfishness and cultivates care and concern for others. He begins to remove old grudges, and he fills us with compassion for people we have found hard to like, much less love. God's economy is not like our economy, and his grace has no limits.

In the Gospel reading from Matthew 16, Jesus calls the disciples to a radical way of life. He calls them to take up their cross and follow him. He declares,

> If any wish to come after me, let them deny themselves and take up their cross and follow me. For those who want to save their life will lose it, and those who lose their life for my sake will find it. For what will it profit them if they gain the whole world but forfeit their life? Or what will they give in return for their life? (Matt 16:24–26)

Like Jeremiah, the psalmist, and the church at Rome who received Paul's letter, we are called to follow the Lord into whatever path he has for us. Jeremiah was rejected by the people because of his message. The psalmist chose to follow the Lord, not succumbing to the wickedness of those around him. The Christians in Rome were called to a radical way of loving and serving others. Jesus calls us to take up our cross and follow him. We do not know what our particular version of "cross-bearing" may look like, but we trust in his steadfast love and faithfulness.

Like God's people throughout the generations, we are not always given answers to our questions, but we are sustained by God's presence. He will give us the grace to endure whatever circumstance we may encounter. He offers his abiding presence on our faith journey. His presence is made known to us through the various means of grace we experience in corporate worship and in personal devotion (word, prayer, worship, community, sacrament, Spirit). We can ask God for his grace to lead us away from temptation so that our souls are not burdened down by the evil of this world.

During this season after Pentecost, may we respond to the radical call of God to take up our cross and follow him. Our hearts and souls long for God's abiding presence, the source of true life. Giving up our lives to gain eternal life in Christ is our greatest desire. By grace, may we follow wherever the Lord may lead us.

QUESTIONS FOR REFLECTION

1. How would you describe Jeremiah's emotional state in Jeremiah 15:15–18? How does God respond to his questions? How does God often provide, not answers, but his sustaining presence in your life?

2. How is the psalmist able to live with integrity? With whom does the psalmist choose not to associate? Where does he truly long to be? Why? Do the people in your life encourage godliness or worldliness? Explain.

3. What does gospel-centered love look like according to Paul? Do you hear the echo of Jesus' Sermon on the Mount (Matt 5–7) in this portion of Paul's Letter to the Romans? Explain. Paul states, "Do not be overcome by evil, but overcome evil with good" (Rom 12:21). How do you live out this exhortation?

4. Jesus calls us to take up our cross and follow him. What does this mean for us today? Describe. What does it mean that we must lose our life to gain it?

PRAYER OF RESPONSE
Based on Matthew 16:24–26; Psalm 26:1, 3

Lord Jesus,
we know that if we want to become your followers,
we must deny ourselves, take up our cross and follow you.
If we truly desire to save our life, we will lose it;
and if we lose our life for your sake, we will find it.
By your grace, may we see the foolishness in striving
to gain the whole world while forfeiting our soul.
Help us to walk in integrity and trust you without wavering.
May your steadfast love be before our eyes
as we seek to walk in faithfulness to you.
In the name of Jesus we pray. Amen.

Proper 18

Sunday between September 4 and September 10 inclusive

LECTIONARY READINGS

> Ezekiel 33:7–11
>
> Psalm 119:33–40
>
> Romans 13:8–14
>
> Matthew 18:15–20

DEVOTION

In the readings for this Sunday, Jesus teaches about the love of neighbor. He teaches how to confront a brother or sister who has wronged us so that he or she may repent and turn back to the Lord. Ezekiel receives the call of God to warn the people of Israel when they have sinned and to call them to repent and turn back to the Lord. The apostle Paul writes about the love of neighbor in his Letter to the Romans. He also teaches about the day of salvation being near and of living in the light. Thus, confronting fellow believers in love and living in light of Christ's return are common themes in the readings for this Sunday.

In the first reading from Ezekiel 33, the prophet receives the message from the Lord that he is to be like a "sentinel" (Ezek 33:7), warning God's people of their wicked ways and calling them to return to the Lord. Speaking for the Lord, Ezekiel declares,

> If I say to the wicked, "O wicked ones, you shall surely die," and you do not speak to warn the wicked to turn from their ways, the wicked shall die in their iniquity, but their blood I will require at your hand. But if you warn the wicked to turn from their ways

and they do not turn from their ways, the wicked shall die in their iniquity, but you will have saved your life. (Ezek 33:8–9)

The Lord is calling Ezekiel to warn the people of God of their sin and wickedness. This is not an easy message to bring to people. No one likes being the bearer of hard news, particularly a message as sobering as the one the Lord is calling Ezekiel to deliver. The warning, however, is a mercy from God. The Lord, through Ezekiel, is giving the people of Israel an opportunity to repent of their ways and return to him.

The Lord does the same for us today. Through the conviction of his word, the witness of the Spirit, the community of other believers, and our own conscience, the Lord seeks to bring us back to himself. This is one of the reasons why being in biblical community is so important.

We all have blind spots, behaviors that we may or may not realize are unhealthy. By being in God's word together with other believers on a regular basis, we put ourselves in a position to hear from the Lord or even to receive loving counsel and/or correction from another brother or sister in Christ. Such accountability is crucial for our journey of faith.

Psalm 119 is the psalm of response. The psalmist sings of following the Lord's commandments. He prays,

> Teach me, O Lord, the way of your statutes,
> and I will observe it to the end.
> Give me understanding, that I may keep your law
> and observe it with my whole heart.
> Lead me in the path of your commandments,
> for I delight in it.
> Turn my heart to your decrees
> and not to selfish gain. (Ps 119:33–36)

It is interesting to note the various phrases that the psalmist uses to express his petitions to the Lord—"teach me," "give me understanding" "lead me," and "turn my heart." All of these phrases reveal the heart and mind of someone who desires to grow, to learn of his shortcomings, to walk in the right direction, and to repent and be transformed. These petitions could easily become part of our own prayer language with the Lord. We all need help in our journey of faith. We all tend to drift. The psalmist reminds us to pray for guidance, to be led in the right direction, and to turn to the Lord and not to our selfish ways.

In the second reading from Romans 13, the apostle Paul teaches what it means to love your neighbor as yourself. He writes,

> The commandments, "You shall not commit adultery; you shall not murder; you shall not steal; you shall not covet," and any other commandment, are summed up in this word, "You shall love your neighbor as yourself." (Rom 13:9)

In this letter, Paul summarizes many of the Ten Commandments by distilling them to love of neighbor. As we grow in our love for others, we will not have the desire to commit adultery, murder, steal, or covet what they have. Such love must come from the Spirit. We cannot create that kind of love on our own; it comes as a gift from God. In our own nature, we tend to use people for what they can give us. Having Christ's love for others does not expect anything in return. Having God's love for other people brings us great joy.

Paul also teaches on the coming of Christ and our need to live in the light. He writes,

> Let us then throw off the works of darkness and put on the armor of light; let us walk decently as in the day, not in reveling and drunkenness, not in illicit sex and licentiousness, not in quarreling and jealousy. (Rom 13:12–13)

Paul appeared to believe that Jesus might return during his lifetime. He is admonishing the people of God to live with a sense of urgency, not giving into the desires of the flesh, but living righteously. Paul uses the analogy of living "decently as in the day," as opposed to sinfully, and we could add, "as in the night." The way people act at night can be quite different from the way they live during the day. Paul is exhorting the Christians in Rome to live in light of their new status as God's children. He is writing to new followers of Christ and is reminding them to live as those baptized in the Lord.

We should receive his admonition as well. If we thoroughly examine our own lives, we will find behaviors that still need sanctification. Paul is encouraging us to live into our own baptismal vows, regularly putting on the Lord Jesus Christ. As children of God, we lay aside the works of darkness and put on the armor of light. Living in biblical community with other believers is a helpful means of being regularly reoriented into God's righteousness.

In the Gospel reading from Matthew 18, Jesus lays out a process of seeking reconciliation with another brother or sister in Christ. First, we are exhorted to approach someone who has wronged us, one-on-one; then, with another witness if needed; and finally, before the church if the first two scenarios are not received well. The purpose of this process is to bring about humility and forgiveness on the part of the offender. Pursuing others in such a way is an act of mercy to bring peace and restoration.

Jesus closes his teaching with the profound statement, "For where two or three are gathered in my name, I am there among them" (Matt 18:20). We also long for the presence of the Lord. Jesus gives us the promise that whenever we are gathered with two or three other believers, he is there with us. This promise expresses itself in the life of small groups, corporate worship (including the sacraments), and in gatherings for prayer and adoration.

During this season after Pentecost, as we learn what it means to live by the Spirit, may we seek the presence of the Lord together. May we learn to live in peace and harmony with our brothers and sisters in Christ, encouraging one another and spurring one another on toward love and good deeds (Heb 10:24–25).

QUESTIONS FOR REFLECTION

1. What was the call that God put on Ezekiel's life? Do you think this was a hard calling to fulfill? How does God call us to warn and admonish one another?

2. What active phrases does the psalmist use in his petitions to the Lord? Do these petitions apply to your own life? Explain.

3. How does the apostle Paul summarize several of the Ten Commandments? Do you struggle with the commandment to love your neighbor as yourself? Describe. What does it mean to "put on the armor of light" or to "put on the Lord Jesus Christ" (Rom 13:12, 14)? How should this characterize the way we live? Why did Paul have a sense of urgency? Do you live with a sense of urgency regarding Christ's return?

4. What is the process that Jesus describes in seeking reconciliation with another person? Have you ever had to go to someone in this manner, or have you been the recipient of someone else's initiative? Explain. What promise does Jesus give us at this close of this passage? How should that promise encourage us today?

PRAYER OF RESPONSE
Based on Matthew 18:15–20

Gracious God,
help us to live at peace with one another.
When we sin against someone,
help us to promptly ask for forgiveness;
and when we are sinned against, give us the courage
to go to our offender and seek reconciliation.
May we fulfill your commandments by loving you
with all of our heart, soul, mind, and strength,
and by loving our neighbor as ourselves.
In the name of Jesus we pray. Amen.

Proper 19

Sunday between September 11 and September 17 inclusive

LECTIONARY READINGS

Genesis 50:15–21

Psalm 103:1–13

Romans 14:1–12

Matthew 18:21–35

DEVOTION

In the readings for this Sunday, we find Jesus telling a parable about forgiveness. In the first reading from Genesis 50, we find Joseph telling his brothers how God brought good out of their intended harm. The apostle Paul teaches about the grace and mercy we should extend to others on matters that are not vital to the faith. Thus, extending forgiveness, grace, and mercy towards one another is a common theme in the readings for this Sunday.

In the first reading from Genesis 50, we find Joseph's brothers pleading for Joseph to be gracious to them. They tell Joseph how their father Jacob pleaded for Joseph to forgive them. Joseph weeps with his brothers and assures them that he is not their judge. Joseph declares,

> Even though you intended to do harm to me, God intended it for good, in order to preserve a numerous people, as he is doing today. So have no fear; I myself will provide for you and your little ones. (Gen 50:20–21)

The mercy Joseph extends to his brothers is to be commended. Although Joseph was in a position of great power, and although his brothers sold him into slavery, he was merciful and kind to them. Joseph could see the bigger picture of God's redemption and did not hold a grudge against his brothers.

God works similarly in our lives today as he did in Joseph's life centuries ago. God is able to bring beauty from the ashes of our brokenness; he is able to redeem us from our sin and from the sins made against us. Like Joseph, we are encouraged to see the circumstances of our lives through the eyes of faith and God's providence. God is able to redeem and restore the trials and tribulations of our lives to bless others, to increase our faith, and to bring us joy.

Psalm 103 is the psalm of response. The whole psalm echoes many of the themes in Genesis 50: God's forgiveness, mercy, benefits, redemption, healing, justice, and compassion. The psalmist sings,

> Bless the Lord, O my soul,
> and do not forget all his benefits—
> who forgives all your iniquity,
> who heals all your diseases,
> who redeems your life from the Pit,
> who crowns you with steadfast love and mercy,
> who satisfies you with good as long as you live
> so that your youth is renewed like the eagle's. (Ps 103:2–5)

We see these traits exemplified in the way God blesses and restores Joseph and in the way Joseph treats his brothers. Joseph could have easily dealt with his brothers in a harsh manner, recounting the way they first thought about killing him, then deciding to throw him into a pit, and then selling him into slavery. Joseph, however, did not bring those crimes before his brothers. He simply acknowledged God's compassion and providence and treated his brothers with kindness. The psalmist knows of this compassion and kindness as well.

We, too, are called to recognize, acknowledge, and praise God for his goodness, mercy, justice, and compassion in our own lives. We are called to "bless the Lord" with our souls and to worship him with all that we are, all that we have experienced, "all that is within me" (Ps 103:1). Living in such a way helps us to respond in a more Christlike manner to those who have wronged us or treated us harshly. Rather than seeking revenge, we ask the Lord for grace to extend love and compassion to our enemies. This is easier said than done, but with God, all things are possible.

In the second reading from Romans 14, the apostle Paul encourages grace and mercy among fellow believers. Though we are diverse, we are called to forgo judgment on matters that are indifferent, not vital to the faith. He writes,

> Welcome those who are weak in faith but not for the purpose of quarreling over opinions. Some believe in eating anything, while the weak eat only vegetables. Those who eat must not despise those who abstain, and those who abstain must not pass judgment on those who eat, for God has welcomed them. Who are you to pass judgment on slaves of another? It is before their own lord that they stand or fall. And they will be upheld, for the Lord is able to make them stand. (Rom 14:1–4)

The church in Rome was like all of the other churches to which Paul wrote. They all dealt with divisions and quarreling and needed to exercise grace and compassion towards one another. Churches and Christians today are no different. We still wrestle with issues and judge others for behaving in a manner we deem as sinful or unfaithful. Paul addresses this topic head on with the church in Rome, recalling the fact that we are not to judge one another, but that each one of us is accountable to God.

Paul is not saying we should act any way we please; however, he is making the point that, in matters that are not vital to the faith, we should not pass judgment on one another. In our day, such matters might include how we educate our children, what shows we watch, how we spend our money, etc. We have to be careful as brothers and sisters in Christ that we do not create our own law and expect others to abide by our standards. We need to live in accordance with God's word and his ways, but we are not to judge others according to our own rules.

Living in biblical community is so important because it reminds us of the differences that exist among us in matters that are indifferent. When we live life together, we receive windows into others' habits, behaviors, values, and beliefs. At times, we may disagree, but we can still maintain love and respect for one another.

When someone is clearly acting sinfully, that behavior should be appropriately addressed. Discerning between a sinful behavior and a behavior or belief that is simply different from our own, however, is precisely where tensions and misunderstandings often exist. Thus, we need to exercise wisdom and prudence in these sensitive matters.

In the Gospel reading from Matthew 18, Peter asks Jesus how many times he is called to forgive another brother or sister in the church who sins against him. To answer him, Jesus shares a parable. In the parable a slave is forgiven a very large debt by his master. Soon after he received his pardon, however, he found someone who owed him a lesser amount of money by comparison. Instead of forgiving him in like manner, he treated him harshly. The first slave's master found about his behavior and made him pay back the money he owed.

The parable teaches us that we are to extend forgiveness to others since we have been graciously forgiven by our heavenly Father. We cheapen God's salvation and redemption when we fail to live mercifully and graciously towards others. Jesus calls us to extend forgiveness lavishly just as he has demonstrated his love for us so abundantly by laying down his own life for us.

During this season after Pentecost, we explore what it looks like to walk in the Spirit in the everyday circumstances of life. By God's grace, may we learn how to forgive and not hold grudges towards fellow brothers and sisters in Christ. May we learn to love others lavishly, just as Christ has loved us.

QUESTIONS FOR REFLECTION

1. Joseph was treated very cruelly by his brothers early in his life. How does Joseph respond when his brothers plead for forgiveness? How is Joseph able to respond in this manner? How do you respond to those who have wronged you? Explain. How would God have us respond to our enemies?

2. The psalmist recounts so many wonderful characteristics of God. Which of these stand out to you? Where have you seen one or more of these divine characteristics in your own life (God's mercy, healing, justice, etc.)? Do you find yourself, like the psalmist, praising the Lord for the various ways he reveals himself in your life?

3. Paul recounts the way believers in Rome judged one another (eating, worship, holy days). What are the issues that can cause division and judgment among Christians today? How would God have us behave toward one another?

4. Jesus offers Peter a parable when asked how often we are to forgive those who sin against us. Summarize the parable. What is the takeaway truth for us in this parable?

PRAYER OF RESPONSE
Based on Matthew 18:21–35; Genesis 50:19–20

Sovereign God,
help us to extend the same mercy and forgiveness
to others that you have given to us.
By your grace, may we not forget
the kindness we have been shown,
but offer Christ's love to our neighbors,
our family members, and friends.
Even when others do us harm,
remind us of your sovereign care,
for we know you are able to redeem
our trials for our good and your glory.
In the name of Jesus we pray. Amen.

Proper 20

Sunday between September 18 and September 24 inclusive

LECTIONARY READINGS

Jonah 3:10—4:11

Psalm 145:1–8

Philippians 1:21–30

Matthew 20:1–16

DEVOTION

In the readings for this Sunday, Jesus offers a parable about the grace and mercy of God. Jonah is upset with God about extending mercy and forgiveness to the people of Nineveh. The apostle Paul writes to the Philippians, encouraging them to remain strong in the faith and of one spirit with one another. Thus, God's steadfast love and mercy towards us and our unity in the faith are common themes in the readings for this Sunday.

In the first reading from Jonah, the prophet is angry with God for showing mercy and kindness towards the people of Nineveh. Jonah prayed to the Lord,

> O Lord! Is not this what I said while I was still in my own country? That is why I fled to Tarshish at the beginning, for I knew that you are a gracious and merciful God, slow to anger, abounding in steadfast love, and relenting from punishment. And now, O Lord, please take my life from me, for it is better for me to die than to live. (Jonah 4:2–3)

We almost find ourselves laughing at Jonah's childlike attitude about God's mercy and compassion towards the people of Nineveh; however, if we look closely at our own lives, I'm sure we will find similar examples of selfish, childlike attitudes towards family members, neighbors, and other acquaintances. We may already have an opinion about how God should treat or respond to a certain person or people group; however, God will not be bound by our conditions for extending love and grace to others.

In the closing section of Jonah, God creates a living parable for Jonah to understand the mercy of God. The book closes with a question for Jonah (and for us): "And should I not be concerned about Nineveh, that great city, in which there are more than a hundred and twenty thousand persons who do not know their right hand from their left and also many animals?" (Jonah 4:11).

The book ends with this open-ended question, leaving us to provide the answer with our own hearts and minds. Are we concerned for those around us who do not know the Lord or those who have drifted from the Lord for any number of reasons? Are we, like Jonah, consumed by our own selfish wants and desires so that we cannot see the bigger picture of God's grace and mercy?

Psalm 145 is the psalm of response. The psalmist sings,

> They will proclaim the might of your awesome deeds,
> and I will declare your greatness.
> They shall celebrate the fame of your abundant goodness
> and shall sing aloud of your righteousness.
>
> The Lord is gracious and merciful,
> slow to anger and abounding in steadfast love. (Ps 145:6–8)

The psalmist knows of the grace, mercy, and steadfast love of the Lord. He knows the Lord who would extend his grace upon a people like the Ninevites. Unlike Jonah, the psalmist wants to praise the Lord for these attributes. These qualities angered Jonah when they were extended to a people that did not deserve them, according to Jonah. At times, we may praise the Lord for his grace and mercy over us, but get angry when he is gracious and merciful to those we deem as enemies. God's character will cause us to stumble when the gospel extends beyond the boundary lines we have erected.

In the second reading from Philippians 1, Paul first articulates his desire to be with the Lord; however, he realizes that it is better for him to labor for the kingdom. He then seeks to encourage the Philippians to remain strong and unified. He writes,

> Only, live your life in a manner worthy of the gospel of Christ, so that, whether I come and see you or am absent and hear about you, I will know that you are standing firm in one spirit, striving side by side with one mind for the faith of the gospel and in no way frightened by those opposing you. For them, this is evidence of their destruction but of your salvation. (Phil 1:27–28)

Paul exhorts the beloved Philippians to live their lives as a reflection of the gospel. He encourages them to persevere in their faith and in their unity. Their steadfastness will be an indictment on their opponents and a witness of their salvation.

Paul's exhortation to the Philippians is for us as well. We, too, should strive to live in a manner "worthy of the gospel of Christ." We, too, are called to remain strong and steadfast in our faith and in unity with other believers. This way of life speaks volumes to those around us. When others witness our faith, it may cause them to wrestle with their own beliefs. Perseverance in the midst of trials and hardship is a powerful witness to the gospel of Christ. In addition, the love and unity of the church can be a powerful influence on the world. Those who are skeptical of the Christian faith may become curious when they witness genuine, mutual love among believers and when that love is extended in grace and through deeds of mercy to others.

In the Gospel reading from Matthew 20, Jesus offers a parable about the kingdom of God. In the parable, a landowner gives laborers equal pay for unequal hours of work. When questioned about the payment by one of the laborers who worked all day, the landowner replies, "Am I not allowed to do what I choose with what belongs to me? Or are you envious because I am generous?" (Matt 20:15).

Jesus closes by describing the economy of the kingdom: "So the last will be first, and the first will be last" (Matt 20:16). Like the laborer who worked a full day, we stumble at times because of the scandalous grace of God and the upside-down economy of the kingdom. The kingdom of God does not operate by the laws and principles of this world. We are accustomed to people receiving what they deserve; we are not prepared for the mercy and steadfast love God shows to those whom we think do not deserve it.

The reading from Jonah, Psalm 145, the passage to the Philippians, and the parable of the kingdom all demonstrate the character of our God and our call to live a life worthy of the gospel of Christ. We are called to extend abundant grace and love towards others because we have been abundantly loved and forgiven by God. During this season after Pentecost, may we not stumble over the grace and mercy of God, but be conduits of his love to others. May our lives be an overflow of goodness and mercy, and may we labor and persevere for the sake of the kingdom.

QUESTIONS FOR REFLECTION

1. Describe the scene in Jonah 3:10—4:11. Why is Jonah acting like a pouting child? What aspect of God's character has Jonah so angry and upset? Why? How do we find ourselves acting just like Jonah?

2. The psalmist does not seem upset by, but praises God for his grace, mercy, and steadfast love. Do you praise God for these character traits only when they are extended to you or also when they are extended to others? Explain.

3. Why is Paul torn in Philippians 1:21–26? Where does he truly want to be? Where does he realize he needs to be? What is the source of faith and love among the Philippians? How are their lives a witness to their opponents? How can the church today exemplify love and unity?

4. Does the parable Jesus shares in Matthew 20 seem unfair to you? Can you hear your own reaction in the voice of the laborer who worked all day? Do you operate more by the world's principles and rules or by the economy and values of the kingdom? Explain.

PRAYER OF RESPONSE
Based on Jonah 4:2; Matthew 20:1–16

Sovereign Lord,
you are gracious and merciful,
slow to anger and abounding in steadfast love.
You do not treat us as we deserve,
but offer us grace and love despite our selfish ways.
Help us to bring your kingdom where we live and work,
demonstrating your love and mercy to others;
and extending grace and forgiveness to our neighbors,
our family, our friends, and even our enemies.
In the name of Jesus we pray. Amen.

Proper 21

Sunday between September 25 and October 1 inclusive

LECTIONARY READINGS

Ezekiel 18:1–4, 25–32

Psalm 25:1–9

Philippians 2:1–13

Matthew 21:23–32

DEVOTION

In the Gospel reading for this Sunday, the chief priests and the elders of the people come to Jesus and ask him a question about his authority. Jesus, knowing their scheming hearts, turns the tables on them and asks them a question regarding the authority of John the Baptist. When they are unable to give an answer, Jesus tells a story revealing the nature of the kingdom of God, sin, and repentance. These themes are common threads throughout the readings.

In the first reading from Ezekiel 18, a proverb is quoted: "The parents have eaten sour grapes, and the children's teeth are set on edge" (Ezek 18:2). The basic meaning is that children suffer from their parents' mistakes; however, Ezekiel exhorts God's people not to use this proverb anymore. Each person is accountable for his or her own actions. He then describes how the righteous shall be punished when they turn away from righteousness and commit iniquity; yet, the wicked shall live when they turn from their unrighteousness and do what is lawful and right (Ezek 18:26–27).

The prophet quotes Israel as saying, "The way of the Lord is unfair." He turns the tables on them, however, and asks, "Is it not your ways that are unfair?" (Ezek 18:29). This passage connects well with the Gospel reading for it emphasizes the role of repentance. In the Gospel reading it is the "tax collectors and prostitutes" who repent and believe. In Ezekiel, it is the "wicked" who shall live when they turn from their unrighteousness. In both cases, the paradoxical nature of God's kingdom is made evident. It is not those with the outward appearance of righteousness who inherit the kingdom, but those who repent and believe.

In Psalm 25, the psalm of response, the theme of salvation is sung:

> Lead me in your truth and teach me,
> for you are the God of my salvation;
> for you I wait all day long. (Ps 25:5)

The psalmist also asks God not to remember the sins of his youth (Ps 25:7). He is pleading for God to be merciful, which, in a sense means, "Do not give me what I deserve." Over and over God demonstrates his mercy and his steadfast love to his people. This is ironic because so often we treat others unfairly, quickly forgetting the kindness and mercy God has shown us. Indeed, the petition from the Lord's prayer articulates this well: "Forgive us our trespasses, as we forgive those who trespass against us." We are to extend to others the same mercy and forgiveness that the Lord extends to us.

In the second reading from Philippians 2, the apostle Paul continues this theme and exhorts us to imitate Christ. He writes,

> If, then, there is any comfort in Christ, any consolation from love, any partnership in the Spirit, any tender affection and sympathy, make my joy complete: be of the same mind, having the same love, being in full accord and of one mind. Do nothing from selfish ambition or empty conceit, but in humility regard others as better than yourselves. Let each of you look not to your own interests but to the interests of others. (Phil 2:1–4)

Paul is exhorting the Philippians to demonstrate the following characteristics: unity, humility, and service. With regard to unity, we are to have the same love, being in full accord and of one mind. With regard to humility, we are to do nothing from selfish ambition or conceit, but in humility regard others as better than ourselves. With regard to service, we are to look, not to our own interests but to the interests of others.

After this exhortation, Paul shares what is thought to be a hymn fragment from the early church. Through these ancient lyrics, the humility and exaltation of Christ are powerfully sung:

> And being found in appearance as a human,
> he humbled himself
> and became obedient to the point of death—
> even death on a cross.
>
> Therefore God exalted him even more highly
> and gave him the name
> that is above every name,
> so that at the name of Jesus
> every knee should bend
> in heaven and on earth and under the earth,
> and every tongue should confess
> that Jesus Christ is Lord,
> to the glory of God the Father. (Phil 2:7–11)

We are called to imitate the life of Christ. Jesus is the one who humbled himself to the point of death on our behalf and was, therefore, exalted. It is the name of Jesus, and no other name, to which every knee shall bend. He is the only King of kings and Lord of lords. Not surprisingly, the values of his kingdom are unlike the values of this world. The kingdom of God is an upside-down kingdom. The first shall be last; to gain your life you have to lose it; and, if you humble yourself, you will be exalted.

The apostle concludes by exhorting us: "Work on your own salvation with fear and trembling, for it is God who is at work in you, enabling you both to will and to work for his good pleasure" (Phil 2:12–13). The takeaway truth in this is that it is God who is at work in us to work out our salvation. God does not leave us to our own resources, but provides the grace and the power to will and to work for his good pleasure.

In the Gospel reading from Matthew 21, the kingdom values from the epistle and from the first reading are echoed: insiders become outsiders; outsiders become insiders. The humble shall be exalted. From Matt 21, we find the question that we all have to answer regarding Jesus: Is he truly who he says he is? If he is, then his authority and kingship changes everything.

Often, like the chief priests and the elders, we approach Jesus with pride and arrogance. We doubt his authority and expect him to cater to our wants and desires. We do not want him to disrupt our lives, call us to repentance, and ask us to follow him. We do not want to be accountable to our Lord Jesus. This is why the chief priests and the elders were so upset. Jesus was shaking things up and disrupting the current mode of operation in the temple.

When the chief priest and elders questioned Jesus about his authority, he cleverly asked them about the authority of John the Baptist. Responding to a question with another question was a very rabbinic thing to do. He put his antagonists on the defensive and caused them to search their own hearts. This is often how Jesus interacts with us. He speaks to us in ways that search out the deep places of our hearts, thus exposing our doubts, our fears, and the places that need repentance. He then told a parable, a story which cut to the heart and further revealed the upside-down nature of the kingdom.

Ironically, the chief priests and the elders, those who should have seen the signs and followed Jesus (insiders), did not do so; however, the prostitutes and tax collectors (outsiders) did recognize him for who he was and the authority he held. The parable revealed the irony, the paradox, and the upside-down nature of the kingdom: those who are first shall be last and those who are last shall be first. Outward appearances are deceiving; righteousness cannot be discerned by human standards. During this season after Pentecost, may we learn to live by the values of the kingdom, and may we seek the humility of Christ in our relationships with others.

QUESTIONS FOR REFLECTION

1. In Ezekiel 18, the people thought God was being unfair. How is God both fair and unfair (in a sense) in his ways with us?

2. In Psalm 25, the psalmist asks God not to remember the sins of his youth. What word best describes how God does not treat us as we deserve? How are we often unfair in our ways toward others?

3. What does it look like to imitate the life of Jesus? Why is the name of Jesus so powerful? Read Philippians 2:12–13. How are we to work out our salvation? What resources do we have at our disposal to will and to work according to God's good pleasure?

4. In Matthew 21, the spiritual leaders question Jesus' authority. Have you settled the question of Jesus' authority in your own life? If asked if you were an "insider" or an "outsider," how would you respond? What would be the basis of your answer?

PRAYER OF RESPONSE
Based on Matthew 21:23–32; Philippians 2:3–8

Lord Jesus,
help us never to question your authority,
but humbly submit to your sovereign care over our lives.
By your grace, may we do nothing from selfish ambition or conceit,
but, in humility, regard others as better than ourselves.
May we not look to our own interests, but to the interests of others.
Give us your mind, your heart, and your desires.
In the name of Jesus we pray. Amen.

Proper 22

Sunday between October 2 and October 8 inclusive

LECTIONARY READINGS

Isaiah 5:1–7

Psalm 80:7–15

Philippians 3:4b–14

Matthew 21:33–46

DEVOTION

In the readings for this Sunday, Jesus tells a parable about a vineyard. The details of his parable have echoes from Isaiah 5:1–7, the first reading. In this passage, Isaiah sings a sad love song between God and Israel, using a vineyard as the key image in the prophetic verse. In the second reading from Philippians 3, the apostle Paul demonstrates how insignificant his credentials are in seeking to justify himself before the Lord. The one thing that is needed is faith in Christ. Thus, living fruitful lives for Christ is a common theme in the readings for this week.

In the first reading from Isaiah 5, the prophet sings about the Lord's vineyard. Isaiah proclaims,

> I will sing for my beloved
> my love song concerning his vineyard:
> My beloved had a vineyard
> on a very fertile hill.
> He dug it and cleared it of stones
> and planted it with choice vines;

> he built a watchtower in the midst of it
> and hewed out a wine vat in it;
> he expected it to yield grapes,
> but it yielded rotten grapes. (Isa 5:1–2)

The prophet's song is about the relationship between God and the people of Israel. He tells of how the Lord had high aspirations for his vineyard, his people, but the vineyard did not yield the fruit the Lord expected. The people of Israel were "rotten grapes," a rebellious people who did not follow the ways of the Lord. Though the Lord carefully and lovingly tended to his vineyard (Israel), his people went their own way. The Lord had to bring judgment upon his people for instead of justice he found "bloodshed" and instead of righteousness he "heard a cry" (Isa 5:7).

The Lord also carefully and lovingly tends to us, but we, like the Israelites, go our own way and do not live justly and righteously. God has to refine us and sanctify us like he did the Israelites. Through the love of Christ and the power of the Spirit, we are drawn back again and again to our beloved. The Spirit is sanctifying us so that our lives bear fruit (Gal 5:22–26).

Psalm 80, the psalm of response, also uses agricultural language as a metaphor for our relationship with the Lord. The psalmist sings,

> You brought a vine out of Egypt;
> you drove out the nations and planted it.
> You cleared the ground for it;
> it took deep root and filled the land.
>
> Turn again, O God of hosts;
> look down from heaven and see;
> have regard for this vine,
> the stock that your right hand planted. (Ps 80:8–9, 14–15)

Similar to Isaiah, the psalmist refers to Israel as a vine that the Lord planted. The imagery is the same, evoking love, care, concern, intimacy, and attention. God prepared the land for Israel to inhabit, but the psalmist laments the trials and hardship that his people are facing.

God cares for his people today. He watches over his own, though, at times, God may feel distant from us. In the midst of our own trials, we may call out for God to turn toward us again. Like the Israelites, we need

God to revive us and restore us. This psalm should also remind us to look to the "true vine" in whom we are to abide (John 15:1–11).

In the second reading from Philippians 3, the apostle Paul list his credentials. He writes,

> If anyone else has reason to be confident in the flesh, I have more: circumcised on the eighth day, a member of the people of Israel, of the tribe of Benjamin, a Hebrew born of Hebrews; as to the law, a Pharisee; as to zeal, a persecutor of the church; as to righteousness under the law, blameless. (Phil 3:4–6)

Though Paul has an impressive list of religious qualifications, he counts it all as "rubbish" compared to knowing Christ (Phil 3:8). Paul no longer seeks a righteousness of his own that comes from the law "but one that comes through faith in Christ, the righteousness from God based on faith" (Phil 3:9). Knowing Christ and realizing what he had done put everything in perspective for Paul. After he encountered the ascended Jesus on the road to Damascus, he was never the same. The zeal he had for persecuting Christians and keeping the law was redirected to knowing and serving Christ. He writes, "I press on toward the goal, toward the prize of the heavenly call of God in Christ Jesus" (Phil 3:14).

Pursuing the heavenly call is our goal as well. Like Paul, knowing Jesus puts everything in perspective for us. Rather than measuring our lives by our external achievements, we find an inner peace in knowing that we can stop all of our strivings. We do not have to have the best job, the perfect family, the most money, or the highest reputation. We can rest in knowing that, in Christ, we already have all that we truly need.

Knowing Christ and the power of his resurrection sustains us through the good times and the hard times. Knowing Christ and the power of his resurrection makes our external goals seem trivial in the scope of eternity.

In the Gospel reading from Matthew 21, Jesus shares a parable about a landowner and his vineyard. He teaches,

> Listen to another parable. There was a landowner who planted a vineyard, put a fence around it, dug a wine press in it, and built a watchtower. (Matt 21:33)

Immediately, we should hear echoes of Isaiah 5 (the first reading). In the parable, the landowner put the vineyard under the care of evil tenants who beat or killed the servants sent to collect the fruit of the vineyard. Ultimately, the landowner sent his son, and the tenants even killed him. Thus, the landowner returned and had the evil tenants put to death and hired tenants who would give him fruit at harvest time.

Jesus concludes by saying, "Therefore I tell you, the kingdom of God will be taken away from you and given to a people that produces its fruits" (Matt 21:43). Matthew gives us the detail that the religious leaders realized that Jesus was indicting them (Matt 21:45).

The chief priests and Pharisees were like Paul before he encountered Jesus. They were all about external achievement, but their lives bore no real fruit. Though they were given authority over God's house, they ultimately killed his Son.

God desires for us to bear fruit for his kingdom (Matt 21:43). Unlike the religious leaders, we do not focus on externals but seek an intimate relationship with Christ. We seek to abide in the vine. Faithful followers are not the prettiest, the wealthiest, or the highest achievers by the world's standards. Faithful followers are those who are concerned about God's kingdom; who seek to know him; and who love others.

During this season after Pentecost, may we seek to bear kingdom fruit. May we stop striving to live by external achievements and place our faith and hope in things of an eternal nature.

QUESTIONS FOR REFLECTION

1. What is significant about the vineyard imagery of Isaiah 5:1–7 as it relates to God and his relationship with Israel? How does this imagery apply to us today as the church and as believers?

2. The psalmist uses the imagery of a vine in Psalm 80. As Christians today, what is our relationship to this vine? See Romans 11:17–24. Where else do we read about the vine?

3. Why does Paul view all of his past accomplishments as "rubbish" (Phil 3:8)? What is the foundation of our faith? Why did Paul so desperately want to "know Christ and the power of the resurrection" (Phil 3:10)? What difference does this make in our lives? What was the goal towards which Paul was pressing? Is that your goal? Explain.

4. What is the nature of Jesus' parable in Matthew 21? How does it connect to Isa 5? How did this parable affect the chief priests and Pharisees? How does this parable speak into your relationship with the Lord today?

PRAYER OF RESPONSE
Based on Matthew 21:33–46; Philippians 3:8

Lord Jesus,
we are like a vineyard which you have planted;
help us, by your grace, to produce kingdom fruit
through lives wholly devoted to you.
May we regard everything as loss compared
to the surpassing value of knowing you as our Lord.
You are the cornerstone, our solid foundation.
Use us for your purposes.
In the name of Jesus we pray. Amen.

Proper 23

Sunday between October 9 and October 15 inclusive

LECTIONARY READINGS

Isaiah 25:1–9

Psalm 23

Philippians 4:1–9

Matthew 22:1–14

DEVOTION

In the readings for this week, Jesus tells a parable of a banquet. It is a picture of the wedding feast that God will share with his people. The first reading from Isaiah 25 also uses the imagery of a rich feast, a prophetic vision of the messianic banquet in the new heaven and new earth. The apostle Paul encourages the Philippians to rejoice in the Lord, the God of peace. Thus, living in light of our future hope is a common thread in the readings for this Sunday.

In the first reading from Isaiah 25, the prophet writes of a banquet feast between the Lord and his people. The poetry of this prophetic verse paints a vivid picture of intimacy, redemption, and hospitality. Isaiah declares,

> On this mountain the Lord of hosts will make for all peoples
> a feast of rich food, a feast of well-aged wines,
> of rich food filled with marrow, of well-aged wines strained clear.
> And he will destroy on this mountain
> the shroud that is cast over all peoples,

> the covering that is spread over all nations;
> he will swallow up death forever. (Isa 25:6–8)

The banquet imagery would have encouraged God's people ages ago with the hope of future victory and restoration. This prophetic imagery should fill us with hope still today. As we await the wedding feast of the Lamb (Rev 19:6–9), we know that our lives will have a beautiful resolution one day. While our lives on earth are full of injustice, death, and trials of many kinds, our future is secure. God will dwell with his people and death will be swallowed up forever.

Psalm 23 is a fitting psalm of response. Here, the psalmist also speaks of a banquet, a table which the Lord will prepare. The psalmist sings,

> You prepare a table before me
> in the presence of my enemies;
> you anoint my head with oil;
> my cup overflows.
> Surely goodness and mercy shall follow me
> all the days of my life,
> and I shall dwell in the house of the Lord
> my whole life long. (Ps 23:5–6)

The imagery of a meal shared between God and his people is prevalent throughout the Bible. From the Old Testament to the New Testament, food and table fellowship are common themes for the covenant people of God. Psalm 23 provides an example in the Writings of the Old Testament. King David is encouraged by the hospitality and protection of God who prepares a table in the very midst of his enemies.

There is no need to fear when the Lord is with you, protecting you and providing for you in the presence of your enemies. The whole psalm is one of peace and protection, a song of how our Good Shepherd blesses and keeps us.

In the second reading from Philippians 4, the apostle Paul encourages the church to a live a life of holiness, prayer, and peace. After highlighting two women, Euodia and Syntyche, who labored in kingdom ministry with Paul, he exhorts the Philippians to be about peace and prayer. He writes,

> Rejoice in the Lord always; again I will say, Rejoice. Let your gentleness be known to everyone. The Lord is near. Do not be anxious about anything, but in everything by prayer and

supplication with thanksgiving let your requests be made known to God. And the peace of God, which surpasses all understanding, will guard your hearts and your minds in Christ Jesus. (Phil 4:4–7)

Paul recognizes the need for rejoicing in the Lord, no matter the circumstances. The same God who spreads a table for us is with us in our trials and our anxieties. Paul is urging the church in Philippi to find their peace through open, intimate, and regular prayer before the Lord.

It is interesting that Paul uses the word "guard" in this context. The practice of prayer helps guard us and keep us from anxiety, fear, doubt, worry, and a host of other emotions. Our hearts and minds will tend to go to worst-case scenarios, and we can soon find ourselves spiraling into fear and anxiety. The God of peace, however, is able to guard and protect us from false narratives and irrational thoughts.

Paul continues to exhort these believers toward a renewed thought life. He writes,

> Finally, brothers and sisters, whatever is true, whatever is honorable, whatever is just, whatever is pure, whatever is pleasing, whatever is commendable, if there is any excellence and if there is anything worthy of praise, think about these things. (Phil 4:8)

In a culture of media bombardment, Paul exhorts us to guard our hearts and minds by only dwelling on things that edify us. We are called to dwell on that which is pure, pleasing, commendable, excellent, and praiseworthy. Paul's list can help us to narrow down what our eyes and ears take in on any given day. Such living will keep our minds healthy and our souls light. Our souls will not be burdened by thoughts and images that are ungodly and unhealthy for us.

In the Gospel reading from Matthew 22, Jesus shares a parable about a wedding banquet given by a king for his son. In the parable, the king becomes enraged as the guests who were originally invited found excuses for not attending. The king replied, "The wedding is ready, but those invited were not worthy. Go therefore into the main streets, and invite everyone you find to the wedding banquet" (Matt 22:8–9). Jesus then shares how the people of the city, "both good and bad," were invited to the wedding banquet, "so the wedding hall was filled with guests" (Matt 22:10).

The parable demonstrates God's love for all people. People from every tribe and tongue, with various backgrounds and stories, and from all walks of life will be guests at the wedding supper of the Lamb. The parable reveals the compassion of God but also the reality of divine election (Matt 22:11–14).

During this season after Pentecost, near the end of the Christian year, we read kingdom narratives concerning the end of the age. We are filled with hope as we reflect on the hospitality of God, the one who will host a banquet for his people. The marriage supper of the Lamb will be a celebration like we have never known. We find peace for today as we set our hope on such eternal realities.

QUESTIONS FOR REFLECTION

1. Do you think the people of God would have been encouraged by the banquet imagery of Isaiah 25? Explain. How does the imagery characterize our relationship with the Lord?

2. The psalmist describes a table that the Lord prepares in the midst of his enemies. What is the meaning of this imagery? How does the Lord protect us and keep us today?

3. What does the apostle Paul encourage the Philippians to do to guard their hearts and minds? Does prayer help relieve your anxieties and fears? Explain. How do the shows, books, movies, and media sources we watch affect our minds and our souls? What should we dwell upon, according to Paul? Do you heed Paul's counsel in your own life?

4. What is the takeaway truth of Jesus' parable in Matthew 22:1–14? Why are meals so significant in the Bible? How do we anticipate the heavenly banquet here on earth? Does this eternal reality fill you with hope for today? Explain.

PRAYER OF RESPONSE
Based on Matthew 22:1–10; Psalm 23:2–4; Philippians 4:8–9

Sovereign God,
you are the Good Shepherd
who leads us beside still waters,
inviting us to feast on your gospel promises.
Yet, too often we make light of them
and live our lives the way we desire.
May we see the mercy you grant us:
when we are weary, you restore our souls;
when we walk through difficult trials,
you carry us and make your presence known to us.
Oh Lord, forgive us and fill us with your Holy Spirit.
Seeking your peace, may we dwell on what is true, honorable,
just, pure, pleasing, commendable, excellent, and praiseworthy.
In the name of Jesus we pray. Amen.

Proper 24

Sunday between October 16 and October 22 inclusive

LECTIONARY READINGS

Isaiah 45:1–7

Psalm 96:1–13

1 Thessalonians 1:1–10

Matthew 22:15–22

DEVOTION

In the readings for this Sunday, Jesus teaches us how to live obediently as children of God and citizens of the world. The prophet Isaiah reveals how God works through the kings and leaders of the world. And the apostle Paul expresses his thanks to the Thessalonians for demonstrating their love of Christ, while living under Roman authority. Thus, God's sovereignty and our responsibility as citizens in this world are common themes in the readings for this Sunday.

In the first reading from Isaiah 45, the prophet declares God's sovereignty over the rulers of this world. Isaiah proclaims,

> Thus says the Lord to his anointed, to Cyrus,
> whose right hand I have grasped
> to subdue nations before him
> and strip kings of their robes,
> to open doors before him—
> and the gates shall not be closed. (Isa 45:1)

Isaiah is prophesying about the Lord's use of a pagan king, Cyrus, in the redemption and restoration of his people. First of all, if we believe that Isaiah lived around two hundred years before the events he is describing took place, then we have to acknowledge the sovereignty of God and the inspiration of the Holy Spirit at work in the lives of the prophets. Isaiah ministered from around 740 to 700 BC. Cyrus defeated the Babylonians and issued an edict for the Israelites to return to Jerusalem in 538 BC.

With this background, we also acknowledge God's sovereignty in using pagan kings and rulers for the good of his people. Isaiah refers to King Cyrus, an enemy king, as the Lord's "anointed." Such a declaration reveals God's ability to sovereignly work through civil authorities and global circumstances to accomplish his divine work of redemption and restoration.

Such an understanding can bring us comfort as we witness ungodly rulers and oppressive circumstances around the world today. We are exhorted to pray and to intercede for all rulers and authorities (1 Tim 2:1–4), and as we do, we acknowledge the ways in which God is able to use those in positions of power to protect and restore his people and to bring peace around the world.

Psalm 96 is the psalm of response. Here, the psalmist sings of the Lord's rule and reign over all the earth and among all the nations. He declares,

> Say among the nations, "The Lord is king!
> The world is firmly established; it shall never be moved.
> He will judge the peoples with equity." (Ps 96:10)

The psalmist declares that there is only one king among all the nations. Though Cyrus was the king of Persia, he was ultimately governed by the Lord Almighty. God chose Cyrus and used him for the good of his own people. We acknowledge the people who are in power in our own lives: mayors, governors, and the president. However, our ultimate allegiance is to our triune God: Father, Son, and Holy Spirit. The Lord, alone, is the recipient of the glory and praise of Psalm 96. The Lord, alone, is the recipient of our worship today.

In the second reading, the apostle Paul expresses his love for and thanks to the Thessalonians. This is likely the earliest letter written by Paul. In it, he praises them for their work of faith, their labor of love, and their steadfastness of hope (1 Thess 1:3). He writes,

> For the word of the Lord has sounded forth from you not only in Macedonia and Achaia but in every place your faith in God has become known, so that we have no need to speak about it. For they report about us what kind of welcome we had among you and how you turned to God from idols to serve a living and true God and to wait for his Son from heaven, whom he raised from the dead—Jesus, who rescues us from the coming wrath. (1 Thess 1:8–10)

Paul reveals the witness that the Thessalonians had to the regions around them. He also expresses how they turned from pagan idols to worship the "living and true God." The Thessalonians are an example of a church that lived faithfully unto the Lord. Though loyalty to Roman authorities was a high value, the believers in Thessalonica stood firm in their faith to Jesus Christ. They were able to live as citizens of Thessalonica who expressed their ultimate allegiance to Jesus Christ.

Our hope is that our own lives and the witness of our own church would have the same kind of reputation. We are called to give our allegiance to the one, true God and to live as examples to the people, neighborhoods, and cities around us of the love and power of Christ.

In the Gospel reading from Matthew 22, Jesus responds to an attempt to stir up controversy. The Pharisees, along with the Herodians, asked Jesus,

> Teacher, we know that you are sincere, and teach the way of God in accordance with truth, and show deference to no one, for you do not regard people with partiality. Tell us, then, what you think. Is it lawful to pay taxes to Caesar or not? (Matt 22:16–17)

Jesus, knowing the evil motivation of their hearts, asks for a coin. He then asks whose head and title is on the coin. He then states, "Give therefore to Caesar the things that are Caesar's and to God the things that are God's" (Matt 22:21). Matthew tells us that the people were "amazed" at his response.

Jesus expects the same of his followers today. As Christians, we are to live as responsible citizens of our country. We pay our taxes; we vote; and we obey the laws of the land. At the same time, we worship one Lord Jesus Christ who is able to work through global rulers and authorities. We are grateful that in the United States, we are able to worship without persecution. We pray for believers in other lands who are suffering for their faith and beliefs.

May we be known as people who exemplify integrity as upright neighbors and citizens and as those who love the Lord Jesus. May our lives reflect the same faith, hope, and love as the Thessalonians who were such a powerful witness to the people around them. During this season after Pentecost, may our lives as individuals and as a church reflect the love of Christ to those around us.

QUESTIONS FOR REFLECTION

1. What lessons do we learn from Isaiah 45:1–7? How did God inspire the prophets in their writings and declarations? How is God sovereign over the rulers of the earth? How does this bring comfort to you as you look at our current, global circumstances?

2. How does the psalmist express the Lord's global rule and reign? In your own prayers and expressions of worship, do you articulate the Lord's global authority or do you tend to focus narrowly on your own life and context? Explain. How can you begin to pray and worship the Lord more broadly?

3. How would you describe the faith of the Thessalonians? What characteristics did Paul specifically point out in his letter? How can we, as individuals and as a church, be inspired by their example?

4. What was the motivation of the Pharisees in asking Jesus about paying taxes? How did Jesus respond? What is the takeaway for us as Christians today? How do we live as responsible citizens and as faithful followers of Christ in the world today?

PRAYER OF RESPONSE

Based on Isaiah 45:2; Psalm 96:7–8; 1 Thessalonians 1:3, 8

Lord Jesus,
we know that you go before us and clear our path.
May we ascribe to you all the glory that is due your name.
Like the Thessalonians, may the world see
our work of faith, our labor of love,
and our steadfastness of hope in the Lord Jesus Christ.
May the good news of the gospel
sound forth from us in our city,
and in every place that our faith in God has become known.
In the name of Jesus we pray. Amen.

Proper 25

Sunday between October 23 and October 29 inclusive

LECTIONARY READINGS

Leviticus 19:1–2, 15–18

Psalm 1

1 Thessalonians 2:1–8

Matthew 22:34–46

DEVOTION

In the readings for this Sunday, Jesus is asked about the greatest commandment. The second reading from Leviticus 19 describes love of neighbor as part of the holiness of the community. In the second reading from 1 Thessalonians 2, the apostle Paul describes the way he, Silas, and Timothy evangelized and nurtured those in Thessalonica. Thus, love of God and neighbor is a common theme in the readings for this Sunday.

In the first reading from Leviticus 19, Moses describes how holiness manifests itself within the community of God's people. God spoke to Moses, saying, "Speak to all the congregation of the Israelites and say to them: You shall be holy, for I the Lord your God am holy" (Lev 19:2). Part of Moses' teaching to the people on holiness includes love of neighbor. He declares,

> You shall not hate in your heart anyone of your kin; you shall reprove your neighbor, or you will incur guilt yourself. You shall not take vengeance or bear a grudge against any of your people, but you shall love your neighbor as yourself: I am the Lord. (Lev 19:17–18)

As it was for the people long ago, so it is for us today. Growing in righteousness and holiness includes loving our neighbors as ourselves. Moses exhorted the people of God not to hold grudges or seek revenge, but to love those around them. We are called to do the same. This exhortation can be a hard one when we think of the many people who have wronged us or hurt us in some way. Loving our neighbors, our family, and those who have sinned against us is a work of the Holy Spirit within us. Such love comes from the grace and mercy of God working in our hearts, transforming us and making us more like Christ.

In Psalm 1, the psalm of response, we are given a vivid image of what it looks like to be in a healthy, vibrant relationship with the Lord. The psalmist describes those who seek after the Lord. He sings,

> They are like trees
> planted by streams of water,
> which yield their fruit in its season,
> and their leaves do not wither.
> In all that they do, they prosper. (Ps 1:3)

The imagery of Psalm 1 reveals the sustenance, stability, and thriving nature of one who walks intimately with the Lord. It does not mean that this person is without sin, struggles, or problems in life, but this person bears fruit and enjoys a healthy and close relationship with God. The imagery is much like the imagery Jesus uses in the upper room discourse. Jesus tells the disciples of the close relationship they are to have with him. He declares,

> Abide in me as I abide in you. Just as the branch cannot bear fruit by itself unless it abides in the vine, neither can you unless you abide in me. I am the vine; you are the branches. Those who abide in me and I in them bear much fruit, because apart from me you can do nothing. (John 15:4–5)

Jesus and the psalmist both describe a closeness and a dependency on God. Like a tree needs water and like a branch needs connection to the vine, so we need regular nourishment and sustenance that can only come from the Lord. Growing in our love for God and for our neighbors can only come from abiding in Christ.

In the second reading from 1 Thessalonians 2, the apostle Paul describes the way in which he, Silas, and Timothy came proclaiming the good news of the gospel to the Thessalonians. He describes how they came, not with arrogance or with a need for man's approval but out of a calling from God (1 Thess 2:1–6). Paul describes how he and Silas and Timothy nurtured and cared for these new believers. He writes,

> But we were gentle among you, like a nurse tenderly caring for her own children. So deeply do we care for you that we are determined to share with you not only the gospel of God but also our own selves, because you have become very dear to us. (1 Thess 2:7–8)

This imagery is beautiful and profound. Paul and his companions loved on the Thessalonians "like a nurse tenderly caring for her own children." This language reveals the depth of relationship that was enjoyed between the evangelists and these young believers. They gave their whole lives for the sake of the Thessalonians. God calls us to love and share the gospel with those around us in this same manner. We are called to love and serve our neighbors and offer ourselves to them. We are not called to give so that we can receive something in return. We are to love as we have been loved by God.

In the Gospel reading from Matthew 22, Jesus is asked about what is the greatest commandment. He answers by saying,

> "You shall love the Lord your God with all your heart and with all your soul and with all your mind." This is the greatest and first commandment. And a second is like it: "You shall love your neighbor as yourself." On these two commandments hang all the Law and the Prophets. (Matt 22:37–40)

Jesus affirms the holiness code of Leviticus 19 and sums up the whole law with two commandments: love God and love your neighbor as yourself. The religious leaders were trying to test Jesus and catch him off guard so that they could bring accusations against him. Jesus is able to silence the Pharisees with his response.

He asks them, "What do you think of the Messiah? Whose son is he?" (Matt 22:42). They give Jesus an answer, which he refutes by quoting Psalm 110:1. Matthew tells us that from that point on, no one dared to ask Jesus any more questions (Matt 22:46).

Our calling as followers of Christ is clear. We are to love God, and we are to love our neighbors as ourselves. Jesus himself says that all the Law and Prophets hang on these two commandments (Matt 22:40). It is simple but hard to obey and live out in our everyday lives. We need the grace of God and the power of the Holy Spirit to love in this way.

Moreover, we learn that we cannot outsmart Jesus. We cannot come to him with our own expectations and expect him to meet our every desire. Though we may not be trying to test Jesus like the religious leaders, we may still have preconceived notions of how he should work in our lives. We have to repent of this attitude and submit to Jesus' authority over our lives. Ultimately, he knows what is best for us and, as a good shepherd, he will lead us in the way of restoration.

In this season after Pentecost, as we learn how to walk in the Spirit, may we grow in our love for God and for our neighbor. May we seek to abide with Jesus and find the nourishment we need through regular time with him in word, prayer, song, sacrament, and community. May we be like a tree planted by streams of living water, flourishing as we find sustenance and grace from Jesus the true vine.

QUESTIONS FOR REFLECTION

1. Why was love of neighbor so important to the call to be holy in the Old Testament? How does that law still apply today?

2. Describe the imagery the psalmist uses in Psalm 1. What phrases stick out to you and why? What does it mean to be like a tree planted by streams of water?

3. Describe the relationship that Paul and his companions had with the Thessalonians. How should that relationship inform the way we engage our neighbors and new believers today?

4. How does Jesus summarize all of the Law and Prophets? Why does Jesus often respond to questions with another question? How did Jesus silence his antagonists? How does Jesus put an end to our questions at times?

PRAYER OF RESPONSE
Based on Psalm 1:2–3; Matthew 22:37–39

Gracious God,
help us to be like trees
planted by streams of living water,
bearing fruit for your kingdom.
May we take delight in all of your commands,
loving you with all of our heart,
all of our soul, and all of our mind;
and loving our neighbors as ourselves.
In the name of Jesus we pray. Amen.

Proper 26

Sunday between October 30 and November 5 inclusive

LECTIONARY READINGS

Micah 3:5–12

Psalm 43

1 Thessalonians 2:9–13

Matthew 23:1–12

DEVOTION

In the readings for this Sunday, Jesus calls out the hypocrisy of the religious leaders. Micah speaks against false prophets and corrupt leaders. Paul reminds the Thessalonians of the integrity of his ministry and how he and his companions treated them with fatherly care. Thus, the theme of leadership, both good and bad, is highlighted in the readings for this Sunday.

In the first reading from Micah 3, the prophet points out the corruption of the religious leaders and the false prophets of his day and how they were leading the people astray. Speaking for God, Micah declares,

> Hear this, you rulers of the house of Jacob
> and chiefs of the house of Israel,
> who abhor justice
> and pervert all equity,
> who build Zion with blood
> and Jerusalem with wrong!
> Its rulers give judgment for a bribe;

> its priests teach for a price;
> its prophets give oracles for money;
> yet they lean upon the Lord and say,
> "Surely the Lord is with us!
> No harm shall come upon us." (Mic 3:9–11)

Writing between 733 and 701 BC, Micah declared the word of the Lord to both Israel (northern kingdom) and to Judah (southern kingdom). He called out the corruption among the rulers, the priests, and the prophets and declared that God would judge them for their toxic leadership over the people. The Lord kept his word as Jerusalem was destroyed nearly two centuries after Micah's prophecy. God cannot overlook sin, particularly the sin of those who are called to shepherd and lead God's people.

The same is true today. Unfortunately, there are wolves in sheep's clothing within the church (Matt 7:15). Jesus himself calls us to be aware and to discern leaders by their fruit. For those who are leaders in the church, we should take these words to heart. Leadership in the church comes in many varieties. Whatever your leadership capacity, lead and serve as gentle, caring shepherds of the flock. Do not lead for money or prestige. Jesus calls us to imitate him as a servant leader (John 13:14–15). As we lead, we are to take up the basin and the towel and wash the feet of those whom we are serving, whether through music, Bible teaching, pastoral care, or deeds of mercy.

Psalm 43 is the psalm of response. The psalmist seeks vindication from corrupt leaders, saying,

> Vindicate me, O God, and defend my cause
> against an ungodly people;
> from those who are deceitful and unjust, deliver me! (Ps 43:1)

Psalm 43 offers us the language and expression of one who has been the victim of spiritual abuse. The psalmist has suffered at the hands of people who are ungodly and unjust. He realizes that God is his place of refuge, yet, he also questions why God had him suffer at the hands of his enemies.

We may be confused about our own lives today. We may question God regarding our grief and loss, which may be the result of corrupt and abusive spiritual leadership. In those moments, we must remember that God is for us. We do not have to doubt his love and his care over our lives.

Though we may not always receive the answers we would like to have regarding our circumstances, God will never leave us or forsake us (Heb 13:5) and nothing can separate us from the love of God in Christ (Rom 8:38–39). People will always let us down, but God is always faithful.

In the second reading from 1 Thessalonians 2, Paul reminds these believers of the way he and his companions came and ministered among them. He writes,

> You remember our labor and toil, brothers and sisters; we worked night and day so that we might not burden any of you while we proclaimed to you the gospel of God. You are witnesses, and God also, how pure, upright, and blameless our conduct was toward you believers. As you know, we dealt with each one of you like a father with his children, urging and encouraging you and pleading that you lead a life worthy of God, who calls you into his own kingdom and glory. (1 Thess 2:9–12)

In contrast to the corrupt leaders mentioned in Micah 3 and Psalm 43, the Thessalonians are reminded of the fatherly care that was demonstrated to them through Paul, Silas, and Timothy. Paul expresses their hard work and their integrity among the Thessalonians. They were never a burden and came with pure motives as they shared the gospel.

Paul and his companions serve as examples for us today. Certainly, church leaders have much to learn from this portion of Paul's letter regarding healthy conduct among the flock. As leaders today, we should not be a burden to the people whom we serve, nor should we live in a hypocritical manner, teaching one thing, but living another way. All believers are called to live honestly before God and others. As Paul states, we are all called to lead lives "worthy of God" (1 Thess 2:12).

In the Gospel reading from Matthew 23, Jesus highlights the hypocrisy of the religious leaders. Regarding the scribes and the Pharisees, Jesus declares,

> They tie up heavy burdens, hard to bear, and lay them on the shoulders of others, but they themselves are unwilling to lift a finger to move them. They do all their deeds to be seen by others, for they make their phylacteries broad and their fringes long. They love to have the place of honor at banquets and the best seats in the synagogues and to be greeted with respect in the marketplaces and to have people call them rabbi. (Matt 23:4–7)

If we are honest, we can probably find ourselves guilty of the same actions as the religious leaders, though translated into twenty-first-century terms. Who does not like to delegate heavy responsibilities to others, to have our piety and faith seen and noticed by others, and to be given distinguished titles? We can easily become lazy and prideful in our ways through these kinds of actions and desires. Jesus exhorts us to remain humble in our leadership capacities. The economy of the kingdom is so different from the values of this world.

Jesus sums up true, godly leadership in this way, "The greatest among you will be your servant. All who exalt themselves will be humbled, and all who humble themselves will be exalted" (Matt 23:11–12). This is the example, the lifestyle we are to imitate. It sounds easy, but it can be very difficult to live out, hour by hour, day by day, year after year.

During this season after Pentecost, may we learn to lead others as Jesus did, washing the feet of those we serve with the grace and love of the gospel. May we not seek fame and fortune, but live humble lives, thinking of others rather than ourselves. For those who have suffered from spiritual abuse, may God be your refuge. May you know his love and kindness, and may he restore you as your Good Shepherd.

QUESTIONS FOR REFLECTION

1. What did Micah prophesy against in his day? Who were the main recipients of his oracles of judgment? Micah also spoke oracles of comfort. How does God deal with us as leaders and as believers today?

2. Where did the psalmist find refuge from spiritual abuse? What sorts of things did he have to endure? Have you suffered from injustice in your own life? Explain. How is God your refuge?

3. How does the reading from 1 Thessalonians 2 compare and contrast with the readings from Micah 3 and Psalm 43? What is a common theme? How can Paul and his companions be an example for us today? What does it mean to lead a life "worthy of God" (1 Thess 2:12)?

4. What one word describes the religious leaders in Matthew 23? How can we demonstrate this in our own lives today? How does Jesus summarize gospel leadership? How can we imitate this in our own lives?

PRAYER OF RESPONSE
Based on Matthew 23:1–12

Triune God,
help us to remember that all
who exalt themselves will be humbled,
and all who humble themselves will be exalted.
May we not be like those who want
all of their deeds to be seen by others;
who seek to have the place of honor
at banquets and gatherings;
who tie up heavy burdens, hard to bear,
and lay them on the shoulders of others.
By your grace, may we practice what we preach,
pursuing justice and mercy, not outward appearances.
Give us the desire to love and care for others
through the power of your Holy Spirit at work within us.
In the name of Jesus we pray. Amen.

Proper 27

Sunday between November 6 and November 12 inclusive

LECTIONARY READINGS

Amos 5:18–24

Psalm 70

1 Thessalonians 4:13–18

Matthew 25:1–13

DEVOTION

In the readings for this Sunday, as we approach the end of the Christian year, we reflect on the second coming of the Lord. The prophet Amos describes the dread and darkness of this day for those who do not know the Lord. Jesus tells a parable about a wedding banquet and bridesmaids, emphasizing the need to be alert, for no one knows when the Lord will return. The apostle Paul teaches the Thessalonians how the dead and the living will all rise to meet the Lord at his return. Thus, Christ's return is a common theme in the readings for this Sunday.

In the first reading from Amos 5, we read of the dread and darkness associated with the Lord's coming. It is a day of both judgment and mercy. For those who do not know the Lord, it will be a dark day of eternal condemnation; for those who do know the Lord, it will be a day of rejoicing and the final restoration of all things. Amos highlights the darkness for those in the northern kingdom because their lives did not reflect lives of true faith and worship to God. Their worship had become empty displays of ritual and sacrifice, and their lives demonstrated no concern for love and mercy and justice. Amos proclaims,

> Is not the day of the Lord darkness, not light,
> and gloom with no brightness in it?
>
> I hate, I despise your festivals,
> and I take no delight in your solemn assemblies.
>
> Take away from me the noise of your songs;
> I will not listen to the melody of your harps.
> But let justice roll down like water
> and righteousness like an ever-flowing stream. (Amos 5:20–21, 23–24)

For the Israelites in the northern kingdom, idolatrous living and a lack of concern for the poor and those in need would bring on God's judgment and exile to a foreign nation. The Assyrian invasion and exile was a short-term consequence of their evil ways. Eternal judgment on the day of the Lord, however, is even more sobering.

In our own day, we must be careful not to drift into idolatry and apathy towards justice and mercy. We can quickly turn to created things rather than the Creator to bring us pleasure, and we can easily turn inward and only be concerned about our own comfort and well-being. Staying in close relationship with other believers, attending corporate worship regularly, having regular spiritual practices that are fervent and alive, and demonstrating Christ's love to others through deeds of mercy are all important in cultivating a real and vibrant relationship with the Lord. These practices can help keep us from drifting from the Lord and turning to sin and idolatry.

Psalm 70 is the psalm of response. In this psalm, we hear the cry of one who seeks a real relationship with the Lord, not one that is characterized by empty rituals and self-absorption. The psalmist sings,

> Let all who seek you
> rejoice and be glad in you.
> Let those who love your salvation
> say evermore, "God is great!"
> But I am poor and needy;
> hasten to me, O God!
> You are my help and my deliverer;
> O Lord, do not delay! (Ps 70:4–5)

The psalmist acknowledges those who truly seek after the Lord. In other psalms, the language is of those who "thirst" for the Lord (Ps 63:1; 42:2). These are men and women who do not show up on Sunday to go through the motions of worship, but people who are grateful for the Lord's salvation in their life; they are thankful for the ways God sustains and sanctifies them.

In addition, the psalmist asks the Lord not to delay in delivering him from his troubles. This plea can also be seen as a prayer for us today, "Come, Lord Jesus" (Rev 22:20). We pray for the Lord to come; we long for his return; we long for him to deliver us from our earthly troubles and to restore all things to their intended glory.

In the second reading from 1 Thessalonians 4, the apostle Paul clarifies some end-times theology for the Thessalonians who were either confused or uninformed about Christ's return. Paul assures them that both the dead and the living will be called to eternal glory with the Lord. He writes,

> For the Lord himself, with a cry of command, with the archangel's call and with the sound of God's trumpet, will descend from heaven, and the dead in Christ will rise first. Then we who are alive, who are left, will be caught up in the clouds together with them to meet the Lord in the air, and so we will be with the Lord forever. Therefore encourage one another with these words. (1 Thess 4:16–18)

At the time of Paul's writing, the early believers thought that Christ could likely return during their lifetime. They were concerned about those who had already died. For us, living twenty centuries after the generation of Paul, we have to be reminded and encouraged that the Lord will return, though the day and hour are unknown. When he does, we will be joined with the countless saints that have gone before us, and we will inhabit the new heaven and the new earth in all of its glory and splendor for eternity.

Sadly, we have lost the anticipation of Paul's generation and have become somewhat numb to eschatological realities. We do not live as though we will one day be citizens of our true home. Paul's letter to these early believers can stir our faith for things beyond just the here and now.

In the Gospel reading from Matthew 25, Jesus shares a parable about a wedding banquet and the ten bridesmaids who were preparing to meet the bridegroom. Five of them were foolish and did not have enough oil for their lamps; five were wise and made sure they had enough oil. The five that were foolish missed the bridegroom's return, while the five who were prepared were able to join him at the wedding banquet. The point of Jesus' parable is to be awake and alert for we do not know the hour of Christ's return. Jesus himself declares, "Keep awake, therefore, for you know neither the day nor the hour" (Matt 25:13).

We must listen to Jesus' warning in this parable and discern our own relationship with the Lord. Are we living apathetically towards God, yet expecting to enter his kingdom? This does not mean we live perfectly, but we are called to live in an honest relationship with the Lord. We are called to seek his kingdom and live as those being redeemed and restored by the power of the Holy Spirit within us. Those who enter the kingdom are those who know the King. We seek to live now as we will when he returns, abiding in his presence.

As we draw near to the end of the Christian year, may we reflect on what is most important in our lives. May we consider our relationship with the Lord. Do we truly know the King, or do we go through the motions of worship and fake our way through the Christian life? Now is the time to settle our relationship with the Lord, for we do not know the day or the hour of his return. May we be ready for the day of the Lord.

QUESTIONS FOR REFLECTION

1. What is sobering about the prophet Amos's description of the day of the Lord? For whom will Christ's return be a day of dread and darkness? For whom will it be a day of entering his eternal presence?

2. In Psalm 70, we find a description of one who is a true worshiper, someone who truly knows the Lord. Describe his relationship with the Lord in your own words. Why does the psalmist say, "Do not delay" (Ps 70:5)? How does this phrase translate in our own lives as Christians?

3. What appears to be the nature of the Thessalonians' confusion? What does Paul have to clarify for them? How does this inform us today as believers in the twenty-first century? The people in Paul's day thought Jesus might return during their lifetime. Do you feel the same way today? Explain. Does your perspective need to change? Explain.

4. Describe the foolish bridesmaids in Jesus' parable. Describe the wise bridesmaids. What was the end result of each? What is the main point of Jesus' parable? How are we to live today when we do not know the day or the hour of Christ's return?

PRAYER OF RESPONSE
Based on Matthew 25:1–13; Amos 5:18–24

Lord Jesus,
may we be ready for your return.
Help us to live in anticipation of the fullness of your kingdom.
In your church and world, let justice roll down like water,
and righteousness like an ever-flowing stream;
and may we be instruments of this kind of love and mercy.
May our expressions of worship not be in vain,
but a reflection of hearts and lives fully devoted to you.
In the name of Jesus we pray. Amen.

Proper 28

Sunday between November 13 and November 19 inclusive

LECTIONARY READINGS

Zephaniah 1:7, 12–18

Psalm 90:1–12

1 Thessalonians 5:1–11

Matthew 25:14–30

DEVOTION

In the readings for this Sunday, Jesus shares the parable of the talents. The prophet Zephaniah offers a sobering depiction of the day of the Lord. The apostle Paul offers an exhortation of how believers are to live in the light of Christ's return. Thus, the nature of Christ's second coming is a common thread in the readings for this Sunday.

In the first reading from Zephaniah 1, the prophet speaks a sobering word concerning the day of the Lord. Speaking for the Lord, Zephaniah declares,

> I will bring such distress upon people
> that they shall walk like the blind;
> because they have sinned against the Lord,
> their blood shall be poured out like dust
> and their flesh like dung.
> Neither their silver nor their gold
> will be able to save them
> on the day of the Lord's wrath. (Zeph 1:17–18)

Zephaniah makes it clear that the Lord will exercise judgment because of the people's sin and rebellion, particularly as it relates to money and wealth. One's money and wealth will be of no value on the day of the Lord's return. The prophet's words should be a strong warning and exhortation to those who have not placed their hope and trust in the Lord. For those who do know Christ, this message should encourage us to share the good news of the gospel to those around us who are lost.

As it was during the time of Zephaniah, people today still put their hope and security in their bank accounts, retirement funds, and possessions. These things are of no use concerning one's salvation. Our money and possessions gain us nothing towards eternal life with God and will be left behind when we die.

Psalm 90 is the psalm of response. The psalmist describes the shortness of our lives on earth in comparison to our eternal life with God. He also speaks of wisdom and the fear of the Lord and how they should guide us in our days on earth. The psalmist sings,

> Who considers the power of your anger?
> Your wrath is as great as the fear that is due you.
> So teach us to count our days
> that we may gain a wise heart. (Ps 90:11–12)

The fear of the Lord should guide our actions and our steps in this life. This does not mean that we are to live afraid of God, but we should maintain a healthy sense of awe, wonder, and reverence towards God, the Creator of all the earth. The day of the Lord, the reality of judgment, and the relatively short span of our lives compared to eternity should awaken us to prioritize our decisions each day in light of heavenly realities.

In the second reading from 1 Thessalonians 5, the apostle Paul instructs these early believers on living in light of Christ's return. He writes,

> So, then, let us not fall asleep as others do, but let us keep awake and be sober, for those who sleep sleep at night, and those who are drunk get drunk at night. But since we belong to the day, let us be sober and put on the breastplate of faith and love and for a helmet the hope of salvation. For God has destined us not for wrath but for obtaining salvation through our Lord Jesus Christ, who died for us, so that whether we are awake or asleep we may live with him. Therefore encourage one another and build up each other, as indeed you are doing. (1 Thess 5:6–11)

Paul exhorts the Thessalonians to "keep awake and be sober" (1 Thess 5:6). He encourages them not to get drunk, but to live ready for spiritual battle. His phrase regarding the "breastplate of faith" and a "helmet" of the hope of salvation foreshadows a more in-depth description of spiritual armor (Eph 6:13–17). The message is clear: we are to live awake and alert, ready for Christ's return and aware of evil and spiritual warfare.

Paul also instructs the believes to build each other up and spur one another on in their spiritual journey (1 Thess 5:11). We should do the same with one another today. We should be intentional about gathering together on Sundays and during the week to edify each other and encourage one another in the context of corporate worship and gospel community.

As we sing together, pray together, open God's word together, and share how God is at work in our lives, we are seeking mutual edification. We are worshiping the Lord, but we are also seeking to edify one another in Christ. This is how we are to live in light of Christ's return. We live awake and alert, sharing the gospel, and edifying our fellow brothers and sisters in Christ.

In the Gospel reading from Matthew 25, Jesus shares the parable of the talents. He describes a person with five talents who made five more, a person with two talents who made two more, and a person with one talent who buried it in the ground. A talent in those days was equal to about twenty years' worth of wages.

The person who buried his talent was basically lazy and regarded the master with unjustified suspicion. When the master asks what he did with his talent, he admits he did nothing out of fear of the master's cruelty had he lost its value. As a result, the master condemns this person for his laziness and misrepresentation and commands that this person's talent be given to the one with ten. He then expresses the main point of the parable: "For to all those who have, more will be given, and they will have an abundance, but from those who have nothing, even what they have will be taken away" (Matt 25:29).

For us, we should hear the exhortation to steward our gifts well and faithfully for the Lord. From Jesus' parable, we should be encouraged to use whatever we have been given in service of God's kingdom. As followers of Christ, we invest our whole lives for the sake of the King and his kingdom. A regular prayer can be "God, maximize my gifts for your kingdom." This is how we are to live in light of the reality of Christ's return.

On the day of the Lord, we desire to hear, "Well done, good and faithful servant" (Matt 25:21, ESV). May we live today seeking that word from the Lord. As we draw near to the end of the Christian year, may the reality of Christ's return encourage us to live wide awake, alert to spiritual warfare, and with a desire to invest our lives and our gifts for the King and his kingdom.

QUESTIONS FOR REFLECTION

1. How does Zephaniah describe the day of the Lord? What was the source of safety and security for the people in Zephaniah's day? See Zephaniah 1:18. Where do we often place our trust and security? How should this passage inform our lives today?

2. How does the psalmist describe the span of our lives relative to God? How does this shed light on our priorities? What does the psalmist ask of the Lord in Psalm 90:12? How does this translate to your life today?

3. In light of the reality of Christ's return, how does the apostle Paul exhort the Thessalonians to live? What contrasts does Paul use to show how we are to live? How does Paul allude to spiritual warfare? What does Paul encourage the Thessalonians to do for one another? How can we build one another up in the Lord today?

4. Briefly explain the parable of the talents. What is Jesus' main point? Do you feel that you are using your gifts for the King and his kingdom? Explain. Do you regularly pray "Maximize my gifts for your kingdom"?

PRAYER OF RESPONSE
Based on Psalm 90:1, 12; Matthew 25:14–30

Faithful God,
you have been our dwelling place in all generations.
Teach us to count our days
that we may gain a wise heart.
Help us to steward the gifts and talents you have given us
for the expansion of your kingdom;
for we know that to all those who have,
more will be given, and they will have an abundance.
As we anticipate the day of your return,
may we live generous and sober lives before you and others.
In the name of Jesus we pray. Amen.

Christ the King

LECTIONARY READINGS

Ezekiel 34:11–16, 20–24

Psalm 95:1–7a

Ephesians 1:15–23

Matthew 25:31–46

DEVOTION

In the readings for Christ the King Sunday, Jesus tells a parable about embodying love to the least. The prophet Ezekiel describes the care and compassion of God our shepherd. The apostle Paul declares the power and authority of the triune God in his prayer to the Ephesians. Thus, the nature of the King and his kingdom is a common theme in the readings for this last Sunday of the Christian year.

In the first reading from Ezekiel 34, the prophet describes the nature of our compassionate God. Speaking for the Lord, he proclaims,

> I myself will be the shepherd of my sheep, and I will make them lie down, says the Lord God. I will seek the lost, and I will bring back the strays, and I will bind up the injured, and I will strengthen the weak. (Ezek 34:15–16)

This passage appears to point to Christ, the Good Shepherd. It tells us much about the way our God cares for us and protects us. This passage can also serve as a description for pastoral leaders in the church. Those charged with shepherding the flock, the people of God, can glean much from this passage. Leaders should not be motivated by power and authority but by care and compassion.

Psalm 95 is the psalm of response. The psalmist sings,

> O come, let us worship and bow down;
> let us kneel before the Lord, our Maker!
> For he is our God,
> and we are the people of his pasture
> and the sheep of his hand. (Ps 95:6-7)

The psalmist makes it clear that we are God's flock, "the people of his pasture" (Ps 95:7). God leads us and tends to us with loving care and compassion. We worship the Lord for he is faithful and loves us with a steadfast love. We can rest in his kingship, for our Lord is not a dictator but our Good Shepherd who tends to his sheep.

In the second reading from Ephesians 1, the apostle Paul prays that the early believers would know the depth of God's grace and power. He prays,

> I do not cease to give thanks for you as I remember you in my prayers, that the God of our Lord Jesus Christ, the Father of glory, may give you a spirit of wisdom and revelation as you come to know him, so that, with the eyes of your heart enlightened, you may perceive what is the hope to which he has called you, what are the riches of his glorious inheritance among the saints, and what is the immeasurable greatness of his power for us who believe, according to the working of his great power. (Eph 1:16–19)

Paul prays that the Ephesians would know the hope, the riches, and the power that are theirs in Christ. Christ our King has blessed us beyond measure. Because of Christ's death, resurrection, ascension, and sending of the Spirit, we have spiritual blessings that bring us hope and power for the challenges we face.

Our triune God has not left us alone to fight our spiritual battles. We have the Father, the Son, and Holy Spirit to go before us and protect us. As the head of the church, Christ has all power and dominion and protects and preserves his people from all evil.

In the Gospel reading from Matthew 25, Jesus tells the parable of the sheep and the goats. On the day of judgment, Jesus will separate those who truly know him from those who do not. Those who will inherit the kingdom on the day of Christ's return are those who demonstrated love towards the poor, the hungry, the thirsty, the sick, and those in prison

(Matt 25:34–40). Seeking to love our neighbor is a mark of those who know Christ and the gospel of grace.

As we celebrate Christ the King Sunday, we reflect on God our shepherd who cares for and protects his people. May we reflect this same care and compassion to those around us, seeking to love the least of this world.

QUESTIONS FOR REFLECTION

1. Describe the shepherd-king in Ezekiel 34. What characteristics stand out to you? How can you manifest some of these characteristics in your own life towards others?

2. What motivates our joyful worship of God? We are described as the people of God's pasture. What does this say about our relationship to God?

3. What does Paul pray for the Ephesians in his letter? How can you appropriate these petitions in your own life? How can the hope, the riches, and the power we have as believers inform your everyday life?

4. Explain the parable of the sheep and the goats. What is the main takeaway for us? How does this parable influence the way you love and serve those around you?

PRAYER OF RESPONSE
Based on Matthew 25:31–40

Christ our King,
we know that on the day that you come in your glory,
you will gather all the nations and separate people,
one from another, as a shepherd separates the sheep from the goats.
May we be counted among the sheep,
the righteous ones who demonstrated your love to others:
giving food to the hungry; offering drink to the thirsty;
welcoming the stranger; clothing the naked;
taking care of the sick; and visiting those in prison.
For what is done unto the least of these,
your brothers and sisters, is done unto you.
In the name of Jesus we pray. Amen.

Appendix

Summary of My Doctoral Thesis: Inspiration for Parents and a Challenge to Worship Leaders[1]

INTRODUCTION

I am including a brief summary of my doctoral thesis to provide inspiration for parents and a challenge to worship leaders. For parents, I hope you will see the spiritual fruit that can come from the steady rhythms of engaging God's story in the home during the week. For worship leaders, I hope you will see the great benefit of building a bridge between church and home through worship and the role that you can play in this endeavor.

My doctoral work was through the Robert E. Webber Institute for Worship Studies in Jacksonville, Florida. The action research for my thesis was conducted at Covenant Church in Palm Bay, Florida, where I have served as the director of worship since 2015. In discerning the direction for my thesis, I decided to explore the theological truth that engaging God's story nurtures faith.

TITLE

"Implementing a Lectionary-Based Resource for Households during the Season after Pentecost at Covenant Church: A Bridge between Church and Home through Worship"

---

1. Jeancake, "Implementing a Lectionary-Based Resource," 69, 70–71, 91–93, 96, 99–100, 102–5, 110–11.

ABSTRACT

To help parents at Covenant Church engage God's story, I provided eleven participants with a lectionary-based resource that was used in the home for five weeks during the season after Pentecost. Data from surveys, interviews, and focus groups revealed an increase in the participants' conviction that they are the primary agents of faith formation in their children and growth in their understanding of the vital relationship between the church and home. Participants also experienced unity as a family as well as increased prayer, biblical literacy, and spiritual conversations as a result of regular spiritual practices in the home.

IDENTIFYING THE NEED AT COVENANT CHURCH

A preliminary survey (conducted June 12–19, 2024) revealed that many parents at Covenant Church acknowledged the importance of their role in the faith formation of their children. However, less than half of the parents actually exercised this role in the home during the week. In addition, many parents expressed various challenges in effectively nurturing faith in their child or children such as feeling intimidated, ill-equipped, overwhelmed, too busy, or more reliant on church leaders and ministries than their own abilities.

ADDRESSING THE NEED: TEACHING SESSIONS AND IMPLEMENTATION OF A LECTIONARY-BASED DEVOTIONAL RESOURCE

To address this need, I assembled eleven participants, representing eight families at Covenant Church. These participants were parents of children, between ages two and seventeen years old. I provided these eleven participants with eight hours of teaching on three foundations (biblical, historical, theological) related to how engaging God's story nurtures faith. These teaching sessions were held on August 31 and September 7, 2024.

I also provided the participants with a lectionary-based devotional resource to engage God's story during five weeks of the season after Pentecost (September 15 through October 13, 2024). This resource served to cultivate spiritual practices in the home during the week while also preparing families for corporate worship with the church on Sundays. The Scripture texts and prayers within the resource correlated with the liturgical texts on Sunday morning. To collect and analyze data, I had the participants take a pre- and a post-implementation survey, and I conducted one-on-one interviews and two focus-group interviews.

The pre-implementation survey was taken before the first teaching session. The post-implementation survey and interviews were conducted over several weeks following the implementation (October 14 through November 4, 2024).

RESULTS OF THE TEACHING AND IMPLEMENTATION

Growth in Their Conviction of Being the Primary Agents of Faith Formation

After eight hours of teaching and five weeks of implementation of the lectionary-based resource in the home, the participants grew in their conviction that they are the primary agents of faith formation in their child or children. The post-implementation survey revealed a 45 percent increase in the number of participants who strongly agree that they are the primary agents of faith formation in their child or children (see Figure 1).

Figure 1. As a parent, I am the primary agent of faith formation in my child or children.

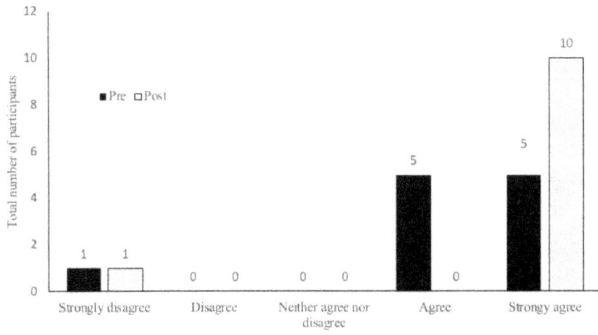

Growth in Confidence

Moreover, the participants grew in their confidence level and felt equipped to engage God's story with their child or children during the week. The post-implementation survey revealed a 45 percent increase in the number of participants who strongly agree that they feel equipped to teach their child or children about the story of the Bible (see Figure 2). The participants also articulated the various ways their faith influences the faith of their children.

Figure 2. I feel equipped to teach my child (or children) about the story of the Bible.

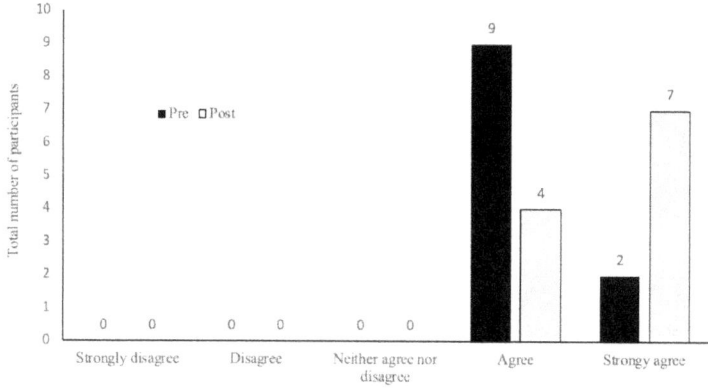

Ability to Overcome Challenges

The participants recognized many of the challenges in consistently engaging God's story and cultivating regular spiritual practices in the home. Through the structure and regularity of the devotional resource, however, they were able to overcome many of these obstacles over the five weeks of implementation.

Growth in Their Understanding of the Vital Relationship between Church and Home

The participants grew in their understanding of the vital relationship between the church and the home and in their appreciation of how the church helps to equip them in nurturing faith in their child or children. They expressed how the church provided resources as well as the time and energy of their leaders to help equip them. The most commonly expressed source of equipping, however, was the relationships that the church provided. These relationships took various forms: peer relationships, older leaders in their life, and the cohort itself. Moreover, some of these relationships supported the parents, others supported the child, and others supported both.

Participants acknowledged how spiritual practices in the home prepared them for or influenced their experience of corporate worship on Sunday. Many expressed how their children were more engaged because they were already familiar with the liturgical texts, songs, and corporate prayers. The impact of children hearing the same message from multiple places (church and home) was a notable discovery with regard to worship. Reinforcement helps a child trust the truth being expressed in word, song, or prayer.

In addition, some participants expressed how their children grew in their understanding of worship; others articulated how spiritual practices in the home during the week made them more present throughout the corporate worship experience.

Manifestation of the Fruit of Regular Spiritual Practices among Children and Families

Some of the most encouraging data came from how families and children were affected by regular spiritual practices in the home. Many dynamics were expressed, including peace and unity in the home, increased prayer, increased spiritual conversations, and increased comprehension of the Bible as a whole. Participants acknowledged less bickering between siblings, more heart-filled prayers, and increased outreach to their friends. The post-implementation survey revealed a 36 percent increase in the number of participants who strongly agree that they see the fruit of regular spiritual practices in the life of their child or children (see Figure 3).

Figure 3. I see the fruit of regular spiritual practices in the life of my child (or children).

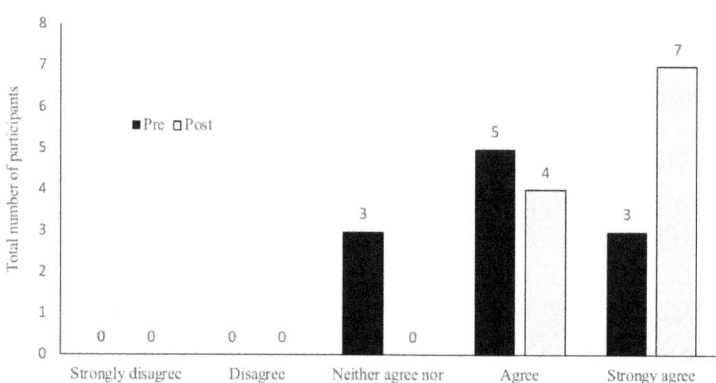

Growth in Their Understanding and Experience of Following the Christian Year and the Revised Common Lectionary

The most striking data came from the participants' understanding and experience of following the Christian year and the Revised Common Lectionary (RCL). Prior to the teaching and implementation, most of the participants had no knowledge of the RCL and limited experience with following the Christian year. The post-implementation survey revealed a 45-percent increase in the number of participants who strongly agree that following the cycles and seasons of the Christian year is a helpful way to engage God's story as a family (see Figure 4).

Figure 4. Following the cycles and seasons of the Christian Year is a helpful way to engage God's story as a family.

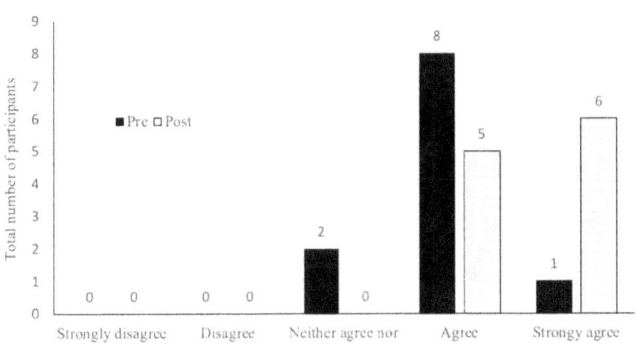

In addition, after the teaching and implementation, 36 percent of the participants agreed and 64 percent of the participants strongly agreed that the RCL was a helpful tool for consistently engaging God's story (see Figure 5).

Figure 5. The Revised Common Lectionary is a helpful tool for our family to read consistently from the Scriptures each week.

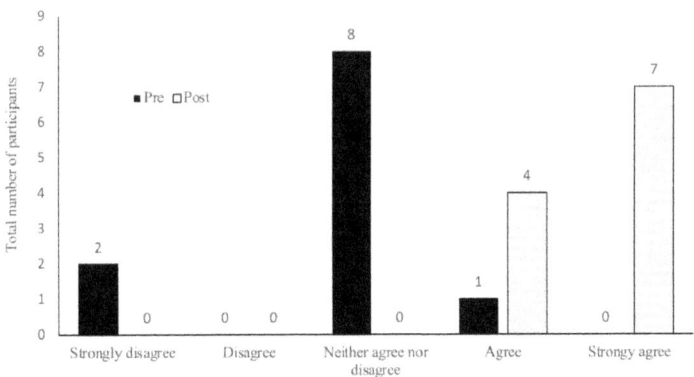

The learning and growth that took place in these two areas (Christian year and RCL) was very encouraging. This data was exciting and significant to me because, as a whole, my denomination (Presbyterian Church in America) does not endorse a lectionary approach to engaging God's story. This doctoral study demonstrated that participants without prior knowledge or exposure to the Christian year or the RCL could find them to be very helpful tools for engaging God's story consistently during the week as a family. The participants articulated how the Christian year and the RCL revealed the covenant faithfulness of God and helped them to see the "overall picture" of God's story.

INSPIRATION FOR PARENTS

I hope these results provide some inspiration for you as a parent. I know that the obstacles and challenges of consistently opening the word as a family are real, but they can be overcome. I pray that as you begin to use this resource in your own home, you will see spiritual fruit in the lives of your children and your family as a result of the steady rhythms of engaging God's story.

A CHALLENGE TO WORSHIP LEADERS

I believe that a notable discovery from this study was that the Christian education and spiritual formation of children should not fall solely under the scope of children and youth ministries, but should be a part of the worship ministry of a local church. Cultivating healthy families and fostering spiritual practices in the home should be part of the scope and pastoral interest of the worship leader.

This doctoral study helped me understand how worship can be the bridge between church and home. When liturgical texts for the congregation are coordinated with devotional resources for parents in the home during the week, both parties can benefit. The home can be edified through the weekly interaction with lectionary-based Scripture texts and lectionary-based prayers as well as a lyric sheet for the Sunday songs and hymns. Moreover, the overall engagement in corporate worship by the family (and the congregation as a whole) can be heightened due to familiarity with the liturgical texts. This is a win-win scenario for church and home that can be fostered by the worship leader of a local church.

Ministry to families can be cultivated through the coordination of the worship ministry and the children and youth ministries. The level of synergy and coordination can vary from church to church, but I believe a worship leader should have responsibilities, not just in planning the *experience for Sunday* but in helping to *build a bridge between the church and the home.* Worship leaders should be intentional about cultivating lifelong worshipers and in assisting parents in this endeavor. This focus would help fulfill the Great Commission by first making disciples within the home.

Bibliography

Adam, Adolf. *The Liturgical Year: Its History and Its Meaning After the Reform of the Liturgy.* Collegeville: Liturgical, 1981.

Consultation on Common Texts. *The Revised Common Lectionary.* Minneapolis: Fortress, 2012.

Gardiner, John Eliot. *Bach: Music in the Castle of Heaven.* New York: Random House, 2013.

Green, Joel B., et al. *Connections: A Lectionary Commentary for Preaching and Worship.* Louisville: Westminster John Knox, 2019.

Gross, Bobby. *Living the Christian Year: Time to Inhabit the Story of God.* Downers Grove: InterVarsity, 2009.

Jeancake, Paxson. "Implementing a Lectionary-Based Resource for Households during the Season after Pentecost at Covenant Church: A Bridge between Church and Home through Worship." Doctoral thesis, Robert E. Webber Institute for Worship Studies, 2025.

———. *Lectionary Journey: Worship Aids for the Christian Year.* Eugene, OR: Wipf & Stock, 2021.

Jeancake, Paxson, and Allison Jeancake. *You Keep Hope Alive.* CD and digital format. Released Jul. 9, 2020.

Long, Kimberly Bracken, ed. *Feasting on the Word Worship Companion: Liturgies for Year A.* Vol. 1. Louisville: Westminster John Knox, 2013.

Mitman, F. Russell. *Worship in the Shape of Scripture.* Cleveland: Pilgrim, 2001.

Peterson, Eugene H. *A Long Obedience in the Same Direction.* Downers Grove: InterVarsity, 2000.

Ryken, Philip Graham. *Exodus: Saved for God's Glory.* Preaching the Word. Wheaton: Crossway, 2015.

Webber, Robert E., ed. *Music and the Arts in Christian Worship.* Vol. 4.1 of *The Complete Library of Christian Worship.* Edited by Robert E. Webber. Peabody: Hendrickson, 1994.

Subject Index

accomplishments, earthly, 307, 309–11
adoption, 35, 37, 247–49
Advent, xviii–xix, 5–20
apostles, 89, 207
Ascension of the Lord, xx, 181–86
Ash Wednesday, xx, 107–11

baptism, 117, 119–20, 177
Baptist, John the
    ministry of, 9–12
    messengers from, 15
    testimony of, 53, 55
Beatitudes, the, 65–67

calling of the disciples, 53, 55
Christ the King, 349–52
Christian year, the, xviii–xx
Christmas, xix, 21–39
church, the, 43, 171–72, 177, 224, 226, 271–74
citizenship, earthly and heavenly, 319, 321–23
confession, Peter's, 271, 273–75
covenant
    promises, 218–19
    with Abraham, 117–20
    with Israel, 255–57
creation, 201–04
cross, take up their, 277, 279–81

Day of Pentecost, xx, 193–97
day of the Lord, 337–41, 343–47
defilement, 265, 267

Easter Sunday, xviii, xx, 153–56
Eastertide, 157, 153–197
Epiphany, xix, 41–103

faith
    example of, 320–23
    justified by, 121, 123–24, 211, 213, 219, 223, 225
    righteousness of, 118–19
    righteousness through, 93, 95
    saving, 219
fall, the, 113–14
fasting, 107–09
forgiveness, 289–90, 292–93

gifts, spiritual, 193, 195, 271, 273
God
    care of, 205–09, 232–33, 349–51
    character of, 256–59
    generosity of, 295–99
    grace of, 295–99
    judgment of, 87–89
    love for, 326–29
    love of, 87–90, 205–08
    peace with, 223, 225, 313–17
    power of, 349–50
    reconciled to, 107, 109–10, 123–24
    shepherd, 165–68
    sovereignty of, 157–58, 289–90
    steadfast love of, 29, 33, 94, 108–09, 111, 132–33, 170, 212–13, 230–31, 234, 236, 278, 281, 290, 295–96, 299
    wisdom of, 65
    with us, 17–20

SUBJECT INDEX

Good Friday, xx, 147–50
Good Shepherd, 18, 49, 88–90, 130, 165–68, 206–08, 261, 314, 317, 334, 349–50
gospel, 17–20, 95–97, 213–15
grace, 235, 237
Great Commission, the, 201, 203–4
Great Fifty Days, the, 157, 153–197
greatest commandment, the, 325, 327

heritage, spiritual, 271–72, 274
Holy Spirit
    gifts of the, 193, 195, 271, 273
    life in the, 243–45, 302–03, 327–28
    life-giving power of the, 131, 133–35
    ministry of the, 251–52, 254
    of truth, 177–79
    our Advocate, 177–79
    wisdom of the, 69, 71–72
hope, living, 157–58, 160
hospitality, 235, 237–38
house of prayer, 265–66

Immanuel, 17–20

Jesus Christ
    Adam and, 113–14
    ascended, 169
    ascension of, 181–85, 187–88
    authority of, 301, 303–05
    baptism of, 47, 49–51
    birth of, 21–24
    blood of, 162
    comfort and protection of, 190–91
    cross of, 147–52
    death of, 147–52
    eternal Word, 25, 27–28, 35, 37
    exaltation of, 303
    followers of, 127–29, 277, 279–81, 297–99, 309–11, 314–15
    high priest, 29, 31, 149
    hope in, 9–12
    humility of, 302–03, 305
    King, 240–41, 349–52
    Lamb of God, 53, 55–56
    light of, 59–62
    mystery of, 41, 43
    post-resurrection appearances of, 157, 159, 181–82, 184–85
    raised with, 153–54
    reflection of God's glory, 25–26
    resurrection of, 153, 155
    righteousness of, 114–15
    second coming of, 5–9, 337, 339–41, 343–47, 350, 352
    shepherd, 18, 49, 165–68, 349
    suffering of, 147–51
    temptation of, 113–15
    transfiguration of, 99–102
    union with, 229, 231
    way, the truth, and the life, the, 169, 172–73
judging others, 291
judgment, final, 350–52
justification, 93, 95, 121, 123, 211, 213, 219, 223, 225

kingdom, 14–15, 225–27, 251, 253, 296–99, 301, 303–04, 309–10

leadership, godly, 325–27, 331–35
Lent, xx, 107–40
light
    children of, 127–29
    in the darkness, 59–62
    of the world, 69, 72
living, godly, 127–29, 277, 281, 283–87, 295–99, 302–05, 314–15, 317
Lord's Supper, the, 141–44
love
    for God, 326–29
    for others, 161–63, 277, 279–80, 283, 285–87, 289, 291–93, 302, 305, 325–29

magi, 41, 44–45
Maundy Thursday, xx, 141–45
miracles
    calming the stormy sea, 259, 261–63
    feeding of the five thousand, 255, 257–58
    walking on the water, 259, 261

SUBJECT INDEX   367

Palm Sunday, xx, 137–40
parables
    hidden treasure, a, 251, 253
    laborers in the vineyard, the, 295, 297–98
    mustard seed, the, 251, 253
    net, a, 251, 253
    pearl of great value, a, 251, 253
    sower, the, 243, 245–46
    talents, the, 343, 345–47
    ten bridesmaids, the, 337, 339–41
    unforgiving servant, the, 289, 292–93
    wedding banquet, the, 313, 315–16
    weeds among the wheat, the, 247, 249
    wicked tenants, the, 307, 309–11
    yeast, the, 251, 253
patience, 13–16
prayer, 107, 109, 252–54
predestination, 37

reconciliation, 283, 285–87
religious hypocrisy, 331–35
responsibilities, earthly and godly, 319, 321–23
rest, 239, 241–42

Revised Common Lectionary, the, xx–xxii
righteousness
    of faith, 118
    of God, 109
    through faith, 93, 95, 211, 213
road to Emmaus, 161, 163–64

sacrifice, living, 273
salvation, 118–19, 161–62, 259, 261
sanctification, 237, 302–03
Scripture, 10
Season after Pentecost, xx, 201–352
Sermon on the Mount, 63, 65–69, 72–73, 75, 77–79, 81, 83–85, 87, 89–91, 93, 95–98, 205, 208–09, 211, 213–15
sin, 237, 239–41, 244–45, 265, 267
suffering, 123, 225

testimony, 176–77
transfiguration, the, 99–102
Trinity, 201–04
Trinity Sunday, 201–04

warfare, spiritual, 187, 190–91
water, living, 121, 124–25
worship, 124, 273

Scripture Index

Genesis

1:1—2:4a	201–02, 204
2:15–17; 3:1–7	113–14, 116
12:1–4a	117–18
50:15–21	289–90, 293

Exodus

12:1–14	141–42
17:1–7	121–22
19:2–8a	223–24
24:12–18	99–100

Leviticus

19:1–2, 9–18	81–82
19:1–2, 15–181	325–26

Deuteronomy

11:18–21, 26–28	93–94, 97, 211–12, 215
30:15–20	75–76

1 Samuel

16:1–13	127–28, 130

1 Kings

3:5–12	251–52, 254
19:9–18	259–60, 263

Psalm

1	326, 329
2	100, 103
8	202
15	64
16	158
22	148
23	128, 130, 166, 168, 314, 317
25:1–9	302
26:1–8	278–79, 281
27:1, 4–9	60
29	48–49
31:1–5, 19–24	94–95, 211–13
31:1–5, 15–16	170
32	114, 116
40:1–11	54
43	332–33
47	183–84
50:7–15	218
51:1–17	108, 111
65	244
66:8–20	176
67	266–67, 269
68:1–10, 32–35	188–89
69:7–18	230–31, 234
70	338–39
72:1–7, 10–14	42
72:1–7, 18–19	10, 42
80:1–7, 17–19	18
80:7–15	308
85:8–13	260–61

Psalm (continued)

86:11–17	248, 250
89:1–4, 15–18	236, 238
90:1–12	344, 347
95	122–23
95:1–7a	350
96	22, 320, 323
98	26
100	224–25
103:1–13	290
104:24–34, 35b	194–95
112:1–10	70–71
116:1–4, 12–19	162
116:1–2, 12–19	141–42
118:1–2, 14–24	154
118:1–2, 19–29	138–39
119:1–8	76
119:33–40	82, 284
119:129–36	252, 254
121	118
122	6
130	132–33
131	87–89, 205–07
138	272
145:1–8	295
145:8–9, 14–21	256, 258
145:8–14	240, 242
146:5–10	14
147:12–20	35–37
148	30

Isaiah

2:1–5	5–6
5:1–7	307–08
7:10–16	17, 19
9:1–4	59, 61, 62
9:2–7	21–22, 62
11:1–10	9–10, 12
25:1–9	313–14
35:1–10	13–15
42:1–9	47–48, 51
44:6–8	247
45:1–7	319–20, 323
49:1–7	53–54
49:8–16a	87–88, 205–6
51:1–6	271–72, 275
52:7–10	25–26
52:13—53:12	147–48, 151
55:1–5	255–56, 258
55:10–13	243, 246
56:1, 6–8	265–66, 269
58:1–12	69–70, 73
60:1–6	41–42
63:7–9	29–30, 33

Jeremiah

15:15–21	277–78
20:7–13	229–30
28:5–9	235–36
31:7–14	35–36

Ezekiel

18:1–4, 25–32	301–02
33:7–11	283–84
34:11–16, 20–24	349
37:1–14	131–32, 135

Hosea

5:15—6:6	217–18, 221

Joel

2:1–2, 12–17	107–8

Amos

5:18–24	337–38, 341

Jonah

3:10—4:11	295–96, 299

Micah

3:5–12	331–32
6:1–8	63–64

Zephaniah

1:7, 12–18	343–44

Zechariah

9:9–12	239–40

Scripture Index

Matthew

1:18–25	17, 19–20
2:1–12	41, 44–45
2:13–23	29, 31–33
3:1–12	9–12
3:13–17	47, 49–50
4:1–11	113, 115–16
4:12–23	59, 61–62
5:1–12	63, 65–67
5:13–20	69, 72–73
5:21–37	75, 77–79
5:38–48	81, 83–85
6:1–6, 16–21	107, 109
6:24–34	87, 89–91, 205, 208–09
7:21–29	93, 95–97, 211, 213–15
9:9–13, 18–26	217, 219–21
9:35—10:23	223, 225–27
10:24–39	229, 232–34
10:40–42	235, 237–38
11:2–11	13, 15–16
11:16–19, 25–30	239, 241–42
13:1–9, 18–23	243, 245–46
13:24–30, 36–43	247, 249–50
13:31–33, 44–52	251, 253–54
14:13–21	255, 257–58
14:22–33	259, 261–63
15:10–28	265, 267–69
16:13–20	271, 273–75
16:21–28	277, 279–81
17:1–9	99, 101–02
18:15–20	283, 285–87
18:21–35	289, 292–93
20:1–16	295, 297–99
21:1–11	137–38, 140
21:23–32	301, 303–05
21:33–46	307, 309–11
22:1–14	313, 315–17
22:15–22	319, 321
22:34–46	325, 327–29
23:1–12	331, 333–35
24:36–44	5, 7–8
25:1–13	337, 339–41
25:14–30	343, 345–47
25:31–46	349–52
28:1–10	153, 155
28:16–20	201, 203–04

Luke

2:1–20	21, 23–24
24:13–35	161, 163–64
24:44–53	181, 184–85

John

1:1–18	35, 37–38
1:1–14	25, 27–28
1:29–42	53, 55
3:1–17	117, 119–20
4:5–42	121, 124–26
9:1–41	127, 129–30
10:1–10	165, 167–68
11:1–45	131, 133–35
13:1–17, 31b–35	141, 143–44
14:1–14	169, 171–73
14:15–21	175, 177–79
17:1–11	187, 190–92
18:1—19:42	147, 150
20:19–31	157, 159
20:19–23	195–97

Acts

1:1–11	181–82
1:6–14	187–88, 192
2:1–21	193–94, 197
2:14a, 22–32	157–58
2:14a, 36–41	161–62, 164
2:42–47	165–66
7:55–60	169–71
10:34–43	47, 49, 51, 153–54
17:22–31	175–76

Romans

1:1–7	17–19
1:16–17; 3:22b–31	93, 95, 211, 213
4:1–5, 13–17	117–20
4:13–25	217–19
5:1–11	121, 123–24
5:1–8	223, 225
5:12–19	113–14
6:1b–11	229, 231
612–23	235, 237

Romans (continued)

7:15–25a	239–41
8:1–11	243–45
8:6–11	131, 133, 135
8:12–25	247–50
8:26–39	251–54
9:1–5	255–57
10:5–15	259, 261
11:1–2a, 29–32	265, 267
12:1–8	271, 273
12:9–21	277, 279–80
13:8–14	283, 285
13:11–14	5–7
14:1–12	289–91
15:4–13	9–10

1 Corinthians

1:1–9	53–55, 57
1:10–18	59–61
1:18–31	63, 65
2:1–16	69, 71
3:1–9	75, 77
3:10–11, 16–23	81–83
4:1–5	87, 89, 205, 207
11:23–26	141, 143
12:3b–13	195
13:11–13	201–4

2 Corinthians

5:20b—6:10	107, 109
13:11–13	201–02, 204

Ephesians

1:3–14	35, 37, 39
1:15–23	184, 186, 349–50
3:1–12	41, 43
5:8–14	127–29

Philippians

1:21–30	295–98
2:1–13	302–03, 305
3:4b–14	307k 309, 311
4:1–9	313, 315, 317

Colossians

3:1–4	153–54, 156

1 Thessalonians

1:1–10	319–23
2:1–8	325–27
2:9–13	331, 333
4:13–18	337, 339
5:1–11	343–45

Titus

2:11–14	21–23

Hebrews

1:1–2	25–27
2:10–18	29, 31
4:14–16; 5:7–9	147, 149

James

5:7–10	13–16

1 Peter

1:3–9	157–60
1:17–23	161–63
2:2–10	169, 171
2:19–25	165–66
3:13–22	175–78
4:12–14; 5:6–11	187, 189–92

2 Peter

1:16–21	99–101, 103